LABOR AND CAPITAL ON THE AFRICAN COPPERBELT

Class and Culture
A series edited by Bruce Laurie and Milton Cantor

Labor and Capital on the African Copperbelt

Jane L. Parpart

Temple University Press
Philadelphia

Temple University Press, Philadelphia 19122
© 1983 by Temple University. All rights reserved
Published 1983
Printed in the United States of America

Library of Congress Cataloging in Publication Data

Parpart, Jane L.
    Labor and capital on the African Copperbelt.
    (Class and culture)
    Bibliography: p.
    Includes index.
    1. Copper miners—Zambia—History. 2. Labor and
laboring classes—Zambia—History. 3. Class
consciousness—Zambia—History. I. Title. II. Series.
HD8039.M72Z342   1983   331.7'622343'096894   83-9170
    ISBN 0-87722-325-4

To my daughters
Laura and Lee

CONTENTS

Maps and Tables

Maps

Tables

Abbreviations

AA	Anglo-American Corporation
ALAB	African Labor Advisory Board
AMAX	American Metal Climax Inc.
AMWU	African Mineworkers' Union
ANC	African National Congress
CO	Colonial Office
DC	District Commissioner
LME	London Metal Exchange
MASA	Mines African Staff Association
MCM	Mufulira Copper Mines
MOSSA	Mine Officials and Salaried Staff Association
MWU	European Mineworkers' Union
NCCM	Nchanga Consolidated Copper Mines
NILAB	Native Industrial Labor Advisory Board
NLA	(Northern Rhodesian) Native Labor Association
NRCM	Northern Rhodesian Chamber of Mines
PC	Provincial Commissioner
RACM	Roan Antelope Copper Mines
RC	Rhokana Corporation
RST	Rhodesian Selection Trust
TUC	Trade Union Congress
UMHK	Union Minière du Haut Katanga
UMU	United Mineworkers' Union
UNIP	United National Independence Party
ZANC	Zambia African National Congress

PREFACE

A considerable body of literature already exists on the Northern Rhodesian Copperbelt during the colonial period, most of which centers on the two copper companies that dominate the Copperbelt, and their relationship with the Northern Rhodesian government and the British empire. For the most part, the Africans who labored in the copper industry have been seen as pawns in a larger game. Improvements in working conditions and even labor organization have been largely credited to benevolent outside forces rather than the efforts of the workers themselves. Preoccupied with the ethnic ties and partial proletarianization of the African miners, scholars have for the most part rejected the existence of an African working class on the Copperbelt during the colonial period. While agreeing that the Copperbelt miners never became a working class in the classic Marxist tradition, a more processual approach to class consciousness and action reveals the gradual emergence among the African mineworkers of a common identity and unity of purpose based on class lines. This book will examine this development in order to better understand the impact of industrial labor on a group of African workers and the role they played in the class struggles of the period.

The research for this book has taken me to three continents, numerous archives, and many individuals. The mines have generously permitted me to examine their excellent records. I found important data at the Copper Industry Services Bureau, formerly the Northern Rhodesian Chamber of Mines, and the Nchanga Consolidated Copper Mines, Centralised Services Division Technical Library, both in Kitwe, the Rhodesian Selection Trust archives at the Central Services Division in Ndola, as well as records in the personnel offices at Rhokana, Roan Antelope and Mufulira mines. Personnel at all the mines were uniformly helpful and supportive, but I owe a special debt of thanks to the intrepid archivist at Central Services Division in Ndola, James Moore. I also examined government records pertaining to the mines at the Zambian National Archives and the Public Records Office in London. The Rhodes House

Collection in Oxford provided several useful documents, as did the American Heritage Center at the University of Wyoming. I examined records of the United Missions in the Copperbelt at the University of London's School of Oriental and African Studies, the Methodist Missionary Society Archives in London, and the Mindolo Ecumenical Center in Kitwe. Small collections in Zambia, particularly the University of Zambia Special Collections, the Institute for African Studies, UNIP headquarters, and the Zambian Mineworkers' Union headquarters in Kitwe, produced various pieces of useful data. A. L. Epstein and J. Clyde Mitchell's data from 1950s Copperbelt surveys were particularly helpful. Both scholars graciously permitted me to examine these records during a recent visit to England.

Numerous informants in England, Zambia, South Africa, and America gave generously of their time and memories, and this study could never have been completed without them. Most miners interviewed had been early trade union leaders, staff association members, or employees in personnel departments. The interviews investigated African attitudes and communication systems in the mines, matters rarely discussed in the records. Corporate officials were interviewed to check information against written documentation and to clarify corporate attitudes and policies. A number of very busy executives spoke to me at length. Former employees in the African personnel department also added their unique perspective to this study. Several former labor officers explained how they mediated conflicts between the miners, government, and/or company demands. Their experiences added an important dimension to this study. A few members of the United Missions in the Copperbelt also provided important first-hand information of the mine townships.

Participant observation supplemented written and oral data. During my field work on the Copperbelt, daily observation provided a "feel" for life on the mines. Tours underground and in the mine compounds sharpened the impact of written records. During periods at each mine, research at the old personnel department centers allowed the researcher to observe daily routine. Many changes have occurred since the colonial period, but much of the general ambience remains the same. One could almost feel the presence of the old compound managers lurking in the background. These observations profoundly affected the conclusions of this study.

I am indebted to many people and institutions for help in the preparation of this study, but particularly to the Copper Industry Services Bureau and the Rhodesian Consolidated Mines, Central Services Division. In Zambia, the staff at the Institute for African Studies deserves a special thanks for their support, both for myself and for my two children. Professors Sara Berry, Robert Rotberg, Steve Baier, Frederick Johnstone, Sharon Stichter, Fred Cooper and Robin Fincham read the manuscript at various stages and provided crucial advice and support. Numerous other friends and scholars contributed much needed counsel and succor during the many years this manuscript has been in progress. Bruce Laurie and Temple University Press deserve a special thanks, as do my daughters, Lee and Laura, for their patience with an often impatient mother, Cathy Conrad, for her excellent typing, and Tim Shaw, for making life more worthwhile.

LABOR AND CAPITAL ON THE AFRICAN COPPERBELT

INTRODUCTION

In the late nineteenth century, the European powers abandoned the concept of informal empire and partitioned Africa into a number of colonial states. This political domination enabled the metropolitan governments to draw Africa ever more firmly into the orbit of the global economy, and the continent increasingly became an exporter of raw materials and mineral commodities to the industrial centers. The need for black labor to work in these industries rose accordingly. As a result, during the nineteenth and twentieth centuries, the colonial authorities pushed large numbers of Africans into the wage labor market.

The consequences of African participation in wage labor have been a matter of considerable debate. Certain similarities between the attitudes and behavior of European and African workers, particularly the forms of labor protest and the phases of their development, suggest parallels with the development of the working class in Europe. However, some important differences occurred as well. For one, colonial workers rarely became fully proletarianized because colonial officials and employers fostered a migrant labor system which placed much of the cost of labor reproduction on Africans in the rural areas. Racial divisions in the labor force, the dominance of foreign capital, and the nature of the colonial state also contrasted with conditions in the industrial nations.

Because of these differences, some scholars deny the relevance of class analysis for the African context. They argue that economic divisions in Africa are still blurred by ethnic and racial divisions which make class terminology premature. Such scholars prefer social and cultural pluralism, elites, or "situational selection" and network theory.[1] Other scholars, who accept the existence of African workers, insist that labor's ties to the land make comparisons with workers in the developed world misleading, and that "labor migration . . . delays the process of consolidating Africans into a class-conscious proletariat."[2] These approaches have a number of problems, but what they ignore most of all is the process of class formation over time.

3

Recently scholars have begun to use class analysis for examining wage labor in colonial and post-colonial Africa.[3] Although the importance of political and ideological factors in class identity/determination remains in dispute,[4] these scholars generally agree that the class experience and thus the source of class consciousness and class action is "largely determined by the productive relations in which men are born—or enter voluntarily," and that participation in the capitalist mode of production tends to create an awareness of common interests and class opposition among workers.[5] The resulting attitudes (consciousness) and behavior, however, vary with the nature of the class struggle in a given social formation over a period of time. This approach assumes worker consciousness and action in any given situation and period must be analyzed in relation to the specific social and historical circumstances in which they are situated and out of which they emerge, rather than in terms of some abstract linear evolutionary theme.[6]

This study seeks to show the relevance of class analysis for understanding the development of attitudes and behavior among the African mineworkers on the Northern Rhodesian Copperbelt during the colonial period. In this respect, it differs from a considerable and important body of literature on the Zambian miners, which focuses on government, corporate, and traditional African institutions to explain worker behavior.[7] It asserts that the attitudes and behavior of the copper miners are best understood as a form of class consciousness and class action. By analyzing the objective interests of the different occupational groups on the mines, and the manner in which these interests are perceived and acted upon in the colonial period, it avoids economic reductionism,[8] extends understanding of the constraints operating for or against the development of class consciousness and class action on the Copperbelt, and provides one more case study examining the link between class structure and behavior.

This is a study of black miners on the Copperbelt. It examines the interrelationship between management strategies, the work process, living conditions, and worker responses in the Northern Rhodesian copper industry during the colonial period. The emphasis is on process, on the manner in which mineworkers recognized shared economic concerns within a new social formation, and their willingness to act together in defense of class interests. Broader political and class allegiances are only examined as they relate to this setting.

CLASS, CONSCIOUSNESS, AND ACTION

As is well known, Marx's prediction of proletarian revolution has rarely been realized. Workers in the industrialized nations have generally been content to negotiate short-term gains within the capitalist system, rather than challenge the system as a whole. Marxist theorists have created a number of explanations for this deviation or "false consciousness."[9] One group of workers has been singled out for its lack of revolutionary zeal—the highly skilled stratum or "aristocracy" of labor. Marx and Engels located much of British proletarian apathy in this stratum of the work force. Lenin placed all workers in the developed world in this category, and concluded that only a revolutionary political party could move them beyond mere trade union consciousness.[10] Gramsci, on the other hand, stressed the role of ideology in the formation of class consciousness and class action. The dominant or hegemonic class uses a variety of mechanisms, particularly religious and educational institutions, to impose its vision on society as a whole. Like Lenin, Gramsci believed an alternative vision of society would only develop among the subordinate, or corporate, classes under the leadership of a revolutionary elite, although not necessarily political activists. Unlike Lenin, Gramsci saw consciousness as largely rooted in production, and held that "the economic base sets, in a strict manner, the range of possible outcomes, but free political and ideological activity is ultimately decisive in determining what alternatives prevail."[11]

There are a number of problems with these approaches. The labor aristocracy thesis assumes structural class position defines behavior. While class identification is important, it is clearly not the sole determinant of the class experience. Recent studies emphasize the fluidity of worker consciousness and the basic working-class orientation of the "labor aristocrats."[12] When examining working-class elites, the connection between behavior and class structure has to be the question, not the answer. Ideology and political factors influence class behavior as well. The question at issue is the relative importance of political, ideological, and economic factors on the class experience. A deterministic emphasis on ideology leads back to an Hegelian interpretation of history, while focusing on politics reduces the impact of the relations of production on consciousness. Both interpretations stray significantly from Marx's assertion that the production process shapes consciousness.

Poulantzas has recently developed a model incorporating politics and ideology into the analysis of social class. While agreeing that economic position is the principal determinant of social classes, he maintains that political and ideological relations of domination and subordination also play an important role. He rejects the notion that social classes exist as economic units and then enter into a class struggle; rather, "social classes coincide with class practices, i.e. the class struggle, and are only defined in their mutual opposition."[13] The working class perform productive labor, are manual rather than mental laborers, and hold non-supervisory positions. It is distinct from the new petty-bourgeoisie who are unproductive laborers, supervisors, and mental rather than manual labors. According to Poulantzas, the traditional and new petty-bourgeoisie are one class because both represent the political domination of capital over the working class. Thus the objective interests of the proletariat and the petty-bourgeoisie can be understood and identified on political, ideological, and economic levels by understanding the reproduction of the social division of labor.[14]

Pulantzas' definition of class identity, however, tells us little about the actual behavior of classes, or class fractions. He rejects the comparison between classes-in-themselves (an economic class) and classes-for-themselves (a class conscious of its class interests), but in fact creates a similar dichotomy. He too is left trying to explain the difference between the objective interests of a given social class, and the behavior of that class, or class fraction, in a specific situation. Like Marx and Lukács, he posits a correct form of consciousness and behavior given the objective conditions of a particular social class, and implies that any deviation from this position is somehow a failure, or false consciousness. This continued allegiance to an ideal class position forces him to explain deviations, diverting analysis from behavior. Political and ideological inputs remain primarily descriptive categories derived from economic position. Little consideration is given to the influence of archaic ideological and political structures upon changing production patterns, and to the impact of decisions and actions by individual actors. Although structural analysis is valuable, it can only define limits and pressures on class behavior.

What then can we say about the relationship between class membership and behavior? Rather than focus on process, the studies mentioned above either lapse into pessimistic gloom about the revolutionary potential of the working class, or assume that structure will win out in that social classes will eventually perceive and act on their objective class interests.

Neither voluntarism nor structural determinism provide adequate approaches to the study of class behavior. For an alternative strategy, we turn to a number of recent writings.[15] First, the historic and relational nature of this task must be understood. Classes and class fractions, like the social relations from which they arise, exist in antagonistic and dependent relations to each other. The expression of class consciousness and class action is located in the relations between classes during a specific historic conjuncture. We need to know the objective interests of the different social classes as they struggle to better or maintain their position in a specific social formation. The objective interests of different groups in the social division of labor will affect the interests and possible range of actions of each group. "Capital does have certain requirements in relation to the reproduction of labor power. . . . This process of reproduction, then, is always a contested transformation. Working-class culture (and behavior) is formed in the struggle between capital's demand for particular forms of labor power and the search for a secure location within this relation of dependency."[16]

In the capitalist mode of production, the tension between capital and labor thus tends to create an awareness of opposition between those who own and control capital and those who do not. The position of the working class in the production system generally pushes workers toward an understanding of their identity of interests against capital and the need for collective action (both ideological and political) against capital in order to protect worker interests. Following the work of Olin Wright, we reassert the primacy of economic position in both class membership and class behavior, and agree that those groups in contradictory class positions are most likely to act contrary to their objective class interests.[17]

The economic structure of a society and the social division of labor are thus the essential framework shaping the objective interests which a social class, or class fraction, will tend to understand. We can say then that class consciousness and class action among workers in the capitalist mode of production tends to unfold in the following stages:

1. Workers must be aware of their common interests as a group within industry and accept the relative permanence of this status (worker identity).
2. At the level of consumption, workers must recognize that they are exploited by management through the wage relationship and are not receiving a fair share of the socially-produced surplus in the form of wages (worker opposition).
3. Workers must recognize that their collective class interest is antagonistic to that of management and must be willing to engage in class conflict, e.g., striking, in order to secure their class interests (worker consciousness).
4. Workers must be willing to form organizations to pursue class interests, regardless of prior status or social origin of fellow workers (trade union consciousness).
5. Workers become aware of the class structure on a societal level (class consciousness).
6. At a societal level, workers must recognize the need to engage in political activity in order to create the conditions that will secure their class interests (political class consciousness).
7. Workers recognize the need to engage in political activities which will alter the social formation in which they live (revolutionary class consciousness). This, as we have stated earlier, is rarely achieved.[18]

At the same time, no necessary linearity can be posited for worker attitudes and behavior in a particular social formation. Class behavior and class membership must not be conflated. Behavior by any class, class fraction, or economic group varies with the nature of the class struggle at a given historical conjuncture. The mode of production, and the need to reproduce it, limits the range of choices available to social actors. Within a given industry, moreover, economic and technical constraints alter the relations between workers and management. Those industries needing larger components of skilled labor generally have to be more responsive to labor demands, while industries with large unskilled labor forces can more easily replace recalcitrant workers. Thus, the opportunities for effective labor action vary with industry's labor needs and labor supply. The position of an industry in the world market also affects management's ability to offer concessions to workers. High profits can be used to buy off worker protest, while low profitability forces management to confront and stymie demands for higher wages and better working conditions.

Both worker and managerial organizations play a crucial role in the struggle between labor and capital as well. Trade unions and professional associations can protect workers and petty-bourgeoisie wage earners from management, both by organizing collective action and by espousing ideas of class opposition. The internal structure of these organizations, and their ethnic, craft, skill and community ties, can affect the capacity of class or class fractions to organize in opposition to capital. Managerial institutions provide information and a base of cooperation among capital against labor. They also help justify capital's domination, both to other capitalists and to the dominated classes.[19]

The class struggle is embedded in political relations as well. Labor and capital act within a larger political context. In the capitalist mode of production, capital looks to the state to help maintain the social division of labor, especially its control over labor. However, this is rarely a passive process. The state, while seeking to maintain the social division of labor, and therefore the dominance of the capitalist class, must maintain the unity and cohesion of the social formation as a whole. This task is complicated by divisions within the bourgeois class. The state must mediate between these antagonistic groups, usually establishing a power bloc in which a fraction of the bourgeois class dominates the society. In order to do this, to find allies for this bloc, and to maintain harmony among all classes in a given social formation, the state requires a degree of relative autonomy. This autonomy enables the state to play off the various contending forces in a social formation in order to successfully reproduce itself. Support for the power bloc can be achieved by rewarding certain classes, or class fractions, particularly peasants, petty bourgeoisie, and skilled workers. The state's need for support and harmony gives the dominated classes some leverage and can result in state support for some of their goals despite opposition from the dominating class. This can alter the perceptions of class interests and class strategies of the dominated classes, encouraging economism rather than class conflict. The impact of the state on a particular class struggle must, of course, be examined in its specific historic context over time.[20]

The class struggle is also waged on an ideological level. In order to maintain the social division of labor in the capitalist mode of production, the capitalist class uses ideology to ensure its dominance. To maintain harmony between capital and labor, the dominant, or hegemonic, class portrays itself as the purveyor of reality for society as a whole. Once again, however, this is not a simple process. As Miliband points out, "The discussion of hegemony and class consciousness more than ever requires the inclusion of the concept of a battle being fought on many different fronts and on the basis of the tensions and contradictions which are present in the actual structures or work and of life in general in capitalism. . . . The ideological terrain is by no means wholly occupied by the ideas of the ruling class: it is highly contested territory."[21] The ideology of the dominated classes is not simply a reflection of the hegemonic class, it emerges from the struggle between capital and labor, and thus, on some level, challenges the hegemony of the ruling class. These ideas are embedded in and often, but not always, facilitated by working-class culture— "the common sense or way of life of a particular class, group, or social category."[22] The study of both working-class culture and ideology is thus crucial for understanding the actual working out of the class struggle in a given social formation. Linked with economic and political relations, an understanding of the ideological struggle between capital and labor helps avoid structural functionalism without lapsing into the empiricism so common to cultural studies.

CLASS ANALYSIS IN AFRICA

Considerable literature on class formation in Africa has been published in recent years. Informed by the French structuralists, a number of studies, most notably by Gavin Kitching and Robert Davies, seek to delineate the objective structure of class and production relations rather than class behavior.[23] Classes are seen as relations which emerge in the reproduction of the social division of labor in a specific social formation. While sometimes disagreeing over exact criterion for class membership, this approach contributes to a more fundamental identification of classes in Africa, one based on objective similarity of interests in the social division of labor rather than merely observed inequalities. It has also encouraged closer examination of the forms of accumulation, the class struggle, and the role of the state in Africa.

The state emerges as the fundamental political force establishing and maintaining class formation in Africa. Following recent work by Berman and Lonsdale, the colonial state may be seen as a special form of the twentieth-century capitalist state, designed to maximize the transfer of surplus to the metropole, while also maintaining political reproduction— that is, the pattern of class domination and subordination within the state. This necessitates not only intervention in class struggles, but also involvement in a range of ideological activities to justify the existing system. It also demands a certain level of autonomy in order to maintain the illusion of concern for the social order as a whole, and is complicated by the need to restructure the precapitalist mode of production to fit the new colonial economy. The social engineering involved is complex, often necessitating the use of force as well as persuasion. However, since the colonial state has only limited access to the surplus it helps generate, its ability to create and control an African working class is hampered by the need to maintain social control for minimal cost.[24]

The role of the settler and the post-colonial state in class formation is a bit more complicated. The settler-dominated state often opposes large transfers of surplus to the metropole, and instead "manages to retain an increasing proportion of the surplus in order to build an infrastructure, reproduce specific forms of labor power, and foster indigenous capital accumulation." As a result, the settler state has more resources to establish and control the African working class so necessary to its reproduction and expansion. The post-colonial state, on the other hand, is more integrated into the global economy, and its ruling class is highly dependent on foreign expertise. As a result, the governing class uses the state to protect its class interests by making the ex-colony attractive to foreign investment. In order to do this, the state frequently intervenes to guarantee production and contain labor protest. The penetration of the state into the production process transforms industrial struggles into political struggles against the state, with important implications for worker consciousness and action.[25]

The growing literature on class, class formation, and the state in Africa is certainly a welcome change from the earlier rejection of class. When examining class behavior, however, many of these studies fall into the trap of structural determinism. As Kitching points out, much of "Marxist work on Africa has been hopelessly ensnared by attempting simultaneously to grapple with what is often called the 'objective' structure of class and production relations and the 'subjective' structure of consciousness, ideology and political factions. . . . A persistent conflation of these two entirely different theoretical problematics has been the principal hallmark of much of the neo-Marxist work on Africa."[26] Working-class behavior is inferred from the degree of proletarianization or position in the division of labor. Although some debate continues over the definition of a proletarian,[27] much of the scholarship on African labor assumes that the greater the dependence upon wage labor, the more class conscious the workers. Thus, the limited consciousness and action of migrant workers are the result of structural dependence upon both capitalist and non-capitalist production modes.[28] The absence of revolutionary class consciousness and behavior among African workers is explained in structural terms as well. According to Arrighi, Saul, and Fanon the privileged skilled workers, or "labor aristocrats," are alienated from other Africans. They become the "bourgeois" fraction of the colonized people, dependent on the colonial authorities, and, as a result, unwilling to align themselves with the colonial system rather than with revolution.[29]

These studies overemphasize structure, neglect the impact of historical circumstances, and consequently overlook some important aspects of the class experience in Africa.

A growing number of scholars are now examining class formation and class consciousness among African workers in both the colonial and post-colonial periods in a somewhat different way. They focus less on structural class position than on worker values and practice,[30] and emphasize the process whereby persons involved in wage labor become "a group groping for self-expression and the creation of a corporate identity." Workers are seen as active agents in the creation of their own group solidarity, consciousness, and action.[31] In agreement with E. P. Thompson, these studies see class as "a happening expressed in shared values, feelings, interests, life experiences, and set in concrete historical events and processes."[32] They emphasize the special factors affecting class formation and class consciousness in Africa, without assuming a linear progression towards a preordained form of class consciousness. Looked at this way, worker consciousness and organization are altered by the mode of production and mediated by the slow and partial character of African proletarianization, racial and ethnic divisions, and the nature of the class struggle at a particular historic conjuncture. Much of this research is concerned with worker behavior before the development of sustained working-class organizations. For example, Charles van Onselen and Ian Phimister look to "the less dramatic, silent and often unorganized responses" of workers for early expression of worker consciousness among Rhodesian gold miners.[33] Other studies examine more explicit expressions of class action, such as work stoppages, for despite the lack of formal working-class organizations, strikes did occur in colonial Africa, particularly among railwaymen, dockers, and mine workers.[34] Recent studies on African labor organizations have taken a more grassroots approach as well, analyzing trade union activity as an expression of worker solidarity and class action.[35] They see the inequalities experienced daily and repetitively by laborers in capitalist production as the driving force behind worker organization. At the same time, the variety of African labor protest, ranging from simple economism to concerted and sustained efforts to overthrow a particular regime, affirms the futility of grounding worker behavior in structural terms and arrangements alone. This more eclectic approach recognizes that in certain instances, particularly those severely repressive, reformism and populism are most likely to emerge.[36]

One promising approach to be followed in the present study is the in-depth analysis of workers in a specific industrial setting. This allows one to examine the impact of participation in the industrial mode of production in greater detail. It permits an analysis of daily life within a particular political-economy with a view toward uncovering class-based loyalties and their various expressions. Its focus is the world of work on the one hand, and the process and dynamics of the transition from "class in itself" to "class for itself" on the other. In this respect it is congruent with most current studies which have identified participation in industrial production as a determining factor in the development of consciousness. As Lubeck discovered in Kano, "At the place of work, organizational pressures tend to homogenize differential ethnic statuses into a common class identity that derives from common inequality relationships and common class interests. . . . During early industrialization, communal loyalties begin to erode, at least in work situations, in favor of class-based loyalties."[37] And yet, we have seen that the development of class consciousness and class-based action is not a linear process. Even for fully proletarianized workers, consciousness and class action are shaped by the historical circumstances in which they work and live. The interrelationship between daily experiences in industrial production and external forces impinging on them, and its effect on the development of class consciousness and class action, needs further investigation. By looking in detail at workers in one industry, this study focuses on what actually happened in the work place, and how work experiences shaped the complex process of class formation, consciousness, and struggle.

The first chapter outlines the development of the copper industry in Northern Rhodesia during the colonial period. Chapter 2 describes corporate labor strategy before and after the Depression, emphasizing the correlation between labor supply and corporate policy. The next two chapters analyze the impact of stabilization on worker attitudes and behavior, particularly the growing willingness to strike for better work and living conditions. The fifth chapter shows how the stabilized miners gradually recognized the need for a broadly-based worker organization to protect their interests. Chapter 6 traces the spread of trade unionism throughout the mine work force. The last chapter examines the struggle between management and the union, the triumph of management, and the subsequent adoption of more economistic behavior by the mineworkers. It also investigates miner attitudes during this period, and concludes that well-developed class consciousness continued to exist, despite changes in behavior.

1

The Copper Industry in the Colonial Period

THE SETTING

When the British South Africa Company (BSA) took over Northern Rhodesia in 1889, the Copperbelt was a sparsely inhabited, narrow strip of country, about 80 miles long, in the north-central section of the country. About 4,000 feet above sea level and approximately 13° south of the equator, the rocky infertile soil discouraged productive farming. The infertility, however, was compensated for by the rich mineral deposits, particularly copper ore,[1] which had been worked by the local Lamba people since the seventeenth century. By the late nineteenth century little mining occurred, and visitors described the area as a "flat, barely undulating land, covered with mile upon square mile of thin but tall forest, which for the most of the time obscures a traveller's view and tends to give an impression of ever-expanding monotony."[2]

By the end of the colonial period in 1964, the Copperbelt had five bustling industrial centers, three smaller mining towns, and a population of about 544,000 people. Ndola (pop. 89,000) was its manufacturing and commercial center as well as the provincial capital. The largest city on the Copperbelt, Kitwe (popl. 90,000), had grown up around Rhokana (Nkana) mine. Due to its central location, Kitwe developed more retail, service, and administrative functions than the other mining towns. Smaller mining centers developed at the three other large mines on the Copperbelt: Chingola (Nchanga copper mine), Mufulira (Mufulira copper mine), and Luanshya (Roan Antelope copper mine). In 1964 these towns had populations of 48,000, 73,000, and 62,000 respectively. Smaller towns grew up at Chambeshi, Kalulushi, and Chililabomwe, but they were purely mining centers.[3]

Clearly a major transformation had occurred on the Copperbelt during the colonial period, a transformation that altered both the Northern Rhodesian economy and the working world of many Northern Rhodesians. This study will examine the impact of the transformation on the attitudes and behavior of those Northern Rhodesians who worked in

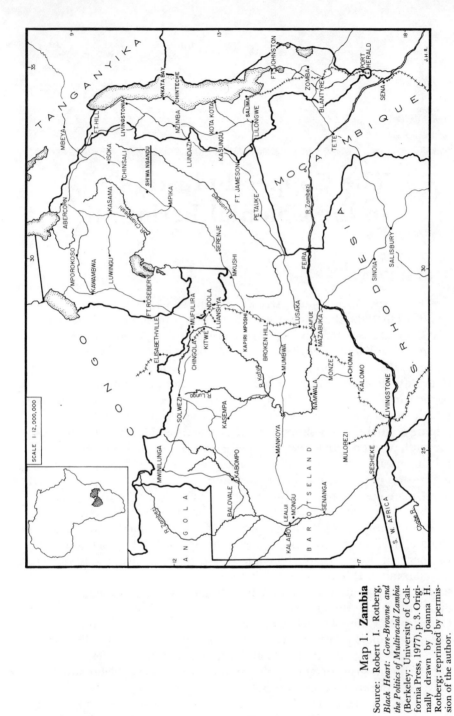

Map 1. Zambia

Source: Robert I. Rotberg, *Black Heart: Gore-Browne and the Politics of Multiracial Zambia* (Berkeley: University of California Press, 1977), p. 3. Originally drawn by Joanna H. Rotberg; reprinted by permission of the author.

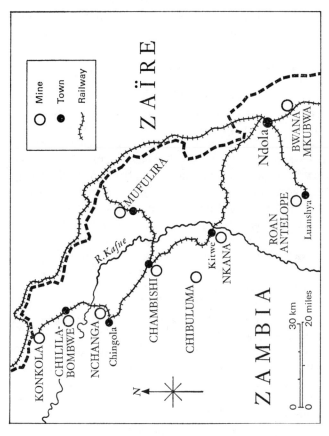

Map 2. The Copperbelt
Source: Andrew Roberts, *A History of Zambia* (London: Heinemann, 1976). p. 187. Reprinted by permission of the author.

the mines, with particular emphasis on the gradual development of class consciousness and class actions among the copper miners.

HISTORICAL BACKGROUND

When the British first entered Northern Rhodesia, they encountered five major peoples: the Lozi, Tonga, Bemba, Ngoni, and Kazembe. Centered on the Kafue flood plains, the Lozi Kingdom was a hierarchical state based on cattle, agriculture and trade, and extensive use of slave labor. The Tonga in the south practiced mixed farming, and lived in large unfortified villages with central enclosures for their cattle. Using Zulu war tactics, the Ngoni had set up a powerful state in southeastern Zambia, where they augmented agriculture and cattle herding with raids and tribute from neighbors. In the nineteenth century the Bemba had turned their warrior tradition to good use, and raided far and wide for slaves and ivory. The Kazembe of the Luapula region also joined this trade to the east, but they declined in importance relative to the Bemba, who became the terror of the northeastern plateau.[4]

At the Berlin Conference in 1885, the British successfully pressed their claim for central Africa. Eager to block Portuguese and Belgian expansion, in 1889 the British government gave Cecil Rhodes a charter for his British South Africa Company, which gave him mineral rights and the authority to make treaties with African rulers giving the Company administrative powers. Rhodes, who had made a fortune in South African diamonds, immediately sent Company representatives north to take over the area's potential riches. By 1891 border disputes had been settled, the Company's occupation rights had been recognized, and in 1897 the area was officially named Northern Rhodesia.

The Company set about administering the territory for its own profit, but soon realized the low-grade ores discovered at Broken Hill and Ndola (Bwana Mkubwa mines) would never yield significant profits. Company officials began to see Northern Rhodesia as a labor reserve for mines in Southern Rhodesia and Katanga, where the Belgian copper company, Union Minière du Haut Katanga (UMHK), provided jobs and freight traffic on the BSA-controlled railroad linking Katanga with South Africa. In order to force Africans into wage labor, the Company levied taxes and permitted corporate recruiting. It also encouraged white farmers and traders to settle in the territory to supply food and trade goods to the mines, and the settler population slowly increased, reaching 3,500 in 1921.[5]

The European settlers resented the Company's restrictive land and mineral policies, and soon began agitating for an end to its rule. In an effort to reduce expenditures, Company officials suggested amalgamating the two Rhodesias, which only increased settler opposition. Assuming they could exert more power if Northern Rhodesia became a Crown

Colony with a legislative council, the settlers appealed to the Colonial Office for help. Weighed down by administrative expenses, the Company agreed to hand over Northern Rhodesia as long as they could retain mineral rights in the northwest—a seemingly minor concession which would eventually yield enormous profits. In 1924, the Colonial Office took over the colony and set up a legislative council, which, although dominated by government officials, included five members elected by a predominately European franchise.

Colonial Office rule did little to change Northern Rhodesia. Britain was mainly concerned that the colony support itself and strengthen links with southern Africa. In order to encourage white settlement, the first governor set aside blocks of land for European use. It was mainly along the line of rail, which had the best soil and access to markets. African reserves were set up, mostly on inferior land. Overcrowding and food shortages soon plagued the reserves, pushing more Africans into wage labor. The new Copperbelt mines (started in 1926) and the European farms quickly absorbed this increase. Indeed, labor shortages plagued central Africa until the Depression.

After the Depression, the Northern Rhodesian economy expanded as did the size and affluence of the settler community. By 1943, the mines employed 32,805 Africans and 3,566 whites. European farming and trading expanded as well and by 1951 there were 37,097 Europeans in the country. That same year, the mines employed over 5,000 Europeans.[6] The European miners organized a union to protect themselves from African competition, and joined other settlers pressing for greater representation in the Legislative Council. The settlers resented the way BSA royalties and British tax levies drained the colony's resources and inhibited development. After the war non-officials gained a majority, but only because government nominated more of them. The settlers began to talk of amalgamating with the larger and more powerful Southern Rhodesian settler community, but the Colonial Office steadfastly refused a solution so inimical to metropolitan profits.

Africans in Northern Rhodesia opposed amalgamation. Unlike the mines to the south, the Copperbelt companies stabilized their more skilled black mineworkers. These men led two major strikes, fought for worker representation, and in 1949 became the leaders of the newly established African Mineworkers' Union (AMWU). They knew about labor conditions in Southern Rhodesia, and did not want them brought north. The African petty bourgeoisie developing in the towns harbored similar fears, and the two groups set about establishing welfare associations to protect African interests in the towns. In 1946 these associations convened to discuss territory-wide political problems, and formed a Federation of African Societies. Two years later this became the Northern Rhodesian Congress, a forerunner of African nationalist political parties.

Frustrated by their inability to control the colonial state, and their fear of the growing African petty bourgeoisie and proletariat, leading settlers cast about for new solutions. They discovered that while Britain rejected amalgamation, it would accept a federation. The labor Government wanted only a guarantee that African political power would increase. In 1951, the Conservatives came to power. Less concerned about African interests, the Conservatives wanted the settlers, rather than Britain, to deal with African pressures for political and economic advancement. Once convinced by the mining companies and settlers that British interests would not be jeopardized, federation seemed an attractive solution.

Instead of appeasing Africans, the threat of federation stimulated an African drive for political power. Africans sensed that Southern Rhodesia would be the dominant partner, and feared an extension of Southern Rhodesian institutions into Northern Rhodesia. Everyone rallied to the cause. Political activity centered around the Northern Rhodesian Congress, which was renamed the Northern Rhodesian African National Congress (ANC) in 1951. A former teacher, Harry Nkumbula, was elected president, and Congress set about organizing opposition to federation. The AMWU cooperated until the threat of massive dismissals forced it to abandon ANC plans for a national prayer against federation. Despite African protests, in August 1953 the Rhodesias and Nyasaland became the Central African Federation amidst promises of equal partnership and prosperity for all.

Initially, federation seemed promising to whites in Northern Rhodesia. African resistance had failed. Copper prices rose, creating more jobs; by 1956 over 7,000 Europeans worked on the copper mines. Prosperity attracted immigrants, and the white population rose from 49,000 in 1953 to 72,000 in 1958. The Europeans, however, could not stimulate expansion of trade and industry alone. African buying power would have to increase as well. A number of Europeans understood this, but faced formidable obstacles. The harsh land and sparse African population (4 million in 1975) inhibited growth. More importantly, Southern Rhodesia used its dominant position to monopolize the economic benefits of federation. Northern Rhodesian revenues were funneled into Southern Rhodesian projects, and by 1963 the territory had lost more than £97 million to the rest of the Federation. The economic arguments for federation diminished among Europeans and even more so among Africans. Increasingly, only fears of a black government kept Northern Rhodesian whites tied to the Federation.[7]

The Africans resented their inferior position in the Federation, and African nationalism soon revived. Radical mineworkers called for political action, and in 1954 Congress supported the union's campaign to stop management from removing its more skilled members. Management won with state support, and effectively forced the AMWU out of national politics until the early 1960s. Despite this dissaffection, by 1958 African public opinion against the Federation had been aroused, and Congress branches once again sprang up throughout the country. Support broadened as falling copper prices and declining construction constricted economic opportunities. New leaders determined to create an independent African state joined Congress and began to challenge Nkumbula. Led by Kenneth Kaunda, the young radicals split from ANC in 1958 and formed a new party, the Zambia African National Congress (ZANC). In 1959 the party was banned and several leaders were jailed, but this only inflamed public opinion, and another party was soon formed, the United National Independence Party (UNIP). Kaunda was released from jail in early 1960, and took over the leadership.

By this time, British officials and far-sighted settlers recognized the inevitability of majority rule in Northern Rhodesia. The Federation was crumbling under pressure from African nationalists and independence-seeking Southern Rhodesian whites. Some leading Northern Rhodesian whites realized African rule would be better than continued Federal maltreatment. The Colonial Office preferred a dependent black government in Northern Rhodesia to the headstrong settlers running the Federation. In 1961, the Colonial Office deliberately proposed a Northern Rhodesian constitution which would establish an African majority in the legislature. The Federal prime minister managed to get this revised, but only at the price of a UNIP civil disobedience campaign. After some violence, the 1962 constitution was revised again and UNIP agreed to participate. In October 1962 UNIP and ANC won two-thirds of the vote. The Federation broke up in late 1963, and soon afterwards UNIP won a decisive majority in the first election based on universal suffrage. The new government convinced the BSA Company to surrender its mineral royalties, and on 24 October 1964, Northern Rhodesia became the independent nation of Zambia with Kenneth Kaunda as president. ANC and other opposition parties continued until 1972, when Kaunda declared Zambia a one-party state.[8]

THE DEVELOPMENT OF THE NORTHERN RHODESIAN COPPER INDUSTRY

Cecil Rhodes' dream of establishing a second Rand had proved an empty hope in the barren hillsides of Northern Rhodesia. Edmund Davis,[9] an associate of Rhodes, discovered lead and zinc in 1902 at Broken Hill (now Kabwe) just below the Copperbelt region, and staked copper claims called Roan Antelope, Rietbok, and Bwana Mkubwa in the area which was to become the Copperbelt. But these prospects were overshadowed by the discovery of more easily treated ore in neighboring Katanga. Under the control of the Belgian mining company UMHK, Katanga was soon producing large quantities of low-priced copper.[10]

No attempts were made to utilize Northern Rhodesian copper until the rise in copper prices in the world market in the 1920s. The price rise induced Davis to seek more capital for his struggling Northern Rhodesian copper mine, Bwana Mkubwa. He managed to interest A. Chester Beatty,[11] an American mining financier based in London, whose holding company, Selection Trust Ltd., provided some funds in 1920.[12] In 1924 Sir Ernest O. Oppenheimer,[13] founder of the Anglo-American Company of South Africa (AA), provided further assistance.[14]

New prospecting soon revealed large deposits of sulfide ore at workable depths just below the topmost layers of oxide ore. Following the discovery in 1911 of a flotation method drastically lowering the cost of processing sulfide ores, the Copperbelt ores became a highly lucrative investment opportunity, and systematic mining began.[15]

The early capital for Rhodesian copper production came primarily as a result of European and South African reaction to the American strangle hold on the world copper market. In 1926, eighteen major American copper producers and ten foreign associates had agreed to limit production and control sales through a new organization, Copper Exporters Inc. (CEI). It fixed the export price of American copper, and acted as a clearing-house for foreign transactions. Between 1927 and 1929, CEI controlled 85% of world copper production, and in 1930–31 it boasted 78% of it. European buyers answered with a strike against the Americans in 1929, and also poured investments into Northern Rhodesian copper properties in the hope of selling directly to the European market without American interference.[16]

Two mining interests were firmly established on the Copperbelt by 1928. Beatty, backed by large infusions of capital from American Metal Company, formed the Rhodesian Selection Trust (RST) as a holding company for multifarious activities in Northern Rhodesia.[17] American Metal sent Arthur D. Storke, one of their senior mining engineers, to watch company interests in London. Throughout the colonial period, American Metal representatives participated in RST board meetings and technical advisors visited the Copperbelt four or five times a year to check on the mines and give technical advice. This was all done with a light touch. "American Metal's policy was to let the RST companies manage themselves," although the Chairman, Harold Hochschild, influenced RST at a number of crucial points.[18]

That same year, AA Company grouped its various interests under a new holding company, with capital of £2,500,000, called Rhodesian Anglo-American Ltd. Finances were arranged in London, while technical, buying, and other services were organized by AA headquarters in Johannesburg.[19] In 1931, the refinancing of the AA holdings brought in new capital and talent through the addition of Rio Tinto headed by Sir Auckland Geddes[20] and the Messrs. Rothschilds. Geddes provided the Company with important connections in the British Government and Washington, and encouraged cooperation between the Rhodesian Selection Trust mines and AA holdings. The Rhodesian AA Company changed its name to Rhokana Corporation Ltd. in 1931, with Geddes as Chairman, Ernest Oppenheimer and Edmund Davis as Deputy Chairmen, and Leslie Pollak and S. S. Taylor as managing directors in South Africa and London, respectively.[21]

The new copper mines were soon divided between the two major investors on the Copperbelt. Beatty's Selection Trust incorporated the Roan Antelope and Mufulira mines in 1927 and 1930 respectively. The AA Company established the Rhokana Corporation in 1931 to manage Nkana mine. In 1937, after a series of difficulties, Anglo-American incorporated the Nchanga Consolidated Copper Mines Ltd., which eventually became the second-largest open pit copper mine in the world.[22]

RHODESIAN COPPER AND THE WORLD MARKET

By the time Northern Rhodesia copper entered the world market in 1931, the Depression had drastically cut overall world demand. Copper accumulated in the producer countries during the slump. Prices dropped precipitously from £112.635s per ton in 1929 to £27.25s per ton in February 1932, and a 4¢ per pound tariff on copper imports effectively closed the American market to foreign production. Both Nchanga and Mufulira closed, and the two remaining mines sharply cut back production.[23]

Because of the low costs of both the sulfide production process and African labor, Rhodesian copper still had a competitive advantage on the world market. The earliest copper from Rhodesia (blister copper) could be landed in Europe for 3.5¢ per pound (£23 per long ton). Comparable copper from America cost 9–10¢ per pound, while South American blister copper could be landed in New York City for 9.96¢ per pound.[24] This gave Rhodesian producers an important competitive edge, which Oppenheimer claimed could even withstand a price war with other copper producers. Indeed, by 1935, copper from Northern Rhodesia could be produced and landed in London for £20 per ton, with further expansion and efficiency promising even lower prices in the future.[25]

Gradually the Depression lifted and the mines began to recover. Mufulira reopened in October 1933, and production facilities expanded at all three major mines. Rhokana began construction on an electrolytic refinery.[26] Total production on the Copperbelt rose from 6,000 long tons in 1929, to 68,000 long tons in 1932. By 1935, the mines were producing 153,790 long tons, or 10% of the free-world production.[27]

But fluctuating prices and erratic demand pushed even the competitively advantaged Northern Rhodesian copper mines into cooperation with other copper producers. In 1935, the Northern Rhodesian companies initiated a scheme to limit production in order to raise prices. They were joined by Rio Tinto, Katanga's Union Minière, Kennecott's Chilean subsidiary, the Braden Copper Company, and three foreign subsidiaries of Anaconda, which collectively established production quotas of 20% and 30% on 1 May 1935 and 1 June 1935. The cartel encouraged "a large output sold at a moderate price, rather than restricted production at a higher price." When copper reached £45 per long ton restrictions would be removed.[28]

As the world moved towards war, the demand for copper rose briskly and prices followed accordingly. By the end of 1936, production lagged behind demand and all restrictions were removed. Except for a brief period from December 1937 to September 1938, Rhodesian production increased dramatically, and by 1938, Rhodesian mines supplied 13.42% of the free-world market,[29] ranking sixth in the Empire for value of mineral production.[30] The cartel remained in operation until 1939, when the British government assumed control of production and distribution. Copper prices were set at £43.50s per long ton, and production expanded rapidly to supply the equipment of war. In 1943 Rhodesian production peaked at 251,000 long tons, or nearly four times the 1932 output. The next few years were plagued by technical difficulties, and demand declined quickly with the end of the war, so that in 1946 only 182,000 long tons of copper were produced. The Copperbelt's share of the free-world market fell to 11.05%, and the mines prepared for the "inevitable" postwar slump.[31]

Much to the surprise of the companies, demand for copper shot up after the war. The 1949 devaluation of the pound raised copper prices overnight by 44%, and the price of copper on the world market doubled between 1945 and 1947, moving from £62 to £131 per long ton. By 1955, copper sold for £352 per long ton on the London Metal Exchange, owing to demand from reconstruction projects designed to rebuild from the ravages of war.[32] Although costs for producing Rhodesian copper had risen to £33.12s.50d per long ton by 1945, the world price sustained the competitiveness of Rhodesian copper.[33] By 1954, production on the Copperbelt reached a record 379,000 long tons, or 16.16% of free-world production. Two new mines, Bancroft and Chibuluma, opened, and Nchanga and Mufulira were enlarged; their production levels soon overtook the two older mines, Roan and Rhokana. By 1960, Northern Rhodesia was the world's second largest producer of copper and in 1964 Zambia entered the world as a leading copper supplier with a yearly output of 633,000 long tons valued at £164,300,000.[34]

PROFITABILITY OF THE MINES

Profitability of mining industries has always been limited by price fluctuations, the wasting nature of the asset, and the high risks. This has led mining investors to demand high returns on investment. The Northern Rhodesian copper mines were no exception to this pattern, but initial investments provided few dividends. For example, Nchanga Consolidated Copper Mines Ltd. closed during the Depression and paid no dividends for thirteen years. Roan Antelope did not declare a dividend until 1935. The copper companies were not free of funded indebtedness until 1938, but by 1936 dividends began to increase. In 1937–38, Rhokana paid a 62½% dividend, and Roan paid dividends of 80% and 20% in the same years.[35] However, most of the profits were reinvested in the mines. Before 1941, the shareholders' total return had been about £17,000,000 after taxes on an investment of £25,000,000, a fact which pressured management to minimize production costs.[36]

Profits soared after WWII. World demand pushed up the price of copper to its peak of £420 per long ton in March of 1956. That year Roan Antelope paid 100% dividends, Mufulira 125%, Nchanga 150%, and Rhokana 200%. The slump in copper prices in 1957 and 1958 reduced profits temporarily,[37] but markets recovered in 1959. By March 1960, copper prices were £250 per long ton. Profits increased accordingly. Nchanga reported an increase of 175% that year, with the effective net dividend rate up 124%.[38] When the new government of Zambia came to power, the mines were well-established and highly profitable enterprises that paid high dividends and owned rich ore reserves.[39] The future of the industry seemed secure. Despite partial nationalization of the industry in 1969, Anglo-American (now Nchanga Consolidated Copper Mines) and RST (now Roan Consolidated Copper Mines) continue to mine copper in cooperation with the state holding company, the Zambia Industrial and Mining Corporation Limited (ZIMCO).[40]

THE COPPER INDUSTRY AND LABOR

Corporate labor policy in the copper industry has always been constrained by the nature of the production process and the position of copper in the global economy. Unlike gold mining, copper cannot be profitably produced by unskilled labor in small mining operations. Rather, it depends on having sufficient accessible high-grade ore, enough capital to develop it, and a reliable skilled labor force capable of mining and producing the copper. Of course, all mining companies strive to minimize costs, especially during periods of global economic contraction, but mining costs can be reduced most efficiently by improving labor skills, and then rationalizing labor through improved technology. This constant need to upgrade the skills of copper miners shaped corporate labor policies of the mining companies. It led to stabilization and expansion of African skills, and eventually to the substitution of some African miners for more expensive European mine labor, all of which had important implications for the development of the Northern Rhodesian working class.[41]

Initially most African labor in the copper mines was unskilled.

Although there were 30,000 workers by 1930, labor arrangements were still fairly simple. African employees lived in compounds which were owned and controlled by the mines. The compound manager supervised all aspects of African labor. Although a small number of skilled miners worked for longer periods, most miners left within a year. Men contracted to work on the ticket system, in which they worked thirty days out of thirty-five or forty. The Africans were organized in gangs of ten to twelve men, with an African supervisor, or boss boy, acting as intermediary between his gang and the immediate European supervisor. Some of the boss boys even had blasting licenses.[42]

In 1941 a new wage structure was created to provide greater inducements to skilled black workers by widening the differentials between the highest and lowest pay categories. Grade A included all workers who had undergone some training, those in highly responsible jobs, and those literate in English. Boss boys holding blasting licenses and first aid certificates, senior clerks, drivers, carpenters, and electric motor drivers were in this category. Grade B was an intermediate group with a certain amount of mechanical skill and knowledge, such as boss boys with blasting licenses, second-grade clerks, second-grade artisans, police corporals, and others. Grade C covered unskilled labor and all black workers not in higher grades.[43]

In response to impending African unionization, in 1948 the companies established a more elaborate system of labor classification which provided for seven groups and a special group for surface employees, and eight groups and a special group for underground employees. Groups 1 and 2 were composed entirely of unskilled laborers, and made up more than half the labor force. Groups 3 and 4 were laborers, and served as promotion groups for less-skilled long-service miners. Group 4 included most African mine police, watchmen, caretakers, and other experienced workers. Groups 5 and 6 were semiskilled, such as carpenters, bricklayers, and other artisans without apprenticeships, while Groups 7 and 8 were the boss boys and mine clerks. In the special group were a few highly trained workers whom management hoped eventually could be promoted to replace expensive European miners.[44]

In 1954, the companies finally forced the European Mineworkers' Union (MWU) to permit African advancement into formerly European-controlled jobs. Those jobs remaining with the MWU were listed as "Schedule A," and those released to Africans were "Schedule B." Intermediate posts were created to bridge the gap between African advancees and the established African grades. Those grades were extended to 13, with 1–3 being unskilled, 4–7 semiskilled, and 8–13 skilled. The companies differentiated between supervisory, staff, and daily-paid miners. Supervisors' main function was "to direct, control, inspect and assist the work of subordinate employees, although they may on occasion carry out manual or semiskilled work." Staff employees' "work mainly involves either the application of some degree of skill in clerical, health, welfare and training departments or calls for special trust in the handling of money or confidential matters or whose work, or the responsibility involved therein, is of a similar general nature to that performed by European staff employees."[45] Despite violent protests by the African union, supervisory and staff employees were pushed into a separate association, the Mines African Staff Association (MASA). Since most advancees fell into these categories, this strategy weakened the union and put many of the most experienced miners in an organization without a strike clause.

Despite friction between MASA and the union, in 1961 the two joined forces to demand a unitary wage scale for black and white miners. The government appointed a Commission, chaired by Sir Ronald Morison, which suggested increasing wages in order to close the gap between African and European wages. Progress in this direction came to a halt in 1964, when the mines were permitted to base their Zambianization plans on a dual-wage scale with separate rates for Africans and Europeans.[46]

THE IMPACT OF THE COPPER INDUSTRY ON THE NORTHERN RHODESIAN POLITICAL ECONOMY

The copper industry was confined to a very small segment of the Northern Rhodesian economy. The highly technical nature of the industry and its export orientation limited the growth of secondary industries. Mining equipment was usually purchased abroad; the skilled European labor force spent much of their large salaries on expensive imported goods; and transportation difficulties and poor land limited economic opportunities outside the line of rail. The secondary industries that did develop catered to the small expatriate communities along the line of rail. Copper dominated the export market, being responsible for 86.5% of the value of all exports between 1945 and 1953 and roughly the same proportion during the Federation years.[47]

This dominance inevitably linked the financial status of the Northern Rhodesian Government with the prosperity of the copper industry. The mines were the largest taxpayers in the country, and when corporate profits fell so did government revenue. In the 1930s the industry even bailed out the government with early income tax payments. This relative dependency increased after WWII when corporate taxes to the government nearly doubled.[48] When the Anglo-American and RST companies moved their headquarters from London to Salisbury in 1951 and 1953 respectively, the government share of revenues rose once again. But this windfall was soon swallowed up by the Federation, as Northern Rhodesia subsidized the rest of the Federation at an average annual rate of £8 million.[49] The British South Africa Company royalty rights also deprived

Northern Rhodesia of much needed income.[50] Nonetheless, what revenue Northern Rhodesia had remained firmly tied to the prosperity of the copper industry.

The dependence upon copper revenues shaped Northern Rhodesian government and Colonial Office policies. While settler complaints spurred the Colonial Office takeover of Northern Rhodesia in 1924,[51] the colonial state was primarily concerned with facilitating primitive accumulation and the transfer of surplus to the metropole. Since the copper industry was far and away the most important source of surplus for the government and for British stockholders, the Northern Rhodesian government was closely attuned to its needs, especially by the late 1930s when the long-term viability of the mines became more apparent. Not surprisingly, most government development projects after 1935 directly assisted the copper industry. Infrastructures relating to copper production and distribution received priority, and government townships were built near the mines to provide services which would attract a European labor force. When settlers, particularly the white mineworkers, opposed corporate policies, the Colonial Office generally supported the corporations. Even policies created to help the Africans, such as the Development Plan of 1947–57, were diverted to serve the needs of the European sector.[52]

Like all states, however, the colonial government in Northern Rhodesia had to mediate between competing fractions of the dominant class. The settlers exerted some pressure through representatives on the Legislative Council, and some of the settlers and many of the missionaries had influential friends in London. Government officials often had little use for settlers, especially the Afrikaners, but they could not entirely ignore them.[53] As a result, the state made certain concessions to the settlers, as in 1928–29, when native reserves were set up to limit African access to land near important markets. A Maize Control Board, established in 1936, kept the maize price artificially high, which protected European farmers from small-scale African competitors. And while both settlers and African farmers suffered during WWII, settler influence increased in 1948 with the achievements of an elected majority in the Legislative Council.[54]

The Northern Rhodesian government tried to placate both the mines and the settlers by providing them with sufficient cheap controllable African labor. To that end, the state limited opportunities to earn cash in the rural sector by creating "native reserves," neglecting transport facilities outside the line of rail, and controlling African access to European markets. Taxation drove men into the wage labor market, where they could obtain cash which was not available in the rural areas. Migration out of the rural areas further eroded the rural economy, and led to an ever-expanding need for participation in wage labor.[55] The state also supported a labor recruiting agency until the Depression created a glut on the labor market. In the wage sector itself, laws regulating labor organization and labor contracts gave Europeans some legal power over African employees. The state also permitted employers to control labor through Northern Rhodesian variants of the South African compound system, and in the early years virtually left the governance of the mine compounds to the copper companies.

Government officials offered limited services to Africans and cited these as proof of colonial benevolence. "A generalized, simple, yet persuasive ideology of imperial governance was fostered,"[56] which, however, ignored the fact that African taxes paid for most programs that directly benefited European employers.[57] Education provided the necessary skills for jobs not reserved for Europeans and health facilities increased worker productivity and reduced the danger of disease for European workers. Even the limited agricultural extension services subsidized labor costs. Although the early stabilization of mine labor gradually moved much of the burden of labor reproduction to the mine townships, the mines still benefited from the rural economy's capacity to absorb the costs of retired and injured workers. The mines also reduced stabilization costs by tying wages and living standards for African miners to rural standards. More generally, the subsistence economy absorbed the mass of Africans not directly involved in wage employment and subsidized the costs of domestic servants, contract employees, and farm labor. This lowered the cost of living, increased the attractiveness of the Copperbelt to Europeans, and allowed the Europeans to claim the towns as their own.[58]

On occasion, however, the colonial state had to oppose the short-term interests of both the mines and settlers in favor of the Africans in order to maintain social control. Some idealistic government officials, who took Colonial Office paternalism seriously, openly criticized European exploitation of the Northern Rhodesians. Officials concerned with "native" education and welfare were especially supportive of services for Africans.[59] In the 1940s, a labor department and African trade unions were established despite protests from the European community and even some government officials. Here, the Colonial Office took an active role. After WWII, the government expanded developmental programs for Africans and sought to co-opt the emerging African petty bourgeouisie.[60] While this behavior no doubt partially reflected a genuine concern for Africans among some Colonial Office personnel, it was largely the result of the colonial state's need to maintain social control over the increasingly conscious and organized groups of Africans thrown up by the penetration of the capitalist mode of production in Northern Rhodesia.

The mines continued as a major force after the creation of the Federation, but the balance of forces changed. The Federation funnelled copper revenues into the expansion of Southern Rhodesian settler capital, reducing the economic and political position of the Northern Rhodesian settlers. The mines further weakened the Northern Rhodesian settler community by launching a campaign to substitute expensive white mineworkers with cheaper African labor. The companies moved their headquarters to Salisbury, and identified mining interests with the welfare of the Federation as a whole. The mines assumed they could neutralize African resistance to federation by improving rural conditions and co-opting the emerging African petty bourgeoisie, both in the mines and other sectors of the economy. The corporations and the Federal government underestimted the degree of hostility to federation, and the capacity of Africans to organize opposition. In the end, the very class of Africans created by the colonial state, especially the mining industry, spearheaded its downfall. The mines had wanted a multi-racial Federation to succeed, but they ultimately adapted to post-colonial Zambia and the vagaries of neo-colonial politics.[61]

CONCLUSION

The development of the copper industry in Northern Rhodesia had important consequences for the country's political economy and its citizens. Those Africans actually employed by the mines were most directly affected by the copper industry. The next chapters will focus on the gradual development, or lack thereof, of new loyalties and actions based on the shared experiences of miners as they worked and lived on the mines in colonial Zambia.

2

Labor Supply and Corporate Strategy, 1926–1936

INTRODUCTION

The profitable operation of the mines required large quantities of capital and labor. We have seen how and why capital became available. This chapter focuses on the manner in which a competitive wage labor market shaped the labor strategies of the mines, altering the South African system of labor mobilization and control in ways which, it is argued in later chapters, had important consequences for the development of black worker consciousness and action on the Copperbelt.

BEFORE THE DEPRESSION

Labor Strategies of South African Mining Capital

Initially, the Copperbelt mining companies, particularly those owned by Anglo-American, considered emulating South African mining capital's system of labor mobilization and control. This system minimized labor costs in various ways by establishing a recruiting monopsony over African labor. "Servile labor measures," such as the closed compound system, pass laws, and legislation against breach of contract, protected South African employers against potential organization and protest by black workers. This system of "exploitation color bars"[1] virtually destroyed opportunities for black workers to bargain with employers over their wages and other benefits.

The compound system was first established in the 1880s in South Africa in order to prevent diamond stealing by black labor. The mine owners enclosed workers in compounds surrounded with barbed wire. All employees were searched before and after work. By 1885, the De-Beers compound was a quasi-military enclosure, surrounded by a corrugated-iron fence ten feet high, with a single large gate as an entrance.

African workers entering the DeBeers compound lost all access to the outside world for the period of their work contract. Wives and children were barred. Management regulated daily life in the compounds to maximize exploitation of the work force. Thus, the compounds minimized costs through economies of scale and uniformly low living standards, and facilitated control over the work force. This system was soon copied by many other South African industries, particularly the gold mines on the Rand, and it became one of the cornerstones of the South African system of labor exploitation.[2]

Labor Supply and Demand

Conditions in central Africa ruled out replicating the South African compound system. As a result, the South African pattern of labor mobilization and control had to be altered to fit specific circumstances on the Copperbelt.

Unlike gold mining, which used largely unskilled labor, copper mining demanded higher proportions of skilled and semiskilled labor. The exact proportions of each varied with the nature of the ore deposits. Roan, for example, needed more skilled and semiskilled labor (hoist drivers and blasting license holders) to work its predominantly flat (scraping) stopes. Mufulira's orebodies (three orebodies superimposed on top of each other) called for extensive use of unskilled lashers, which increased the size of the black unskilled work force. Nkana Central and Mindolo orebodies were more accessible and permitted greater use of unskilled labor.[3]

Skilled white miners could find work in Europe, South Africa, and North America. The poor health record and meager facilities on the Copperbelt thus held little attraction for them. In order to attract sufficient skilled labor, the mines hired experts to eradicate health hazards, built good houses and recreational facilities, and offered high wages. Gradually, the number of European miners increased from a mere 304 in 1926 to 2,934 in January of 1931.[4] Men came from all over the world. "The new white communities . . . were composed of all sorts and conditions of men—Texas drillers, hardbitten Afrikaners, Yugoslav timbermen, fitters and turners from South Africa, smeltersmen from Wales, American construction experts with experience in the copper mines of Arizona or Latin America, Cornishmen and others."[5] Their one common goal was the search for high living standards.

Since white labor was both expensive and scarce, the mines recruited Africans for semiskilled and unskilled work. Large numbers of unskilled laborers were needed for mine construction and many of these were hired by contractors for limited periods. More and more surface and underground miners were brought on in the late 1920s, when construction declined and extraction began in earnest. In 1927 the mines employed about 10,000 African construction workers, but by 1930 there were nearly 30,000 production workers.[6]

Before the Depression the copper companies were hard pressed to obtain sufficient African labor, especially experienced underground black labor, which was in short supply all over southern Africa. As readiness for production approached, both mining companies became increasingly concerned about their labor supply. In 1929, two shafts at Mufulira even closed temporarily because of insufficient personnel.[7] A year later, visiting mining engineer Sydney Ball warned that "this labor supply . . . with certain of the Companies at least, may retard appreciably their attainment of a large copper production."[8] The general manager at Mufulira reported a "grave shortage of boys, particularly for work underground." The situation was so desperate that he advised "any reasonable expenditure on training, better food or better living conditions in the compounds is alright if it helps get labor underground."[9]

Such difficulties were not due to an insufficient labor supply. Northern Rhodesian men had worked in the mines of Katanga, Southern Rhodesia, Tanganyika, and South Africa since the early twentieth century, many travelling south in search of the higher Southern Rhodesian and South African wages.[10] The Southern Rhodesian gold mines recruited labor from the north through the Rhodesian Native Labor Bureau, and the Katanga copper mines obtained Northern Rhodesian labor through the Bourse du Travail du Katanga and Robert Williams and Company. In 1920 and 1921, approximately 9,000 members (or 56.1%) of the Union Minière work force were from Northern Rhodesia. Thousands of Northern Rhodesians voluntarily migrated to Elisabethville as well,[11] and a small but regular number of Northern Rhodesians worked in the Lupa gold fields of Tanganyika.[12]

Northern Rhodesians employed in southern Africa had developed their own networks which conveyed information on labor conditions. News travelled rapidly along the established labor routes, and conditions on the mines of Katanga, Southern Rhodesia, Tanganyika, and Northern Rhodesia were well known. Most Northern Rhodesians understood the relative rewards available to them at various places of employment, and they made decisions based on that knowledge. The general labor shortage of the 1920s in central Africa put skilled workers in a relatively good bargaining position in the labor market.[13] Jobs were plentiful, experienced workers were in short supply, and employment information networks enabled miners to compare the potential rewards for their labor. Northern Rhodesian workers knew they could change jobs easily, and they did. The Africans avoided recruitment, preferring "to find their own way to the Copperbelt and to apply for work under the particular boss or department which appeals to them at the mine they have chosen. . . . [This gives them] a much greater choice of conditions of work." Many workers preferred working for contractors because of "the loose system of control they exercised over labor at work and in the compounds."[14] Even recruited labor could, and did, choose between working in or outside Northern Rhodesia.

Small wonder that when the mines began construction in 1926, Northern Rhodesians did not flock to them. They compared Copperbelt wages, working and living conditions with those of other employers, and many continued to work elsewhere. As late as 1929, 50,000 Northern Rhodesians were still employed outside the country, most of them in Southern Rhodesia. Some went simply because of proximity, but many more were drawn by higher wages.[15] Better working and living conditions also drew Northern Rhodesians to Union Minière, which employed some 10,500 Nothern Rhodesians in 1929. Union Minière's shift to stabilized labor in 1926 had been accompanied by a dramatic upgrading of living conditions for their workers. By the end of the decade African workers in Elisabethville enjoyed the best food and housing in central Africa. As a result, Union Minière recruiters had no difficulty obtaining Northern Rhodesian labor. In fact, many Northern Rhodesians went to Katanga on their own instead of working on the Copperbelt.[16]

Within Northern Rhodesia, Broken Hill and Bwana Mkubwa mines competed with the Copperbelt companies for labor. These proved to be the mines of choice because they allowed workers to bring dependents to the mines and provided housing and rations for them. Broken Hill was especially popular because it offered miners five-acre plots to supplement rations and wages. On the other hand, Copperbelt mines with poor reputations, such as Nkana, had difficulty obtaining sufficient voluntary labor.[17]

Labor Strategies and Labor Supply

The companies adopted a number of strategies, both jointly and separately, to attract labor. Because voluntary labor remained at the mines longer and cost less than recruited labor, the mines preferred to employ voluntary labor as much as possible.[18] In this period, about two-thirds of the companies' labor force came to the mines voluntarily.[19]

The companies joined forces with local European farmers and pressed the Northern Rhodesian government to help them secure more control over the labor supply by placing immediate limitations on foreign recruitment. However, government officials refused to cut off completely this established pattern of worker migration for what they considered the still uncertain future of the copper industry. Katanga continued recruiting until 31 July 1931, although in slowly decreasing numbers. The flow southward into Southern Rhodesia did not diminish until the Depression, and was due then to market factors rather than legislation. Labor policies in Southern Rhodesia, Northern Rhodesia, and Nyasaland were not coordinated until 1936, when an agreement established the priority of each country's labor needs.[20] Thus, despite some efforts to help the mines acquire and control labor, during the 1920s the Northern Rhodesian government did not yet accept the importance of the mining industry to Northern Rhodesia and England, and refused to grant the copper mines exclusive control over Northern Rhodesian labor.

Lack of control over the labor supply aggravated the conflict between competitive self-interest and potentially beneficial cooperation between the Northern Rhodesian copper mines, for the companies had to struggle against each other for labor as well as against foreign competitors. However, interlocking directorates between the two companies and an appreciation of the dangers of unchecked rivalry prevented competition between the mines from getting out of control. Oppenheimer wanted to amalgamate the two Copperbelt companies because he feared that destructive competition would undercut profits. In 1937 Anglo-American suggested "a fusion where both groups have an equal say but where the control is vested . . . in the 'Chartered' company." Negotiations between the companies bogged down over some misunderstandings and the Rhodesian Selection Trust's disinterest. With improved market conditions in 1937, talk of amalgamation ended, and Rhokana reopened Nchanga as a separate company. Unlike the mines in South Africa and Southern Rhodesia, the copper companies did not establish a Chamber of Mines to enforce cooperation between the mines until 1941. Management in London, New York, and Johannesburg kept in touch over larger issues, but daily cooperation between the companies did not occur.[21]

The mines did establish a joint recruiting agency following the failure of voluntary labor and small private recruiting agencies. Rhodesian Selection Trust hired H. H. Field in 1928 to organize a recruiting depot at Fort Jameson (Chipata) in Eastern Province.[22] Anglo-American contracted for recruits with R. W. Yule, who also worked for Union Minière du Haut Katanga. In 1927, only 12% of Roan's labor force was recruited, but as construction expanded, the need for labor rose dramatically, and with it the need for more effective recruiting. By 1928, 44% of Roan's work force was recruited and Roan's general manager called for the formation of a central recruiting bureau. A year later the two groups met with the governor and agreed to create The Native Labor Association. As an interim measure, both mines agreed to employ Yule. This agreement failed to yield much labor, and labor scarcity soon drove the mines to replace Yule with A. Stephenson, former commandant of the Northern Rhodesian police.[23] In its first year, the Association sent 10,000 men to the mines and in 1931, had 27 agents stationed at strategic points throughout the territory.[24] Like its South African counterpart, the Association arranged for recruits to sign work contracts for set periods of employment, and guaranteed transportation to and from the mines. Although this cooperative venture never supplied all mine labor, recruitment did provide much of the skilled black labor, frequently from outside Northern Rhodesia. In the early 1930s, the Association recruited 2,400 trained Southern Rhodesian miners to upgrade the work force and supplied over 2,000 Nyasaland workers to fill clerical jobs. According to Spearpoint, these men dramatically upgraded the efficiency and productivity of the work force.[25]

Still both mines complained about the quality of their laborers. Said L. Eaton of RST, "The native negro is small and unused to hard physical labor." Mechanization seemed the logical answer, for management believed labor could "be taught to handle simple mechanical equipment or routine work. The supply [of labor] is inadequate and recourse must therefore be had to minimizing methods in which the ore is moved by mechanical or gravity means."[26] Elaborate plans were drawn up to increase mechanization in the future.

However, none of these measures succeeded in overcoming competition between the mining companies for voluntary labor. Because of their need to attract voluntary labor and their failure to monopsonize recruitment, the companies had to offer conditions of employment comparable, or nearly comparable, to those at neighboring mines. This competition led to a situation in which the mines "were all looking for recruits and making offers better than the man next door to get the native to engage."[27]

Wages on the Copperbelt rose as each mine tried to outbid the other for labor. For example, at Mufulira, the general manager wrote the head office in 1929 saying that "Mufulira's pay was a little lower and should be put up with other Copperbelt wages."[28] By this time, the average monthly wage of black workers on the Copperbelt was 18s, while many experienced men earned between 20s and 22s 6d. A few underground workers even started as high as 30s. Skilled underground workers who were in great demand did even better, with some drawing wages of 45s or more per month (see Table 1. for detail). By 1930, the average wages at Roan were 21s per month for surface work and 33s for underground work. In 1932, the average wage at Nkana was 25s for surface work and 32s 6d for underground work.[29] These scales enabled the Copperbelt mines to compete with Union Minière for skilled labor, and to outbid them for unskilled labor. Northern Rhodesian wages were still below those at the sisal estates of Tanganyika and the Wankie mines in Southern Rhodesia, which had average monthly wages of 22s 6d and 32s 6d respectively.[30] However, since Katanga was the nearest competitor for Copperbelt labor, the mines concentrated on competing with Union Minière's wages.[31]

Stabilization

Competition for labor forced the mines to deviate from the South African migrant labor system. They had to recognize that skilled and experienced Northern Rhodesian workers were accustomed to living

Table 1. **African Wages at Roan Antelope, 1929**

Job	Range of Daily Wages (note including bonuses)
Recruiting	5d to 1s1d
Watchman	6d to 1s5d
Compound police	6d to 2s1d
Head police	6d to 2s10d
Office boy	2d to 2s10½d
Bricklayer	7d to 2s9d
Bricklayer's laborer	2d to 8½d
Time office clerk	9½d to 2s10½d
Compound clerk	11d to 2s11½d
Engine driver	8d to 1s3½d
Boss boy	8d to 1s4d
Timbering	8d to 1s

Source: Coleman, *The Northern Rhodesian Copperbelt*, pp. 179–80. Note: These specimen figures are from Rhodesian Selection Trust files.

with their families at Katanga and other local mines. And since the companies preferred experienced black labor to costly white labor, they still had to offer accommodations and rations to attract veteran African miners.[32]

The acceptance of a stabilization policy varied with the differing labor needs and managerial traditions of the two Copperbelt companies. Because of the nature of its orebody, the Rhodesian Selection Trust mine, Roan Antelope, required a relatively high proportion of experienced labor.[33] The compound manager reported that "in the early days it was practically impossible to get labor and so when a native offered himself for work, we were only too pleased to take them together with their wives and families."[34] Many Rhodesian Selection Trust managers came from America and Canada with their traditions of company towns, and consequently were more willing to encourage stabilization. David Irwin, an American mining engineer, was the general manager at Roan and Mufulira for the first five years. Another American, R. M. Peterson, was general manager during World War II. The general managers had considerable freedom to set policy.[35] Irwin "set standards which were based on American mining experience. He insisted on a sensible organization, good engineering, and good conditions for Africans. He favored some industrial training for the Africans. . . . Africans were given purgatives and fed well. Malarial eradication programs were started. All this was to attract European labor as well as Africans."[36]

The percentage of married stabilized workers at the Rhodesian Selection Trust mines increased steadily as management discovered that married labor was "more efficient, healthier, more contented, and remains longer than the single native," and that women in the compounds discouraged prostitution, gambling, fights, and general disorder. In 1931

Table 2. **Percentage of Men Accompanied by Wives**

Mine	1932	1933	1934	1935	1936	1937 to 31st May
Luanshya	37.33	43.43	42.91	57.00	65.11	61.70
Mufulira	—	32.00	28.08	38.85	44.90	—
Nkana	18.91	27.24	28.00	27.04	38.87	—
Broken Hill	44.06	46.00	47.72	47.06	54.87	60.87
Union Minièe	64.30	59.90	51.00	50.43	52.52	—

Source: *The Pim Report*, p. 45.

married miners at Roan stayed an average of 20.25 months, or twice as long as single workers and they could be trained to carry out the more complicated tasks of copper production.[37] Management soon recognized the advantages of married labor, and the percentage of married workers rose steadily from 20% in 1927, to 37.3% in 1932, and to 65.11% in 1936. The percentages lagged at Mufulira, partly because that orebody required fewer skilled workers and partly due to the mine closure during the Depression. Still, both mines remained committed to stabilization, and Mufulira eventually reached parity with Roan (see Table 2.) On both mines, the length of employment increased. The average length of service for surface workers at Roan climbed to 18 months, with 64% of the African employees in 1932 having over a year's employment on the mine, and 8.27% having over two years' employment.[38] Labor turnover at Roan fell from 24.09% in 1927 to 7.5% in 1933 (see Table 3.)

Because of the nature of the orebodies at Nkana and Nchanga, Anglo-American mines needed fewer experienced miners. They were

Table 3. **Married Labor and Labor Turnover at Roan**

Year	No. of Employees	% Married	Average Length of Employment (in months)	% Turnover
1927	1,093	20.00	3	24.09
1928	2,005	20.00	5	22.27
1929	2,999	21.00	5	17.16
1930	3,961	22.00	6	16.71
1931	4,729	26.58	6	11.30
1932	2,317	37.33	14	10.45
1933	3,075	43.43	14	7.50
1934	4,621	50.00	16	7.38
1935	4,513	52.24	23.72	3.17

Source: Spearpoint, "African Natives," p. 53.

Table 4. **Average Length of Stay on the Copperbelt, 1932**

	Nkana		Roan Antelope	
Time	*No. of Employees*	*%*	*No. of Employees*	*%*
Under 1 year	1,862	68.28	1,248	67.86
Between 1 and 2 years	782	28.68	439	23.87
Between 2 and 3 years	65	2.38	82	4.46
Between 3 and 4 years	13	0.48	36	1.96
Over 4 years	5	0.18	34	1.85
Total	2,727	100.00	1,839	100.00

Source: Merle Davis, ed., *Modern Industry and the African*, p. 71.

able to maintain production with voluntary migrant labor or unskilled recruits. As Table 4 reveals, Nkana had significantly less long-term labor than Roan. In 1932, only 18.9% of Rhokana's miners were married, and the average length of employment for married men was 12.9 months as opposed to Roan's 20.25 months. Married men, however, did stay longer than single employees, who averaged 8.6 months of employment.[39] This discrepancy between the mines can be partially explained by the differing managerial traditions of the two companies. Rhokana field management was appointed and closely supervised by South African consulting engineers from the Johannesburg office, who were accustomed to the South African migrant labor system.[40]

Economics, not ideology, was the main issue. When necessary, Anglo-American was just as capable of stabilizing workers as the Rhodesian Selection Trust mines. In 1931 the Rhodesian-Anglo-American Company even petitioned the Colonial Office to permit permanent settlement for several thousand skilled laborers from Nyasaland at Rhokana, and advertised good housing, recreation, medical and welfare facilities, as well as social security benefits. The mines were willing to bear the cost of such benefits if they would guarantee sustained improvements in output.[41] Nevertheless, they preferred lower-cost migrant labor, and retracted this offer when the Depression changed the labor market and a sufficient number of experienced miners accepted short-term employment on the mines in order to remain on the Copperbelt. Before the Depression, therefore, Anglo-American never had as much married labor as the Rhodesian Selection Trust mines. And, when the labor market loosened, Anglo-American was able to further reduce its married labor force and to rely on voluntary migrant labor for both unskilled and more skilled work. Managerial ideology could be put aside when economically necessary, but whenever possible, the Anglo-American mines tried to replicate the South African migrant labor system.

The Compound System on the Copperbelt

The dependence upon voluntary labor, particularly married stabilized labor, forced the copper companies to alter the control and facilities of the South African compound system in ways which, it will be argued below, significantly affected the development of class consciousness and action among the miners.

The voluntary nature of the labor force left the mines vulnerable to employee mobility. As Spearpoint complained, "It was difficult to get a native to engage for work, and once he did so it was equally difficult to keep him."[42] Unlike the South African compounds which were designed to regiment a captive labor force, the Copperbelt compound system had to attract and keep labor as well as control it. With this in mind, the companies set up programs which not only drew workers and their dependents to the mines, but also helped acclimatize them to the working environment.

Northern Rhodesian and Colonial Office officials were only too happy to let the mining companies control their compounds. The perilous financial condition of the Protectorate, and reservations about the long-term prosperity of the mines, made the government reluctant to interfere in company affairs. The government had passed laws pushing Africans into wage labor and keeping them there for the duration of their contract. At the same time, the colonial state legitimized its role as protector of the African people by setting minimal standards for the compounds—standards which the mines had little difficulty meeting. Mine Safety Regulations covered work conditions.[43] Ostensibly, officials were supposed to enforce the regulations through regular inspections of the mines and mine compounds, but government enforcement proved difficult. Provincial Administrators made occasional sweeps through the compounds, but these were infrequent and generally in the company of mine officials. When a District Officer visited the compounds he was more "in the position of an honored guest" than an inspector.[44] In 1929, Ndola District had no European officers available for patrol work in the district or township. Sub-stations with District Officers in residence did not open until 1931 at Nkana, Nchanga, Luanshya, and Mufulira. Police were in short supply, and the only Resident Magistrate resided in Ndola.[45] The Provincial Administrators focused on the problems of the local Europeans and rural Africans. Only a few officers believed urban Africans were a long-term problem. Most government officials considered the mines "exemplary employers." When officials criticized the mines, they did so in private and politely.[46]

Because of these inadequacies, government played a largely passive role in regard to industrial labor in this period, and thus gave the mines a free hand to set the parameters for work and living conditions.[47] The Copperbelt mine compounds developed into self-sufficient townships housing black miners and their dependents during their employment.[48] "Responsibility for the housing, drainage, sanitation, health, discipline, and general welfare . . . [was] vested in the compound manager and his organization."[49]

Compounds were controlled by compound managers, who were quite autocratic. The compound manager had "full authority over all employees except when actually at work; he and his staff receive the new entry of recruits, allocate accommodations, supervise the issue of rations, hear complaints, superintend arrangements on payday, devise and repair housing, washing, and sanitary arrangements, maintain order, and generally control the several thousand natives of whom they are in charge."[50] In the 1940s the compound manager disciplined the African labor force. The "changa changa," as the black miners called him, struck fear in the hearts of the miners,[51] and the general managers took every opportunity to buttress his position. Management warned government officials not to undermine the authority of the compound managers. For their part, the compound managers left no doubt to visiting officials as to who was in control. Spearpoint was even known to spy on government officials because of his "great suspicion of the administration."[52]

The compound managers were assisted by European and African compound staff, which varied in size at each mine. Generally at least one European was in charge of each job division in the compounds, such as sanitation, housing, repairs, and food allocation. The European staff was assisted by African manual laborers and a staff of clerks, many of whom had been trained in mission schools in Nyasaland. They were translators for the Europeans (frequently done even when the staff knew African languages) during discussions with Africans, and they screened cases coming into the compound offices, deciding who should hear each case. The work crews carried out the daily maintenance, checking on housing, sanitation, and other compound problems. As the mines expanded, services for workers broadened, and the compound staff grew accordingly. (Growth was particularly swift in the 1950s with the development of mine welfare activities.[53])

Many early compound administrators came from South Africa. This is not surprising since 60% to 70% of the white laborers on the Copperbelt were South African in the early years. They invariably retained white South African racial attitudes. Most of the compound administrators had worked in South African, Southern Rhodesian, or Katangan compounds before coming to Northern Rhodesia, and many had been in the Northern Rhodesian Police, the British South Africa Company Police, or the army. A military background was considered helpful for quelling potential disturbances. The compound staff was not as well paid as those Europeans directly involved in production, and few of them were highly educated. Experience "handling" Africans was the primary qualification for the job. Many compound officials tried to simply adopt the ideas current in South African compound adminstration. At best this resulted in paternalism which likened Africans to children.[54] At worst, it involved an outright contempt and distaste for anything African. The expectations of deference and obedience common in South African compounds however, had to be modified to fit the Northern Rhodesian labor market. After all, the compound manager had to attract and hold scarce labor, and as a rule he gave veteran workers special consideration.[55] Thus, from the beginning of the copper industry, the labor needs of copper production and the scarcity of experienced labor altered the South African pattern of compound management, forcing greater responsiveness to the demands of labor, or at least to the demands of the more experienced sector of the black work force.

Compound administrations varied to some degree with the personality of the compound manager. Cecil Spearpoint at Roan, who had been a manager in Southern Rhodesia before moving north, was admired for his skill in sports. Both Chris Cook (Assistant Compound Manager at Roan) and Spearpoint were said to be "very liberal. They were very good men."[56] In contrast, the first compound manager at Mufulira, Ben Schaefer, was extremely harsh and unpopular. He had been compound manager of the largest Union Minière compound before coming to Mufulira, and was a strict disciplinarian, dismissing workers for wife-beating and other "moral" offences. He was known to "box laborers on the ears" when considered appropriate.[57] H. H. Field, who followed Schaefer as compound manager, was more popular. He was a "quiet and fair man," although his assistant, Twigg, was "easier to talk to."[58] Both Field and Spearpoint distrusted the more skilled black miners and preferred to buttress the role of traditional elders in the compounds. William Scrivener of Rhokana was more aloof and unapproachable. Having worked at Union Minière before coming to the Copperbelt, Scrivener was an expert on "scientific" compound management, and was roundly disliked by the miners. Workers feared him, avoiding him whenever possible.[59] M. Mwendapole remembered Scrivener as "a very rough man . . . a person who drives some fear into the miners."[60] Gabbitas at Nchanga was more accessible and popular. Miners recalled that "Gabbitas is liked all over the Copperbelt, even in Broken Hill. He has the love of the people, he makes no difference between Europeans and Africans. He is not jealous. Is good to his clerks and his servants. . . . Chamber of Mines listens when he speaks, all the football people like him."[61] All four of these men worked at the mines for most of the colonial period, providing important continuity and giving a distinctive flavor to their compound administrations. But, the differences were more of style than substance. On broad policy issues, the compound managers followed the dictates of upper management, which were shaped by production needs and the position of Northern Rhodesian copper in the world market.[62]

Mine officials were directed to create a village-like atmosphere in the compounds in order to attract labor and ease the transition of African workers and their families to the urban industrial world. By 1930, Field even complained that "it almost appeared now that competitive recruiting has been done away with, the mines were going in for a competitive Compound program."[63] Because Roan needed more experienced labor, it was most directly in competition with Union Minière and thus had to meet Union Minière's standards. Between 1926 and 1927, expenditure per worker at Roan increased by 40%, primarily for housing, food, and social services. In 1932, when Union Minière's service cost for each African employee reached a record 22s5d per ticket, Roan spent 16s5d for each of its African employees. Management at Roan and Mufulira also brought in teams of experts to help improve health standards. Anglo-American, in contrast, spent only 11s64d per ticket on services, hired fewer experts, and was less willing to provide more than the bare essentials for its workers.[64]

Housing on the Copperbelt mines reflected different positions in the wage labor market as well. Those mines needing more experienced workers competed directly with each other, particularly Broken Hill and Union Minière. Of course, even the best housing for African miners was far below European standards. Most mine houses were round one-room structures, built of Kimberley brick with dirt floors, a thatched or iron roof, and often lacked even one window. Single men were often housed in barracks called 10–10's, long buildings with ten small rooms back to back. Housing had only the simplest furniture, and no water or electricity. Overcrowding was common, with seven or eight men sleeping in a house designed for four. The Rhodesian Selection Trust mines did the most to provide conditions which would attract labor. In 1930, Mufulira boasted the best housing on the Copperbelt. Roan compensated for lower-quality housing by allowing employees to build fences around their homes, make hen coops, and keep fowl and domestic animals. Married workers liked this because it supplemented the meager rations provided for wives and children.[65] In contrast, Anglo-American housing at Nkana and Nchanga reflected the need for less-skilled workers and the consequent lack of interest in married labor. Nkana compound, which housed 6,000 laborers on 159 acres in 1931, was "utterly unAfrican in its precision and mathematical regularity."[66] The single men lived in barracks, there were no trees, and the general atmosphere was barren and hostile. Nchanga was similarly stark, despite a 1931 program to build some brick houses with kitchen huts in front. Most units still had only room for either a family or a number of single men.[67]

Health care and accident prevention received systematic attention at the mines in this early period. Both companies had to solve the malaria problem to keep both black and white labor productive. In 1928, often

30% of the European miners were laid up with malaria. Irwin brought in a tropical medicine specialist, Dr. Watson, and within a few years the number of malarial cases dropped dramatically.[68] General medical facilities for blacks improved as well, and in 1931, 17 per 1,000 Roan employees died from illness, while Nkana's death rate was 39 per 1,000. Neither of these figures compare with Union Minière's rate of 8.01 per 1,000, nor the Rand's 12 per 1,000, but the Rhodesian Selection Trust mines were clearly trying harder because of their greater need to attract and hold experienced miners. Both companies sought to minimize accident rates, for accidents interfered with productivity and scared off potential employees. Again, Roan had the best safety procedures. All African gang supervisors (boss boys) were trained in first-aid work. Candidates for blasting certificates at Nkana received similar training.[69]

The mines made no efforts to improve compensation payments, probably because this was a less immediate issue for workers than wages and living standards. The Workmen's Compensation Scales set up in 1929 provided a modest sum to relatives in the event of death on the mines, and compound managers set the award for injured miners. Only a court decision could alter this; consequently few workers contested their awards. Compensation was paid in a lump sum, contrasting with Katanga's system of monthly payments throughout life or the period of disability.[70]

Special advantages were awarded married miners in order to attract and keep them on the mines for minimal cost. Roan gave married miners garden plots to supplement their mine rations, and purchased their surplus produce, buying 30 tons of vegetables from employees in 1931.[71] Beer production also supplemented married workers' incomes. Each mine rotated permits for beer brewing in the compounds. Since women did the brewing, only married workers made beer, which became an important source of income.[72] Brewing was usually done near paydays to maximize sales. It was so profitable that illicit production became an important source of additional cash. Spearpoint claimed that "for every 10 permits issued, there were another 10 people illicitly brewing beer." Police and clerks even participated, or at least "looked the other way" for a small fee or some beer. Illegal brewing continued even after the permit system ended in the early 1930s, when all beer was ostensibly produced in government-run halls.[73]

The companies set up welfare facilities in the compounds to keep miners and their dependents busy and, hopefully, content during their period of employment. Once again, Roan's programs aimed to attract and retain adequate numbers of skilled, educated workers. Many of these men wanted to better themselves through educational programs, and to fulfill these needs Roan hired a welfare officer in 1929. The following year a large recreation hall was completed.

In the main hall provision has been made for letter writing, there are tables and benches placed conveniently, and racks for native newspapers are provided. It is also possible to obtain soft drinks, biscuits, writing paper and envelopes, pencils, tobacco and cigarettes. Hot tea is always available. . . . Another item which is popular is a gramophone with a quantity of records.[74]

The gramophone often did not work, and the reading material disappeared, but the hall still provided a center where more educated miners could come to relax, learn, and communicate with one another. Concerts, gramophone recitals, debates, and indoor games were held in the evenings for more educated audiences. Night school offered classes in English, first-aid, and other subjects of interest to those aiming for self-improvement. While the mines offered few programs for women, there were some activities for children. A small school tried to educate a fluctuating pupil population; a playground with swings and other equipment was fenced in during 1930. And for the mass of the work force, the welfare officer organized sports, cinemas, and traditional dancing. The mines built facilities for the popular physical training classes, football, pushball, and other games. Twice-weekly movies frequently had audiences of over 2,000 people, though films were carefully screened to keep "the native from losing his respect for European women." Mufulira had similar programs.[75] Of course, none of these programs compared favorably with the lavish European facilities. Budgetary considerations severely limited welfare facilities on the African compounds. But, within this constraint, management at the Rhodesian Selection Trust mines supported compound welfare programs, both to attract and improve the quality of experienced labor, and to monitor the leisure time of the entire work force.

The lower percentage of experienced stabilized miners at Nkana and Nchanga held down Anglo-American's investment in welfare programs. Because of the higher turnover, management eschewed programs demanding extended participation. Education, Pathfinder Scouts, debating clubs, and other activities were less appealing to short-term employees. Anglo-American management designed welfare activities to control and amuse workers during their leisure hours, not to keep them at the mines. Consequently, welfare concentrated on sports and cinemas. A welfare officer, H. C. Nutter, ran a small children's school at Nchanga, and taught the miners carpentry and other skills which could supplement wages. He also policed conditions and encouraged hygiene. Nonetheless, Nutter was unpopular because of his reputation for taking advantage of miners' wives while their husbands worked. Despite objections by miners, Anglo-American retained Nutter. Clearly his low salary and money-saving activities were more important than his effectiveness as a welfare officer.

Nchanga had the worst facilities on the Copperbelt before it closed down in 1931.[76]

Labor Control on the Mines

Along with the establishment of programs to attract mine labor, management still worried about maintaining the discipline necessary for maximal output. The mines turned to the Northern Rhodesian government for help, which in turn passed labor legislation similar to that already established in South Africa. A Native Registration Ordinance of 1929 forced all Africans working outside the native reserves to carry identification cards, or citupas. The cards helped identify and regulate workers. They recorded a person's work history, and had to be stamped by employers at termination. This enabled employers to punish workers by refusing to sign a citupa, or writing negative comments on it. Workers could thus be "blackballed" for uncooperative behavior. However, citupas were readily forged. In 1935, the provincial administration estimated that at least *half* of the 7000 certificates it issued were duplicates. Provincial administrators were understandably discouraged with the system, although the mines successfully fought a move to repeal the Registration Ordinance.[77]

Other laws attempted to control African labor. The Employment of Natives Ordinance of 1929 made contract-breaking a criminal offense. Contracts were defined loosely, and verbal contracts were accepted as evidence in court. As a result, employers could take unsatisfactory employees to court for breach of contract, and have them punished by fines and even jail.[78] Thus, government regulations provided a legal structure by which employers could threaten and coerce black laborers to fulfill their contracts. Still, as we have seen, the colonial state was unwilling to stop the flow of African labor to neighboring countries.

Discipline on all the mines, therefore, was limited by the employment mobility of miners before the Depression. The mines discovered that when European supervisors were "too persistent, the following day most of [the workers] had deserted and completely vanished."[79] Although the mines prosecuted deserters whenever possible, this was difficult: workers could change identities easily. A man merely reported his citupa missing at the nearest District Office, and received another. He could then take his new citupa to another employer, and be hired. Voluntary labor worked by the ticket, and was free to leave at the completion of each thirty–day period of employment. In the labor shortage, even unskilled miners could find new jobs relatively easily. Those miners with some training were always in demand, and could readily find work at any of the mines.[80]

This state of affairs forced the mining companies to set up a system for enforcing industrial discipline which did not completely alienate the mine work force. Management designed a daily routine to encourage regular work habits among the miners. Each compound was divided into sections, with several mine police assigned to each one. The police circulated throughout their areas twenty-four hours a day, and woke everyone for work. Scrivener reported that at Nkana "a bell is rung in three places in the compound at 4:30 a.m. and the Police boys go round their sections shouting to the people that it is time to get up and go to work. . . . The underground workers must be at the shaft head not later than 6:45."[81] All miners were checked in at work; absentees were counted, and then investigated by the police. The sick were taken to the hospital, and unexcused absences were reported to the compound manager. A system of bonuses rewarded productive work habits. Each week workers with perfect attendance and high productivity received a 1s3d bonus. If a worker wore his boots and coat all week, he received another bonus of 9d per week. Workers who did not perform satisfactorily received no bonus and were sometimes fined. Roan set up a similar system. Both Copperbelt companies used "loafer tickets" as well, whereby each day European supervisors marked the tickets of their American miners. If a supervisor was displeased with a miner's performance for the day, he gave him a loafer ticket, which entitled the miner to rations but no pay.[82]

The entire compound structure was designed to control the daily life of miners and their dependents as well. A high fence surrounded each compound, and carefully guarded gates monitored the flow of persons in and out of the facility. In order to avoid fights among ethnic groups, the seventy or more groups were deliberately scattered throughout the compounds. Housing was allocated by seniority, occupational level, and family size. Only mine employees, their dependents, and temporary registered guests were allowed to live in the compounds. Mine police kept the peace. Food was supplied daily in carefully monitored feeding lines to all the employees and dependents, and only registered inhabitants could use the health facilities. Beer hall hours were strictly regulated to keep the miners from arriving drunk at work. Welfare programs tried to keep the compound inhabitants busy and out of trouble when idle.[83]

Most disciplining in the Northern Rhodesian mine compounds was conducted without recourse to outside institutions, for the mine police were permitted to make "arrests" on the premises. The police also regularly swept through the compounds searching for illicit beer-brewing and unauthorized visitors.[84] As one informant recalled, "If you opened a door, and the police wanted to search your house, they just opened up and barged through. They took you to the compound manager if arrested."[85] Compound managers heard cases, reached a verdict, and inflicted punishment much like a District Officer. Persons committing first offenses or minor infractions were fined, but serious crimes or repeated offenses brought swift dismissal. Small variations occurred. At Mufulira, Ben Schaefer dismissed men who beat their wives, while the same offense at other compounds brought only warnings or fines. The ease with which compound officials dismissed workers also varied with the labor supply and skill of the miner involved. Scrivener dismissed workers more readily because of Nkana's more enviable labor supply.[86]

In order to maintain the loyalty of the mine police, management deliberately separated them from the rest of the work force. They were given higher wages and special uniforms, were housed in separate areas with better facilities. Every effort was made to isolate them from the influence of friends and relatives in order to avoid corruption. Management emphasized the special position of the police as a favored group, a "junior partner" of the compound administration.[87]

Despite these efforts, the mines never fully trusted the police. Compound administrators believed that "it is not a desirable practice to rely on police boys as a medium of contact with the natives in every phase of life."[88] The companies hired other Africans to spy on the miners. These "undercover agents" went to meetings, listened to conversations in the beer halls, and generally observed daily life around the compounds. Anything deemed a threat to management was reported to the authorities.[89]

In 1931, Spearpoint set up tribal representatives in order to bypass the authority of the African mine police and clerks and to facilitate the solution of small problems in the compound. Each ethnic group with over twenty-five people selected its own representative. These officials were directed to "adjust minor difficulties among the Natives . . . and . . . help the compound manager to keep in touch with any grievances."[90] Spearpoint expected them to "overcome the chance of difficulties about police and/or clerks reporting problems." The representatives received better housing, and some extra rations. They "function[ed] as a contact group between White officials and Natives keeping either side informed about the other," and according to Spearpoint, they were a great success.[91] In contrast, Scrivener refused to follow suit at Rhokana, preferring to keep discipline under his direct control.[92] Once again, Rhodesian Selection Trust labor strategies were shaped by the greater need to attract and keep experienced labor. This pattern holds true until the early 1930s, when the Depression drastically altered the labor market in southern Africa.

THE COPPERBELT, 1931–1936

The Copper Industry in the Depression

The onset of a severe depression in 1931 dramatically reduced the price and the demand for copper on the world market. Prices plummeted from £74 per ton in early 1931 to £24 per ton a few months later. Even Northern Rhodesia's position as a low-cost supplier could not ensure sufficient demand, and its producers had to cut back sharply. Rhokana and Roan alone turned out small amounts of copper; Mufulira and Nchanga became virtual ghost towns.[93]

The cutbacks forced a parallel reduction in employment, and the mines shifted suddenly from a shortage to an overabundance of laborers. The number of European employees fell from 3,326 to 964, and African employees declined from 30,000 miners in early 1931 to 11,636 in January 1932. By December 1932, this number had dwindled to a mere 6,677. Large numbers of unemployed workers drifted around the Copperbelt in search of work, and the government reported a floating population of at least 5,000 unemployed moving between Ndola and the mines as late as 1935.[94]

Suddenly the African laborer lost his leverage in the labor market and the balance of power shifted to the mining companies. As employment opportunities dried up throughout Southern Africa, miners clung fiercely to their jobs. Absenteeism and desertion fell to new lows. In 1932, Roan listed only five absentees daily out of a total average work force of 2,317, a rate of 34 absentees per 1,000. This contrasts sharply with 638.2 absentees per 1,000 in 1929 and 377.4 absentees per 1,000 in 1931. Even Anglo-American mines had no trouble keeping workers.[95] At Nkana mine alone, over 20,000 men applied for 6,723 places in 1935; Roan was swamped with job applicants, reporting over 500 men applying for only 150 jobs in 1936. Skilled and semiskilled miners were easier to come by, for they were more accustomed to urban life, and many remained near the Copperbelt after losing their jobs in hopes of finding employment which would enable them to continue living in town. The mines were even able to set up labor pools of potential employees by feeding and housing the unemployed in the compounds.[96]

The two companies quickly exploited this advantage in the labor market. The lessons of earlier competition had been well learned. Led by Rhokana in 1932, the mines agreed to coordinate a cut in African wages. In 1933, surface rates for new employees were reduced from 17s6d per 30 working days to 12s6d per 30 working days, and underground scales were similarly reduced from 30s0d to 22s6d (at Nkana it was 20s6d) per 30 working days. Increments for experience remained the same, but the maximum levels were reduced.[97] The mines reassured themselves that they were only providing a fair wage in a formerly unrealistic and inflated labor market. The wage cuts were declared "reasonable" and became the foundation of a new labor policy.

In order to further reduce the cost of labor, the mines disbanded the Northern Rhodesian recruiting agency and established a purely voluntary work force. This exposed them to periodic shortages of skilled labor. As a result, the mines still required a force of stabilized experienced labor in order to guarantee smooth production. Roan, with its higher component of skilled labor, continued to rely on married workers, while Rhokana reduced its percentage of such workers.[98] By 1935, 57% of Roan's work force of 4,293 men were married, while only 27% of Rhokana's 6,606 miners lived at the mine with their wives.[99] Roan also encouraged longer periods of employment, and in 1935 its turnover rate for black miners was 57.1% as opposed to Nkana's 108.6%.[100] The nature of the orebody at Rhokana allowed management to maintain higher turnover rates, which it did. Rhokana also took advantage of the labor surplus to abandon its plans for permanently settling some workers.[101] However, at both mines some stabilization continued, although at differing rates.

When Mufulira resumed production in 1934, it too established a core of married stabilized workers. J.D. Tallant, the general manager, and Ben Schaefer, the compound manager, were primarily concerned with getting the mine solidly established. Initially, short-term labor needed for construction projects kept the labor turnover rate higher than Nkana's. However, Tallant's belief that a "definite industrialized population" would be necessary in the long run reflected the more positive attitude of the Rhodesian Selection Trust mines toward longer service employees, as well as Mufulira's technical needs. Mufulira's management thus raised the percentage of married miners from 32% in 1933 to 38.9% in 1935, and by the late 1930s, this figure nearly equalled that at Roan.[102]

Having adequate labor supplies, the mines allowed housing conditions to deteriorate. In 1932, only 220 out of a total of 2,325 houses at Roan had more than one room, and most married workers lived in a single overcrowded room with their families. One informant recalled that it was common for children to sleep in little jury-rigged shelters near the house.[103] Unmarried quarters were even more overcrowded, frequently housing four to six men in one small house.[104] Mufulira had the best housing on the Copperbelt, but its quarters were still cramped.[105] Rhokana's three compounds remained the worst on the Copperbelt, the married quarters being "little more than slums."[106] Even Geddes admitted that "the siting of the married quarters quite defeated him."[107] At the Kitwe compound, overcrowding and lack of privacy were endemic. The new Mindolo compound had separate houses in better condition, but the compound was small and congested.[108] Visitors to the Rhokana compounds were struck by "the more rigid and mechanical atmosphere and less of the personal touch than exists at Roan."[109] After their tour of the compounds in 1935, the Russell Commission (set up to investigate the 1935 strike) declared their "general impression . . . was a lack of shade in the compound and that the huts might be described as austere quarters rather than houses."[110]

Little effort was made to improve the welfare programs at the mines, for the labor supply no longer hinged on such benefits. Nutter continued running his little school, teaching carpentry and generally seeing "to the repairs in the compounds."[111] Both mines maintained small welfare halls, but attendance was low. Roan reported a daily attendance at their welfare hall of less than 10 in 1932. Only the dry canteen was well used.[112] The compound managers had no incentive to improve recreation programs, and dismissed the need for change. They concluded that "you are up against the native apathy towards anything that is done for his recreation. . . . It is solely for the amusement of the Bwanas."[113] Now that labor was abundant, the companies relaxed their programs.

Mining accidents increased in this period, despite government inspections of the mines. With the labor glut, the mines no longer feared loss of labor from increased accident rates. The fatal accident rate rose from 1.33 per 1,000 in 1932 to 3.93 per 1,000 in 1933, back to 1.84 per 1,000 (this due to some efforts at reform after a strike) in 1935. Serious personal injuries also rose, reaching a peak of 13.67 per 1,000 in 1933. Most accidents were underground, and some increase can be explained by initial production problems. However, the companies admitted that more precautions could be taken. Nkana was the worst offender. In 1933, one of Rhokana's directors admitted that Nkana was shamefully behind Roan. He maintained that of the fifteen deaths in the last five months of 1933, ten "should and could" have been prevented by the European staff.[114] Despite such chastisement, no serious efforts were made at reform.

Only those facilities directly affecting productivity, such as rations and health care, remained the same. Rations continued at their pre-Depression levels, and sickness rates improved at both mines, with Roan once again in the lead. African sickness and death rates still outstripped those of the local European community, but the mines made concerted, although rarely equal, efforts to protect both communities. As in earlier years, death rates were highest among miner dependents, especially the children. Crowding encouraged epidemics which swept periodically through the compounds, leaving death and disruption in their wake.[115] Fear of contamination in the European community undoubtedly spurred on company efforts at improvement, but health care for Africans focused particularly on the miners, whose health directly affected production.

In order to maintain productivity in a period of lower rewards for labor, the mines tightened their discipline system. Assaults and beatings increased as miner mobility decreased. The compound manager at Mufulira regularly "boxed employees' ears" as a mild form of punishment. This was not done as frequently at the other mines, but assaults by Europeans on African workers were still tolerated by management, bringing mild rebukes "except in exceptionally brutal cases."[116] Dismissal became a potent weapon much feared by the miners. Management could count upon large numbers of recruits eager to replace dismissed workers. The threat of dismissals kept miners efficient and disciplined. This was especially true for those with families who preferred to stay on the Copperbelt. African miners were well aware of the difficulty of being rehired at other mines after a dismissal for bad conduct. Desertion rates fell rapidly in response to the tight labor market. Scrivener even conceded to the Russell Commission that the policy of dismissal would not maintain discipline if a labor shortage developed, but as long as the labor surplus continued, it was quite effective. The compound manager at Roan also told the Commission that "we find the threat of dismissal and the bonus system fulfills our needs."[117]

Conditions did not deteriorate as much at the Rhodesian Selection Trust because of its dependence upon stabilized labor. Roan, for example, continued to supplement married workers' incomes with garden plots, and maintained facilities for women and children in order to attract and hold experienced miners. Both F. Ayer and C. Spearpoint were cited for "genuine interest in the native."[118] In 1933, Reverend R. J. B. Moore found the general atmosphere at Roan "much better than anywhere else we went. There is a genuine interest in the welfare of the native at least on the part of management."[119] The Roan administration was also more open to innovations. Its general manager even told the Chief Secretary in Livingstone in 1934 that "should you in your travels see any good native movements or schemes which would assist in building up the health and efficiency and contentment of our native organization and native families, I shall appreciate it ever so much if you would drop us a line."[120]

The Colonial State in the Depression

The Northern Rhodesian government willingly acceded to these changes, partly because the Depression severely reduced revenues. In fact, the year 1932–33 left the government £177,041 in debt, and government officials saw little to gain by focusing state policy on the precarious future of the mining companies. The colonial state, after all, was concerned with maximizing the transfer of surplus to the metropole. The way to achieve that in the Depression seemed clear: limit spending on Africans and settlers in Northern Rhodesia and continue to push African laborers into the migrant labor systems to the south. To that end, Governor Sir Ronald Storrs (1932–34) continued colonial taxation and labor legislation, but disbanded his predecessor's projects, particularly those for Africans, fired several department heads, pulled down all the wireless stations throughout the country, and stopped all construction projects. He reduced the provincial administration from 110 in 1932 to 90 persons in 1935, and the number of provinces from nine to five in 1935. Technical, medical, and educational personnel were sharply curtailed as well.[121]

The next governor, Sir Huburt Young (1934–38), followed Storr's policies. Formerly Governor of Nyasaland, Young was an ardent exponent of indirect rule, and like so many colonial officials of the time, believed Africans should remain tied to the land and their traditional cultures as long as they also participated in the migrant labor system. He supported the extension of the powers of rural chiefs and their councils established in 1930. This policy was predicated on the assumption that migrant workers would maintain their traditional loyalties, and return home after employment. Even after the financial recovery of the mines, Young envisioned them as precarious, citing the wasting character of the copper ores and the uncertain future of the base metal market.[122]

This attitude, together with the inadequate financial and manpower position of the provincial administration, led to a poorly defined, ad hoc government policy on the Copperbelt. The much reduced provincial staff improvised policy as problems came along, their efforts shaped by the need to minimize expenditures and maximize revenues. Provincial administrators made regular sweeps through the compounds to collect taxes, but as far as possible left the daily business of running the compounds to the mines.[123] They had neither the resources nor the personnel to intervene in the mine compounds. Even those officials interested in the mines were "so occupied with water-borne sewage versus types of huts, etc., and court work that they have had no time to give to the native."[124] Since the mines had not yet become the primary source of government revenue, they did not appear to warrant much government support. Before and during the Depression, conditions in the mine compounds outshone those in the compounds of smaller employers, encouraging government officials to rely on the mines to provide adequate living standards for their employees. While some government officials were critical, most government reports reflected this trust.[125] For the most part, the mines had a free hand in their compounds.

When problems with the Northern Rhodesian administration did occur, the mines generally tried to resolve them through influential connections in London. Both companies had offices in London, where they maintained regular contact with the Colonial Office and high-level government officials. A number of factors led to "a certain lack of mutual comprehension in the relations between the industry and the Administration," and "a perceptible air of suspicion in the transaction of business."[126] A few government officials, notably Charles Dundas and some Copperbelt officials, found their inability to improve mine compound conditions frustrating, and openly criticized the mines for exploiting black labor.[127] On the other hand, management resented the vacillating policies of Northern Rhodesian officials,[128] the continued belief that Northern Rhodesia was basically a migrant labor pool for the south, and the growing influence of the settlers, particularly the white mineworkers. The companies worried that the white miners might eventually demand a union, and the establishment of a color bar which "would so put up the cost of production that the mines would have to close down."[129] In order to counter any pressures which might threaten their labor strategy, both companies used their influence in London and their crucial role in Northern Rhodesian finances to buttress their position.

This approach worked for the most part during this period. In the early 1930s, the government was too short of money and manpower to significantly threaten the companies. But as the mines began to recover in 1934, the government increasingly came to depend upon the copper industry for revenue. The Colonial Office favored financial self-sufficiency for British colonies, and so also had a stake in the industry's success. Numerous stockholders in Britain used their influence to support the industry. As the mines recovered financially, the colonial state became more supportive. Even when a large and violent strike by the black copper miners in 1935 raised the specter of the "black peril" among settlers and government officials, no serious change in policy occurred. The strike further galvanized settler and government opinion in Northern Rhodesia against permanent urban residence for Africans. However, except for an increase in the police force and official statements against increased stabilization, the government left the companies' labor policies unchanged.[130]

The colonial government did occasionally oppose the mining companies in order to maintain social order. In the early 1930s, for example, the state established public beer halls in the urban areas. Government control over beer production and sales was motivated more by a desire indirectly to "tax" Africans for their own welfare programs than by any concern to provide better services for urban Africans, although government rhetoric would not admit such a thing. The settlers' fear of uncontrolled drinking in the urban areas may have also contributed to the goverment's desire to monitor African drinking. Initially the mines opposed this plan, preferring to maintain beer production as an income supplement for married workers. However, when the government promised to limit drinking hours so as not to undermine industrial efficiency and offered to subsidize some of the mines' welfare programs with the profits, the companies agreed to the change. Government beer halls were established in Luanshya in 1932, and in Nkana in 1934. Mufulira continued on the permit system until later, but only because the government had not yet been able to set up a hall. Mine management soon discovered the beer halls neither increased drunkenness nor undermined discipline, and they came to depend on beer hall profit subsidies for their compound programs.[131]

CONCLUSION

The labor strategy of the Northern Rhodesian copper mines before and during the Depression was significantly affected by production needs and government policy. Unlike mining capital on the Rand, the Copperbelt mines could not convince the Northern Rhodesian government to help monopsonize their labor supply. Market factors, and the options available to black workers, modified both the structure of the work force and capital's control over labor. The mining companies had to devise strategies which would attract and keep adequate supplies of stable and efficient labor. With the sudden onset of a massive labor surplus during the Depression, the mines reduced the returns for labor and tightened discipline without losing labor. However, the companies' decision to abandon recruiting, and the need for some experienced reliable black labor, necessitated some stabilization on the Copperbelt, particularly at Roan. The decision to stabilize a section of the black work force and to modify the compound system had important consequences for the development of worker attitudes and behavior, consequences which will be investigated in the following chapters.

3

The Politicization
of Black Labor:
The 1935 Strike

INTRODUCTION

In 1935 a massive strike among the black mineworkers on the Copperbelt revealed both widespread grievances against the companies and a willingness to protest labor conditions through collective action. The question arises whether this behavior proves a growing consciousness of class and commitment to class action among the mineworkers. Most studies of the period reject this possibility, dismissing the strike as "riots."[1] An important recent contribution by Charles Perrings, for example, concludes that the structural migrancy of the mine work force limited the consciousness and action of the copper miners in 1935. Reacting against Phimister and van Onselen's preoccupation with the work place as the source of African worker consciousness, Perrings stresses the need to understand the limitations placed on consciousness by dependence upon two different modes of production. He explains Bemba militance in the strike as a reaction to constricting economic opportunities outside the mines, and the greater determination of the Roan strikers as a response to frustrations over recent reductions in the work force.[2] Perrings' call to assess the consciousness of migrant workers within the totality of their social existence is well taken. It appears, however, that he ignores a number of important variables affecting worker attitudes and behavior, such as the impact of the compounds and the production process, the skill structure of the work force, the experience of collective action, and government policy. He thus underestimates the consciousness and organizational capacity of the 1935 strikers. The daily experiences at work and in the compounds led to a rapid understanding among the miners of both their common interests and their exploitation by management; despite plans to return to the rural areas, the stabilization policy of the mines created a group of workers who increasingly understood that collective labor action was their most effective weapon in the struggle against capital. The conjuncture of particular historic forces in 1935 enabled these miners to translate this understanding into strike action on the Copperbelt.

THE 1935 STRIKE

Before 1935, both Rhodesian Selection Trust and Anglo-American management believed their black employees accepted, and even liked, working and living conditions in the copper mines. Citing plentiful supplies of voluntary labor, as well as low absentee and desertion rates, management complacently assumed their employees were "perfectly happy." The compound managers congratulated themselves on their contented and peaceful compounds. Schaefer described Mufulira compound as "one of the happiest compounds I've ever had."[3] Even the lowering of wages and living conditions after 1932 failed to worry management. Indeed, Roan's general manager, F. Ayer, insisted that "our wages and bonuses and the things we have done—[are] more than we need to do for [the black miners]."[4]

This complacency was rudely shaken in May 1935, when a massive strike broke out, engulfing one mine after another. Events started at Mufulira on Tuesday May 21st, when the compound clerks, led by Mateyo, spread the word of a tax increase and called for a strike. The Mufulira clerks sent letters to the compound clerks at Nkana and Roan, urging them to join the work stoppage. Mufulira leaders were predominantly clerks and a few mine policemen.[5] Strike leaders held many small meetings throughout the compound urging people not to work. A number belonged to Mbeni and used the Mbeni association to help organize the strike. Fred Kabombo, a Watch Tower leader, urged support by his coreligionists.[6] The response was dramatic. By Wednesday, 600 of the 3,000 miners at Mufulira refused to work, and by that evening, all work had stopped. In an effort to end the shutdown, District Officer John Moffat met with the strikers that afternoon to hear their complaints, and later that night arrested eight of the most outspoken strikers at the meeting. The arrests, along with Moffat's promise of a government investigation into work complaints, convinced the strikers to return to work, and by Thursday afternoon, the 23rd of May, production resumed on the mine.[7]

Meanwhile, the news of the strike had reached Nkana by letter and in person. Stories of victory of Mufulira encouraged the Nkana clerks to start their own strike, and by the 24th, posters calling for a strike blanketed the compounds. Written in Chibemba, which was fast becoming the lingua franca of the Copperbelt, the posters demanded a wage increase and threatened violence to those who refused to strike on Monday May 27th.[8] The compound clerks, particularly Herbert Kamanga, a Nyasa, and Isaac Ngumbo, who had been in the 1927 Shamva strike in Southern

Rhodesia, were key organizers. At Mindolo, most of the leaders were capitaō.[9]

The clerks and other "big people" (mostly experienced workers) held meetings on Saturday. One witness reported a meeting, primarily of mine clerks, held at a nearby stream, and other meetings with larger crowds were held in the compound. As at Mufulira, the leaders used whatever organizations they could to muster support. There were many informal meetings in the compound, and though little is known of them, one witness claimed two leaders on Saturday were preaching violence. Several Watch Tower members were important strike organizers. Mr. Wright, a capitaō and Watch Tower member, preached strike support at meetings of Watch Tower followers. The Mbeni did not figure as prominently as at Mufulira, but the Mbeni organization still assisted the strike.

On Sunday the 26th, four Bemba speakers organized a large meeting. The leaders, several of whom belonged to Watch Tower, addressed the crowd "trying to get people to state definitely that they would start the strike. They also suggested that those who refused to start the strike should be beaten and assaulted."[10] The meeting agreed to strike, and before sunset the crowd marched to the road, and forcibly removed two hundred workers from the concentrator. "Hostility was directed against anyone who wished to work. It was not a personal matter."[11] Despite the arrests of seventy-five ringleaders, on Monday night strikers again blocked the roads to the mine and leafletted the compound. Several lorry loads of scabs broke through the miners' pickets, but production was effectively stopped. However, the arrival of troops from Lusaka to patrol the compound frightened the strikers and the night shift turned out in the normal manner. A few miners tried to keep the strike alive, but with the arrival of the British South Africa Police on May 31st, opposition soon evaporated.[12]

The Roan miners struck after both the Nkana and Mufulira strikes were over. Roan had been relatively peaceful, but visitors from Nkana and Mufulira kept people informed and conceivably urged similar strike action at Roan.[13] On the 28th, a Rhokana worker was seen distributing leaflets demanding a strike. That evening, a large group of workers (Spearpoint claims they were largely Bemba although he was not there) met in the football field to arrange a strike the next day.[14] Notices appeared in the compound claiming that "Nobody must go to work. . . . We shall die. They will kill us."[15]

As at the other mines, strike leaders used every weapon available to organize the strike. They called on ethnic groups, Mbeni, and Watch Tower to mobilize support. Informal meetings throughout the compound enlisted support for the strike, and by the next morning, all but a few miners had joined. Some of the more ardent strikers forcibly kept potential strike breakers from going underground. Several mine police were assaulted; eighty African Northern Rhodesian police soon arrived, and without provocation began to attack both strikers and bystanders. European officials barely restored order as tempers flared on both sides, and with tempers at fever pitch, representatives from both sides agreed to meet on the football field. The shouting and chaos were too much for the officials, and they dismissed the meeting. This angered the strikers, who had expected to reach an agreement which they could then discuss at the Boma (the building housing local government officials). Instead the police drove the strikers to the compound office and then ordered them back to work with ominous threats. Enraged, the strikers began to throw stones, sticks, bottles, and any available sharp objects. In the pandemonium, the police and their white supervisors lost control and opened fire, first above the heads of the strikers, and then into the crowd. Six men were killed and twenty-two wounded.[16] The strikers temporarily withdrew; shortly afterwards, two platoons of Northern Rhodesian Regiment troops arrived from Nkana. For two hours, the strikers, police and troops exchanged insults and threats. The strikers protested loudly about taxes, bad food, low wages, and police brutality. They complained to a government official that "they were trying to talk with the Government, and the Government had killed them like cattle."[17] The crowd finally dispersed when the soldiers fired over their heads. That afternoon, several district officers met with the strikers on the soccer field to discuss grievances. The workers reiterated earlier complaints, particularly the need for higher wages. Since the government wanted more money, they "must tell the mines to give us more money."[18] Emotions ran high, but there were no threats or violence. Keith (DC, Luanshya) mollified the crowd with promises of an investigation, and by late Thursday, most workers had returned to work and the strike was over.[19]

THE STRIKE: A BEMBA RIOT OR EARLY WORKER PROTEST?

Most studies of the strike have accepted the Russell Commission's conclusion that it was basically a spontaneous reaction to a tax increase and was dominated by Bemba-speaking miners. Elena Berger even calls the strikes "the 1935 riots." Both Henderson and Perrings see the strike as an attempt by workers to resist deteriorating living standards. They see the strike as a spontaneous upheaval, "the protest of the desperate," led by that "most coherent and troublesome group in the Copperbelt labor force," the Bemba-speaking peoples. While Henderson accepts the role of the Bemba without question, Perrings further explains Bemba militancy as a response to the Congo border closure, a move which increased Bemba vulnerability to job insecurity and the rising cost of living.[20]

On closer examination of the evidence, the argument for Bemba dominance in the 1935 strike is not convincing. Most accusations against the Bemba came from mine authorities, government officials, or from evidence given by Nyasa and other non-Bemba to the Commission. A careful reading of the strike commission's evidence reveals that many witnesses referred to Bemba speakers, rather than to the Bemba themselves. For example, the so-called Bemba meeting at Luanshya was led by two Bemba speakers, but of the twenty-one leaders arrested at Roan, only four were Bemba. Only 1,500 to 1,600 Bemba miners worked at Roan, out of a total of 4,370.[21] By 1935, many non-Bemba spoke the language. According to Musumbulwa, most Africans could speak "town-Bemba" within a year on the Copperbelt. It is not surprising then, that Mateyo, although a Nyasa, addressed the miners at Mufulira in CiBemba.[22] At strike meetings, whether addressed in Bemba or any other language, appeals were aimed at all workers, not at a particular ethnic group. This was especially true at the large meetings held on the football fields. The leaders asked all workers to join the strike, and animosity was aimed at non-strikers, rather than any particular ethnic group.[23] The Bemba, because of their numbers, and undoubtedly because of their economic insecurities, played an important role in the strike, but to see the strike as a Bemba affair is to agree with District Officer J.S. Moffat, who carried his stereotype of the fierce Bemba into an urban context, developing a new caricature of "the wholly industrialized Wemba . . . a most unpleasant person indeed."[24]

In the first place granting the Bemba a less pivotal role in the strike, can one legitimately claim that the strike was anything more than a spontaneous outburst or riot? Certainly one cannot equate the 1935 strike with the better organized strikes of the 1940s and 1950s. The lack of formal worker organizations limited the chance for long-term gains by the strikers. On the surface, then, the 1935 strike resembled a riot. However, on closer examination, both the attitudes and the behavior of the strikers cannot be explained simply as "the protest of the desperate." Rather, the strike suggests that deeper changes were occurring on the mines, changes which signalled growing worker consciousness among black miners on the Copperbelt.

In the first place, the organization of the strike was more deliberate and complicated than one would expect in a riot. Such organization cannot be explained as a momentary upheaval, a simple spontaneous reaction to a tax increase. The strike leaders used letters, posters, various compound organizations and both large and small meetings to organize the strike. The strike leaders at all the mines unanimously called for worker unity, insisting that all miners stop work until mines increased wages. They turned a deaf ear to all who tried to stop them, including tribal elders. Indeed, at Luanshya the elders took refuge in the compound office with management. Except for the momentary violence at Roan, the strike leaders asked for and mostly obtained a unified response from workers. The strikers intimidated potential strike breakers with threats, but little direct violence. Neither Europeans nor European property was damaged; government and company officials circulated among the miners without fear.[25] As one close observer put it, "The strike was reasonably well organized."[26] It was too well organized to be described as a riot.

The grievances expressed both during and after the strike revealed a developing consensus about the miners' common position in an exploitative set of production relations. Although the tax raise was the proximate cause of the strike, there were deep-seated issues which had caused collective grievances. One miner told the Commission that a strike would have occurred "even if the tax had not been increased, because the hearts of the people were not right."[27] Numerous witnesses before the Commission likewise alluded to general discontent among the workers. One informant recalled "constant complaints among the workers about conditions, especially among the educated people."[28] This is understandable because most of the more educated miners had been in the employ of the mines long enough to observe the disintegration of living and working conditions during and after the Depression. However, whether long- or short-term employees, all miners demanded better treatment. As Sylvester Nkoma recalled, "All the people at that time had a lot of complaints about conditions of employment, about poor wages, about poor housing, and things."[29] When the Bemba paramount chief arrived to talk to the miners, he was told that "we are suffering and we know what we want."[30]

The miners universally condemned both their wages and the system of compensation for accidents and death. Witnesses complained (to the strike commission) that compensation money never reached the relatives of deceased miners. They rejected the award of one year's pay for the loss of a limb, and asked that miners with partial injuries be given some kind of surface employment rather than being dismissed.[31] Long-felt grievances about wage reductions erupted into demands for a wage increase. Isaac Munkhata testified that Roan workers protested that "their wages which had been cut have not been given back to them."[32] Complaints were also lodged against the system of deductions and bonuses, which aggravated and confused miners, particularly as they differed from mine to mine. As Mufulira miners told the Commission, "if we received more money we would not complain about the tax at all . . . our main complaint is money. The people made the noise about the tax because they wanted more pay from the Europeans."[33]

Strikers at every mine also protested inadequate food rations. Even a witness favoring the companies, Lubita Mukubesa, admitted that at Nkana "people do complain about the rations and say they are very small." Bemba Paramount Chitimukulu, in his tour of the mines after the strike, discovered that inadequate rations was a major grievance. Mufulira miners complained about meat supplies, and one witness claimed that "I get more food in the gaol than I get at the mines."[34] Married miners were the most vocal. One witness testified that his family always ran out of food on the weekends, and another reported having to buy food daily for his wife and children.[35] These purchases drained the mineworkers' small incomes. The steady stream of visitors into the compounds only aggravated matters, creating even greater strain on the miners' limited resources.

Compound conditions were roundly criticized as well. The strikers complained about the small houses and general overcrowding. Mukubesa told the Commission that "the houses [at Nkana] are too small, and sometimes there are four or five people in the hut," which brought on sickness. Kambafwile at Mufulira also testified that the houses were too small, noting that workers often had to sleep outside in little shelters. In the Roan single quarters, according to Julius Chattah, "you will find that four, five, or six laborers live in one hut." Miners disliked sleeping in the same house with their children and the badly built latrines which accommodated both men and women under one roof—both contrary to custom. They accused the beer halls of overcharging, selling bad beer, and being poorly run.[36]

Many strikers complained bitterly about assaults and verbal abuse from Europeans. Chola Linyama recalled a lot of Africans "getting knocked on the job" at that time. Witnesses to the strike commission protested the frequent assaults, particularly at Mufulira. Babu Time, a Nyasa at Nkana, testified that "if I make a mistake the European looking after me can make trouble and beat me." Even the Roan medical doctor, Charles Fisher, testified that he had seen four or five miners who had been struck by Europeans.[37]

The strikers unanimously assailed the African mine police for their brutality. The Mufulira mine police were accused of mistreating workers as well as lying to compound officials. A witness claimed that "if you obey the mine police, then you are all right. But if you find it is not good to do what they tell you, then you are in trouble. . . . If you swear at them [the mine police] they take you to the Compound Manager and your work is finished. . . . This happens very often—every day." During the strike mine police were widely suspected of being "company men." The head policeman at Nkana discovered after the strike that people would not tell him the causes of the strike "because they think I will go and tell the Bwana."[38]

In summary, the evidence suggests that by 1935 most miners had developed some awareness of their common interests as a group, and an understanding of their position within the copper industry. The grievances expressed during and after the strike reveal a growing sense of exploitation. But this consciousness remained expressed and understood primarily in racial terms, for the dramatic difference between the living standards and authority positions of European and African mineworkers undermined potential identification among miners across racial lines. The strikers complained bitterly about the abusive language and behavior of the white miners.[39] However, the strikers did direct their complaints toward management, and opposed collaboration between management and the African mine police, showing some recognition that the opposition between management and workers transcended racial barriers. Thus while the evidence in no way suggests a well-articulated class consciousness, it does indicate some awareness of both worker identity and the conflict of interests between management and themselves among the black miners.

SOURCES OF WORKER CONSCIOUSNESS

How can we explain the development of these new attitudes among the miners, despite the fact that most mineworkers were migrant laborers? Certainly many factors impeded the development of worker consciousness. The constant flow of laborers in and out of the compounds, as well as the diversity of ethnic backgrounds among the miners, had an unsettling effect. It encouraged workers to stick with their own kind, rather than identify with their class as a whole. Dependence on the rural economies, moreover, kept short-term workers preoccupied with their rural ties: new employees generally looked for relatives when they first came to the mines. Language and cultural similarities drew those of common backgrounds together in the compounds, creating social ties along ethnic lines. One informant recalled that "the Bemba-speaking people stuck together" in the early years, as did the Lunda and the Nyasa. Certainly much of the daily socializing in the mine compounds centered around ethnic, or at least linguistic, groupings.[40]

Other factors encouraged in both short-term and longer-term mine employees the development of a common sense of identity. The compounds were organized around the concepts of industrial time and work discipline, which all miners had to adhere to. Miners were rewarded for successfully adopting these principles, rather than for their allegiance to traditional values. In fact, ethnic identity and status had little impact on one's position in the mines, both in employment and living conditions. In a subtle but unremitting manner, the process of living and working in the mines forced all black miners to adopt some similar values, at least for the duration of their employment. The internalization of these values generally increased with the degree of stabilization of the workers. Those workers with the greatest dependence upon wage labor and the longest experience in industrial production were the most apt to adopt such values.

Experiences in the work place often emphasized similarities among the black mineworkers. First of all, many black miners were manual laborers, and so did similar work. In the 1920s management rotated these workers from gang to gang, which reinforced their common status. Miners met one another as they waited at the shaft or worked together in the mines. Several informants recalled friendships based on such experiences.[41] The dangers of mining also enforced cooperation among underground miners. The democracy of fear forged bonds of trust which often transcended ethnic and occupational labels, and sometimes even racial divisions. As one informant remembered, "Underground we were all miners together. When danger came, we would help each other like brothers."[42] Thus, the daily experiences in the mine exposed the similarities among the black mineworkers, and indeed all copper miners, and encouraged the growth of class identity.

The structure of the mine compounds also facilitated worker identification. Houses were small, crowded, and crammed closely together. Little privacy existed. Workers were in constant touch with one another in their neighborhoods. "They had to learn about meeting each other, because you remember in the early days each tribe only heard the stories told by their own people. When they came to the Copperbelt they had to meet many new people and hear how they live and so on."[43] The daily activities of the women and children also centered around their neighborhoods. The women met each other on the food lines, in the welfare classes, and at the beer halls as well. Children played together at the welfare centers and playgrounds; men worked and played with those on their shift; everyone met at the cinemas, sports events, and other recreational activities. People came to recognize each other, especially those from the same neighborhood or on the same shift. The miners and their dependents got to know each other in the daily round of life's activities.[44] This constant interaction facilitated the perception of common interests, and encouraged identification among the workers and their dependents.

The pressure to cooperate forced miners and their dependents to overcome many of the language and cultural barriers between the different ethnic groups. Initially, language problems interfered with communication in the compounds, but ingenious solutions were soon found. In the earliest years, each ethnic group informally appointed "interpreters," usually more senior mine employees, who had been on the mines for a while and knew several languages. Some workers used Fanagalo, or Chilapalapa as it was known in Northern Rhodesia. This patois of Zulu and English evolved in South Africa and had become the language of the mines in Southern Africa. Many South African whites knew Chilapalapa, so it was convenient to use in the work place. However, it was created to facilitate European dominance, and was consequently disliked by most Africans. Instead, a form of Bemba known as "town-Bemba" evolved as the common language of the Copperbelt, being used for work, at home, socially, for education, and for public speaking.[45]

Traditional dancing groups on weekends also helped break down barriers between the different ethnic groups in the compounds. Management encouraged these performances, for they appeared to be harmless amusements. The dances were not designed as cross-cultural learning experiences, but they became as much for the workers. On Sundays, each ethnic group would get together to dance in the area designated for it. Spectators moved around the compound watching the different performances. One informant recalled that "we learned to mix freely with the other groups. Say you happened to be a friend of mine, then I [would] have to take you to my tribal group's dances. Then you watch. After finishing there, we go to your tribal dances."[46] Learning about the different foods, dances, and other cultural artifacts of the different ethnic groups became a hobby for many workers and their families. Friendships grew up between people of different backgrounds. One informant recalled "that when I was child of about four years, I remember a person, we were going around together, and I took food from his parents and he had food from my parents. They were Lunda and we were Bemba, and my parents never regarded them as scavengers."[47] The dances symbolized the common bonds between workers. Traditional enemies and allies alike danced next to one another in the mine compounds. Old rivalries turned to friendly competition. If the weekend dances realized management's desire for harmonious compounds, they also inadvertently helped the miners and their families to overcome some of the cultural barriers which could have impeded cooperation at the work place.

This internal communication was supplemented by frequent visits between mines. For example, miners and their dependents regularly trekked between Nchanga and Kitwe on weekends, a walk of about six hours. This inter-mine travel revealed the similarities of life at the different mines.[48]

Within the mine work force, the more skilled stabilized miners, both underground and on the surface, developed a keen awareness of their common interests. These miners were still a small percentage of the labor force. They had worked at the mines long enough to develop a community of interest with each other. Their higher wages, better housing, and supervisory status separated them somewhat from other black miners. Most were married. Many aspired to a European style of living, adopting customs such as tea drinking, European dances, and clothing made in England. The similarities in authority, material culture, and expectations drew the stabilized miners together. Spearpoint reported that they "have a tendency to isolate themselves. . . . These people form a definite social group quite shorn of anything tribal, they live in a world entirely different to the other natives; one finds members of different tribes mixing very freely and all meeting on a common footing." As an informant recalled, "The more educated miners used to stay to themselves a lot, they had their own amusements."[49]

Occupational divisions could have undermined worker identity among the miners, but in this period the mines deliberately adopted a labor strategy which minimized divisions in the work force. The compound managers assumed that a peaceful contented work force was a productive work force. In order to promote harmony, the Copperbelt mines carefully scattered the different ethnic groups throughout the compounds. They allocated housing by seniority, family size, and marital status. With the exception of the mine police, no group of miners lived apart from his coworkers. Despite somewhat better conditions for higher-grade miners, all compounds inhabitants came under the same authority system, one that emphasized similarities rather than divisions in the work force. Even skilled underground miners, mine police, and clerks could be discharged if a European employee accused them of wrongdoing. As one informant recalled, "No one felt safe from the compound manager and his police."[50] All African workers had to live in the compounds. Race defined housing, wages, general living conditions, and job opportunities. The dual wage structure and de facto color bar on the Copperbelt limited the gap between elite and unskilled miners. Even the more skilled miners could only progress a limited way up the mine hierarchy. Consequently, although the stabilized miners developed a strong identity as a group, mine labor policies unwittingly facilitated the perception of similarities, and thus helped to build identification among the mineworkers.

The structure of the mine townships also clarified the common position of the black workers in relation to European employees. Black miners and their dependents lived in clearly demarcated areas separate from the European housing areas. They were not allowed to loiter in the European areas, nor to be there at night. The mine townships exposed the hierarchical division between black and white mine employees. The European townships were permanent and daily symbols of the gap in rewards to black and white mine labor. Black mineworkers and their dependents could see that "the copper mines built cheap houses on the African side, but on the European side you can see they built big houses. . . . The people could see that the whites lived much better." Africans could come to the European football games only if they "didn't sit where the Europeans were sitting." As John Chisata recalled, "The people knew whites are superior and black inferior,"[51] and the townships daily reminded them of that fact.

The visible gap between European and African miners' living conditions exacerbated feelings of exploitation among the black miners as well, particularly the more stabilized miners. While strike complaints reveal that most miners felt exploited, the stabilized miners took rather strong exception to the higher standard of living of the Europeans. More than other black miners, they depended primarily on wage labor for their livelihood, and expected to remain dependent upon wages. Living expenses in town continued to rise, which strained earnings and heightened awareness that the gap in rewards between European labor and themselves did not correspond to the gap in skill levels.[52] Every time they walked through the European townships, or saw a European drive by in a car, the stabilized miners were reminded of their relative poverty. As Eliti

Tuli Phili, a Nyasa clerk at Roan, told the Commission, the mineworkers "have seen that they started work at the same time as the European, and the European at once is able to buy a motor car and he gets a lot of food at the hotel. The natives complain about this. . . . They do the same kind of work."[53] In the same vein, a World Council of Churches' study of Copperbelt labor conditions in 1932 concluded, "That the Rhodesian Native harbors grievances against the White man is unquestioned in spite of his recognition of the values to be gained from the adoption of elements of the White man's culture, and that these grievances are expressed most vigorously by semi-detribalized individuals longest in contact with the Whites is equally known."[54] An explicit understanding of the opposition between management and workers, rather than between racial groups, would develop later; at this point stabilized black miners resented the better living conditions of both white miners and management.

COLLECTIVE LABOR ACTION ON THE COPPERBELT

If one accepts a growing sense of identification and awareness of common exploitation among the black miners on the Copperbelt during this period, why did this awareness not lead to collective labor action long before 1935?

The evidence suggests that most mineworkers before the Depression only vaguely understood the collective nature of their class interests and the potential power of collective labor action in pursuit of class interests (i.e., worker consciousness). In the early years of the mines, the slow development and often partial nature of worker identity and opposition among the miners undoubtedly inhibited the development of worker consciousness. The high turnover rate of labor, the ethnic diversity of the labor force, and the absence of a tradition of collective action against capital impeded the growth of worker solidarity. The competitive wage labor market in Northern Rhodesia before the Depression also reduced the need for workers to understand and carry out collective labor action. The labor shortage permitted miners to improve conditions of employment by simply changing employers. If a worker was dissatisfied, he could simply desert; the mines tried to prosecute deserters, but with little success.[55] Desertions were frequent.[56]

Thus, before the Depression, the political economy of Northern Rhodesia encouraged workers to act individually rather than collectively to improve the rewards for their labor. African workers understood their market value in the wage labor market, and used that knowledge to maximize their earnings. By 1930, many Northern Rhodesians chose to work on the Copperbelt because of the high wages. The *Annual Report* that year noted that "the habit of going abroad to work is already losing its hold."[57] As we have seen, experienced miners gravitated to the Rhodesian Selection Trust mines because of its better conditions. Inexperienced unskilled labor went to the less popular Anglo-American mines. As these workers gained experience, they frequently moved over to the more desirable mines. As one would expect, Nkana had the greatest difficulty obtaining labor. A pattern of mobility developed, in which black miners actively sought to improve their economic position by moving around the Copperbelt. One informant's father worked 3½ years in Katanga in the early 1920s, then went to Nchanga for eight years, to Mufulira for eight months, then back to Nchanga, then to Bwana Mkubwa for six months, and then back to Nchanga.[58] Other informants, and the work histories taken by J. Clyde Mitchell, reported similar experiences.[59] Thus, black miners eagerly pursued their economic well-being, but this pursuit was affected by the nature of the class struggle in Northern Rhodesia at the time. As long as individual labor action brought some rewards, the miners had little incentive to organize more complicated and alien forms of collective action.

The most common expression of labor protest on the job, absenteeism, also discouraged collective labor action. Absenteeism enabled miners to protest conditions without actually leaving. For example, absenteeism at Roan increased sharply when hours were extended. Slow-downs and general uncooperativeness were also frequent on the mines. Spearpoint claimed that the African miner was "a past master at finding means to defeat any rules which have been instituted to encourage regular attendance, regular hours, and regulations for efficiency."[60] These were rarely cooperative efforts, involving at most small groups of miners.

Thus, the ability to improve the rewards for one's labor individually undermined the development of worker solidarity and collective labor action before the Depression. As long as the labor shortage allowed miners to improve their working conditions by desertion and job mobility rather than cooperative efforts, collective struggle was unlikely since there was no incentive for it. As long as this situation continued, circumstances on the mines did little to reveal the power of collective action to protect worker interests. Only when the nature of class relations changed, and individual efforts failed, would workers begin a search for new weapons in the struggle against capital. Out of the search, a new consciousness would emerge.

ASSOCIATIONS IN THE COMPOUNDS

Despite the lack of collective labor protest before 1935, many miners cooperated informally for their mutual benefit. Neighbors frequently shared food and cooking responsibilities. Sometimes organized around ethnicity, these groups often simply included people in the same neighborhood. Neighbors sometimes pooled their wages, with one man drawing two salaries for a month, and the next month the other man getting both paychecks. This provided more cash for purchasing consumer goods, as the better-educated miners organized large orders to England for mail-order clothing. Such cooperation allowed them to escape the carrying charges for individual orders, and often involved quite substantial amounts of money. In 1933, for example, Spearpoint, discovered Roan miners spent £764 on such clothing.[61] Neighbors also helped each other hide illegal beer or guests from the mine police. One informant recalled how his mother brewed beer and sold it in the neighborhood. Once when the police discovered the beer, his mother went to the neighbors, and left him to take the blame. The neighbors pretended the beer brewing was just a prank to protect their beer supply.[62] Similar stories were told about illegal residents. Although on a small scale, these efforts revealed an early ability to cooperate as workers.

Miners also formed organizations for protection and support. Mbeni dance societies, which were established in the late 1920s, provided mutual aid as well as recreation for members. These were confined to ethnic groups, with Kalela being essentially "Bisa," Mganda essentially "Nyasa," and Mbeni essentially "Bemba." Competition remained within each group, rather than between them. The dance teams "contributed to assist members in distress, pay a fare back to a rural area and buy some goods to take back with him if a member is destitute, pay for a box as a coffin to ensure that a member dying in town had a proper funeral." Despite its traditional orientation, Mbeni gave its members the opportunity to "act out" with appropriate costumes and gestures some of the new roles established by colonial society. By playing out these roles, Mbeni members learned behavior appropriate to long-term participation in the emerging colonial society of the Copperbelt. On a more practical level, Mbeni provided mutual aid and fellowship. However, by encouraging members to practice roles appropriate to urban colonial society, Mbeni implicitly advocated African participation in that society. As one might expect, Mbeni attracted members from those miners most committed to urban life.[63]

The Watch Tower movement also had special appeal to miners committed to long-term participation in the colonial economy. Watch Tower spread throughout the Copperbelt in the early 1930s under the leadership of "prophet" Andrew Kasembala. Originally from the U.S. and South Africa, Watch Tower was both anti-white and anti-colonialism, prophesying the eventual end of white domination. Kasembala told his followers that "we natives will soon be mixing with the Europeans, sitting down and eating food at the same table, and they will shake us by the hand. The white men who refuse to mix with us will be told to go home." This message imparted to urban Africans an ideology legitimizing their claims to full participation in the emerging industrial society of the Copperbelt. It probably enjoyed the loyalty of the more stabilized miners who believed they deserved to be accepted in colonial society, and felt most rejected by "the racialist abuse and social exclusivity which typified colonial behavior toward socially aspirant Africans."[64] This elite group, "those who wore European dress, used tables and chairs in their huts, owned bicycles, and frequented Bible classes rather than the beer halls," made up the majority of Watch Tower members. On the mines, Watch Tower galvanized a considerable number of unskilled workers as well. In 1935, the government estimated 50% (perhaps as many as 70%) of the miners were Watch Tower adherents.[65] While undoubtedly inflated to justify blaming the 1935 strikes on Watch Tower, this figure suggests that the Watch Tower message was received by a broad spectrum of miners. For along with being anti-white and anti-colonial, Watch Tower opposed the uneven distribution of wealth in colonial society and proved an important institutional framework for miners critical of the colonial system.

The church groups in the compounds also encouraged acceptance of a western style of life. They stressed living more like Europeans, encouraged learning English, and provided important leadership experience. The African Methodist Episcopal Church, with its South African black leadership and its black American origin, was the most outspoken advocate of racial equality.[66] However, all the churches, including the African Methodist Episcopal Church, expected African equality to emerge slowly under the guidance of benevolent Europeans and "properly enlightened" Africans. Many churches were linked to ethnic groups, which undermined their ability to facilitate worker solidarity as well.

Thus, although miners cooperated both informally and formally before the 1935 strike, their collective life never included the entire work force. None of these organizations advocated unified worker action. Watch Tower, although it did "generate ideas of confrontation and a vocabulary of protest"[67] and an institutional framework for organizing anti-colonial protest, never articulated a proletarian movement in the conventional sense of the term. Conflict was predicted along racial rather than class lines. Nor did Mbeni appeal to the entire work force. Church groups spoke vaguely of the brotherhood of man, but the racial segregation in the churches undermined the practical application of this ideology.

WHY COLLECTIVE LABOR ACTION IN 1935?

Given the lack of either an ideology or institutions based on worker unity before the Depression, we are left with the task of explaining why and how a Copperbelt-wide strike was mounted by the African miners in 1935. What was it about 1935 that caused the miners to protest for the first time on a large scale, how was the cooperation achieved, and what did the strike indicate about the level of class consciousness and action among the black mineworkers?

A number of structural factors certainly heightened the impact of the 1935 tax increase, the most important being the growing dependence of mineworkers on wage labor in an increasingly unfavorable labor market. Opportunities for Africans to earn money in agriculture were being strangled by government protection for European farmers. Tax, land, and labor policies pushed Africans into the wage labor market just when the Depression had created a labor surplus on the Copperbelt. The mining companies now had the upper hand in the labor market and more control over labor. Inefficient or uncooperative workers were simply discharged. Those workers who kept their jobs were increasingly committed to wage labor, particularly longer service miners, many of whom expected to remain on the Copperbelt until retirement or longer. As a Bemba Chief told the Commission, "Many people on the mines had no intention of returning home, and the number of people who are staying here for longer periods is increasing."[68] The women were particularly reluctant to return to the village. "They have a much better time at the mines."[69]

The stabilized miners had come to expect a certain standard of living which was increasingly difficult to attain. They set the pattern for "proper behavior" for all ambitious workers. Indeed, Spearpoint noticed that "natives spend most of their money on purchasing clothing and luxuries in the way of foodstuffs. The men buy a decent suit, hat, and shoes and for their women they buy whatever they can. They hold tea-parties for their friends."[70] Such luxuries became necessities if men were to maintain respect and attract desirable women in the compounds. As a result, miners' small salaries were constantly stretched to the limit, and many workers were in debt. In 1935, a welfare officer at Luanshya reported that "there are few natives in Luanshya who are not in debt."[71] And it looked like conditions would not improve in the foreseeable future.

By the mid-1930s, a crisis of expectations had developed which was only worsened by the recognition that wage reductions made during the Depression had never been reinstated. Meanwhile the cost of desired goods continued to rise. Every visit to the fully-stocked shops in the townships heightened awareness of the miners' reduced spending power, causing even more rancor. This was all the more difficult to accept when the African miners compared themselves to their more affluent European colleagues. Indeed, the Inspector of Police at Ndola believed this "universal envy of Europeans" would have led to disturbances "if not now, later."[72]

Widespread dissatisfaction among the miners was further aggravated by dramatic cuts in the mine work force in April 1935, due to production restriction. Roan was the hardest hit. Between April and June of 1935, its labor force fell by one-third. The other mines continued their construction programs although even they were cutting back inefficient workers.[73] When the new tax increase for urban dwellers was announced in early May, miners were already feeling the press of hard times. The tax added yet another burden. In a time of minimal job security, the levy aggravated an already volatile situation and led those most severely affected into a desperate strike for higher wages.[74]

This explanation is sufficient if one accepts the 1935 strike as a spontaneous upheaval or riot. However, although objective economic circumstances can explain the miners' strong reaction to the new tax, they cannot, by themselves, explain how this reaction developed into an organized strike. For this we must look at the class struggle in Northern Rhodesia in this period. As we have seen, no compound organizations embraced the entire black work force, nor had there ever been a large strike. Before the Depression, African miners had improved their position through individual action. But this form of labor protest lost its effectiveness in a declining world economy, and workers had to negotiate within the industrial system, or leave it altogether. Limited collective action became one of the few means of protesting conditions for those miners unwilling to leave employment. Small groups of workers downed tools to dramatize their complaints, refusing to work until a particular problem had been solved. In order to maintain production, management generally tried to straighten out disagreements with limited concessions if they involved scarce experienced mineworkers.[75] Thus, growing dependence on wage-labor in an increasingly competitive labor market drove workers towards limited collective action.

However, a number of factors stymied the development of more broadly-based labor action. The concept of collective action, such as a strike, was still foreign to most miners. Only a few workers who had been employed in Southern Rhodesia or South Africa had ever been involved in a large work stoppage, most notably the 1927 Shamva Strike in Southern Rhodesia. Some of the clerks and underground workers also learned about strikes from their European supervisors, and they brought some knowledge of strike action to the mines. It is not surprising that one of the few abortive strikes on the Copperbelt was organized in 1933 by Henry Chibangwa, a miner who had been in the Shamva Strike and was a member of Watch Tower.[76] Thus, although some black miners had strike experience, for most miners the strike was still an unfamiliar weapon.

Management did everything it could to discourage collective labor action as well. The increased commitment of African workers to wage labor, and the large pool of surplus labor, allowed management to dismiss dissidents. Nkana managers deliberately hired young workers because they were more amenable to discipline. Management also discouraged collective protest by refusing to meet with groups of workers. Instead, they dealt with individuals only, claiming that it was necessary to maintain control in the compounds.[77] Spearpoint supposedly allowed workers to protest through their tribal representatives, but such protests were strictly confined to domestic matters. On all the mines, workers were denied an institutional framework through which they could present group protests, and individual protestations were blocked by the threat of dismissal. As much as possible, the mines closed legitimate avenues for worker unity.

Public policy did little to encourage worker solidarity and collective labor action among the black miners. The government emphasized traditional ties among Africans. Urban residence was permitted solely for the purpose of wage labor, and African workers were treated as members of an ethnic group first and as workers last. All problems were referred eventually to traditional leaders. Although the district commissioners were supposed to help Africans, in fact they had limited access to the mine compounds, and left discipline primarily to the compound managers.

Considering the pressures on miners not to engage in collective labor action, and the insecurity of the labor market, how does one explain the 1935 strike? One would expect a tendency to persevere except under the most extreme provocation. Indeed, this is what happened at the mines until 1935. In order to explain how this stoicism was transformed into at least a sporadically organized strike, we need to discover the mechanisms that brought the workers together, despite the absence of both a well-articulated ideology of worker solidarity and collective action, and institutions based on that ideology. The strike overcame this formidable barrier. The question is: how?

As we have seen, the answer lies largely in the nature of the compound, the common experiences of workers, and the leadership of the relatively skilled, longer service workers. It should be recalled that the compounds housed all African workers, which encouraged bonds of mutuality. The compactness of the compounds enabled information to spread rapidly and easily throughout the work force. Meetings in the compounds could be arranged quickly through word of mouth. Strike leaders were able to spread strike information through whatever groups they identified with, be they ethnic, religious, or any other type. According to witnesses, such meetings, as well as small informal meetings among neighbors and friends, were common during the strike. Larger meetings at the compound football fields enabled the strike leaders to bring all the workers together to organize strike action.[78]

Organizers planted followers at strategic routes in order to funnel as many people as possible into the large meetings. Indeed, when Muwamba arrived at Luanshya, he was directed to the meeting at the football field, despite being a complete stranger. Posters were put up all over the compounds for those who could read. The compound not only assisted the spread of strike information, it made it easy to identify and coerce those unwilling to strike. It thereby assisted the organizers in creating identification and loyalty among workers, and also made anyone not a part of this group automatically an outcast. It helped momentarily crystallize worker consciousness and a sense of commonality not ordinarily felt by most miners. Because the compound was the one institution based on the African work force as a whole, it became the means by which certain militants organized a mass strike.

Rather than dismiss the role of the Nyasa clerks as mere "slogan-writers and advisors,"[79] it seems they were the essential ingredient in the strikes. Both A. T. Williams (District Commissioner, Nkana) and Scrivener blamed the Nkana disturbances on the Nyasa clerks. Reverend Moore claimed that "the Mufulira clerks wanted a wage hike, and used the tax to make a row." Then, "the Mufulira clerks wrote the Nkana clerks telling them to strike."[80] These elite workers, the clerks, the capitaō, a few mine policemen at Mufulira, and the more skilled underground miners supplied not only the communication and organizational skills necessary for coordinating the strike, but also a sense of solidarity needed to pull together the many disparate groups in the work force.

These miners had worked on the mines for longer periods, were accustomed to urban life, and many planned to remain on the mines for the forseeable future. More than any other miners, they were able to see beyond ethnic divisions to a future based upon participation in the colonial economy. Although not conscious of themselves as a class in opposition to other classes, they had a growing sense of pride and group identification. They envisioned their future, and their children's future, within the new colonial structure. "They wanted their children to get more education, so they could have a better future."[81] Because of this commitment, such workers were able to identify with each other as fellow workers, rather than as members of a particular ethnic group. As one informant recalled, "The educated people, they were all together. They understand things, and they were not happy."[82] It was this class feeling which provided the rhetoric of worker unity necessary for a successful strike.

Corporate labor policies unwittingly motivated the stabilized miners to extend this class feeling to the work force as a whole. In 1935, no opportunities existed for the more experienced miners to improve their standard of living. Compound administrations deliberately minimized divisions within the compounds. Because of both factors, the more ambitious workers could not separate their well-being from the mass. When the tax increase eroded their already meager financial status, they could not successfully fight for changes by themselves. Large-scale labor protest could only occur if they joined forces with the rest of the miners. As Chisata recalled, "In my view, they [the elite miners] realized that if they united [with other miners] they could be much stronger." Indeed, Scrivener perceived this when he told the Commission that the Nkana strike was the result of "a band of avaricious clerks and fairly well educated people, who expected that if rises in wages were obtained they would also benefit." Similarly at Mufulira, Moffat concluded that a few mine police and a certain number of clerks organized the strike.[83] Thus corporate labor strategy left the elite miners no choice but collective action; no other avenue promised to improve their position on the mines.

The stabilized miners used their prestige in the compounds and their leadership in compound organizations to obtain the cooperation of the rest of the miners. They had a disproportionate influence in the compounds. According to Spearpoint, "These are the natives who will, and in fact are, molding the minds of their less coherent fellow tribesmen in the industrial areas."[84] They led various "tribal dance societies," welfare activities, and religious groups, and used their leadership positions, particularly in Mbeni and Watch Tower organizations, to spread information about the strike and mobilize support. Such organizations became important mechanisms for forging a consensus on tactics. However, neither Mbeni, Watch Tower, nor any other compound organizations provided an ideology of worker solidarity or a mechanism for organizing the entire work force. Watch Tower encouraged rebellion against authority, but this rebellion was not framed solely around worker interests. The Mbeni "were used . . . as a sort of agent, acting on instructions, and somewhat reluctantly."[85] Both organizations were used by strike leaders to mobilize support, but ethnic groups and informal and formal meetings in the compounds were equally important. The stabilized miners' determination to use compound organizations for strike mobilization explains the effectiveness of the miners, not the organizations themselves.

The behavior of the strikers at the different mines also suggests the more skilled stabilized workers were the key ingredient in the strikes. If the strikes merely reflected a dislike of mine conditions, then Mufulira, with its harsh compound administrators, or Nkana, with its inferior compound conditions, should have had the most serious episodes. If the percentage of Bemba were the critical factor, Mufulira, with its 80% Bemba work force, should have had the best organized strike. On the other hand, if stabilization were the key, then Roan with its higher percentage of stabilized workers should have been the site of the most militant strike.[86] This is indeed what happened. Roan strikers were more unified, more hostile to non-strikers, and more persistent in their demands. Even after the shooting on the 29th, Luanshya miners remained militant. "The mine compound was quiet; but pickets of strikers were placed on the gates to prevent natives from going to work. The natives appeared to be quiet and happy: but they said they were still on strike." At an afternoon meeting on the 30th, they repeated their demands "for the mines to give the natives more wages."[87] Some of this tenacity has rightly been explained by the economic insecurities accompanying cutbacks in the Roan work force. However, the evidence suggests that the stabilized miners at Roan were the more crucial factor. These miners were not only more dependent upon wage labor, many of them understood the need for collective labor action. The organization of the Roan strike reflected the greater understanding and commitment of the stabilized miners. Most miners cooperated with little coercion, and successfully cowed those few who would not go along. The call for worker solidarity seems to have hit a much deeper chord at Roan, which, I believe, is best explained by the higher percentage of stabilized miners at that time. The budding consciousness and organizational capacity of these miners, although still fragile and uneven, provided the cohesiveness and determination for the Luanshya strike.

CONCLUSION

In conclusion, the mining companies and the colonial state inadvertently provided the ingredients necessary for collective labor action on the Copperbelt in 1935. Experiences in the mines and the mine compounds facilitated the development of a sense of identity and exploitation among the black miners. Initially the balance of market forces permitted workers to resist as individuals, but the global Depression and state support for settler agriculture reduced the effectiveness of such measures, and encouraged collective action. Although structural migrancy inhibited this process, corporate labor policies, the Copperbelt compound system, and the production process intensified the impact of industrial labor even on migrant workers. This was particularly true for the more proletarianized miners who had more opportunities to develop a collective identity, and a greater understanding of and need to organize. The more proletarianized miners, and indeed most miners, surmounted the limitations of structural migrancy during the 1935 strike. Thus, historical circumstances on the Copperbelt permitted the development of a degree of worker consciousness and collective action not predictable in purely structural terms.

Clearly, despite the limitations of migrant labor, participation in the industrial process had already changed the attitudes and behavior of many Africans involved. The 1935 strike proved conclusively that African miners under the leadership of the more proletarianized workers could overcome ethnic and occupational divisions in order to support their common self-interest. Now that the miners had stopped production once, a precedent of collective labor protest existed on the Copperbelt that could be used in the future. A small number of workers had already demonstrated they could temporarily arouse the less articulate miners to collective action. No worker institutions had been formed. And yet, the potential for worker organization was now a certainty. The question was not whether African miners could organize, but rather, when and how they would do so in the future.

4

The Politicization
of Black Labor:
The 1940 Strike

INTRODUCTION

In 1940 another massive strike erupted on the Copperbelt. It was considerably better organized than the 1935 episode, for the strikers put forth coherent demands, and demonstrated remarkable solidarity as well as surprising organization. Scholars have explained these changes in a number of ways. While acknowledging that the 1940 strike was clearly an industrial dispute, Berger does little to investigate the roots of its development. Henderson acknowledges the emergence of an industrial leadership from among the underground supervisory miners, but returns once again to Bemba political consciousness for his explanation. Perrings emphasizes the deteriorating economic position of the more skilled miners and their consequent leadership role in the strike.[1] While it is clear that the growing proletarianization of the more skilled black labor on the mines was the key ingredient in the 1940 strike, other factors influenced worker behavior as well. The struggle of the European Mineworkers' Union against capital, the welfare programs, and other experiences at work and in the mine compounds provided the stabilized miners with an understanding of collective labor action and the organizational skills necessary for successful labor protest. The intensity of mine life also increased worker consciousness among even the unskilled miners, making it easier for the more stabilized miners to organize large-scale labor protest. This chapter examines the manner in which these factors shaped the 1940 strike, and assesses the impact of the strike on black mineworker consciousness.

LABOR SHORTAGE, CORPORATE STRATEGY, AND GOVERNMENT POLICY

After 1937, expanding production once again created a labor shortage in southern and central Africa. The removal of copper production quotas that year allowed the mines to increase production. The need for labor rose accordingly, and between 1939 and 1941 the Copperbelt labor force increased by 30%.[2]

In an effort to control the outflow of Northern Rhodesian workers, the companies pressured government officials to limit foreign labor recruitment. Although sympathetic, government officials did not yet feel that the copper industry was sufficiently stable to warrant a complete moratorium on outside recruiting. Government officials still believed migrant black labor was an important source of revenue. While the Katanga border remained closed, Northern Rhodesians were still permitted to work elsewhere. In 1936, the government signed an agreement with Southern Rhodesia and Nyasaland, which declared that national labor needs must be filled before outside recruitment would be permitted. This agreement controlled recruiting, but could not stop the flow of voluntary labor. Southern Rhodesia, with its higher wages and close proximity, appealed to neighboring Northern Rhodesians. As we have seen, despite attempts to control the southward drift, laborers easily crossed the border. In 1937, the Pim Report estimated that 45,000 Northern Rhodesians worked in Southern Rhodesia, and the actual figure was probably higher. South African recruiting was reopened as well, but on a severely limited basis.[3] As in the past, a small number of Northern Rhodesians worked in Tanganyika as well.

The 1935 strike had convinced both settlers and government officials that a settled African labor force in the urban areas was undesirable and even dangerous. Led by Senior Provincial Commissioner T. F. Sandford, government officials pressed the mines to maintain a migrant labor force. The administration also strengthened the Copperbelt police force and increased the amount of time district officers spent among the miners.[4] Officials opposed improvements in wages, living conditions, or welfare and recreational facilities for fear this would draw people to the towns. Indeed, one official insisted that the miners "do not keep these considerable sums of money—they blow them in the stores at once; there is very little saving of cash." Local canteen committees, consisting of the district commissioner and a few interested citizens, controlled expenditure of the beer hall funds to such an extent that even Sandford condemned them for their "cynical disregard of the persons most concerned, namely the African."[5]

Because of their growing contribution to government finances, however, the mines increasingly dominated Northern Rhodesian policy. As a former law officer and district commissioner recalled, "In the 1930s, the mines were regarded as a wonderful thing. . . . The mines were the biggest and most positive thing around at that time from the point of view of the government. They were given a tremendous amount of rope."[6] The mines exploited both local and London contacts to shape Northern Rhodesian policies. For example, the head office interceded with the

Secretary of State for the Colonies in London to ease a law which would have prevented blatant use of labor on Sunday at Roan. Company representatives dominated the Native Industrial Labor Advisory Board (NILAB), created in 1936 to advise government on questions directly or indirectly connected with the employment of labor under industrial conditions. The general managers even went to meetings to advocate company interests. At one NILAB meeting, for example, the Roan general manager convinced the Board to let Roan hold paydays on Sundays (to keep down absenteeism) over the strong objections of idealistic government officials. The companies routinely threatened less revenue to the colony if they didn't get their way, which carried more weight in government circles than the need to placate African labor.[7]

Small wonder then, that when the mining companies decided that increased stabilization was their best answer to the labor shortage, the government reluctantly agreed to lend its support. NILAB adopted a laissez-faire policy on stabilization, and eased sanctions against keeping children on the Copperbelt. In 1937, the government expanded welfare facilities for urban workers, and as part of this program, limited the use of beer hall profits to medical and welfare facilities, reorganized the local beer hall committees, and set up a Central Native Welfare Advisory Committee to oversee the establishment of new programs.[8]

In order to allay government and settler fears of urbanized Africans, the mining companies adopted a policy of "stabilization without urbanization." This explicitly denied stabilized miners the right to become permanent urban dwellers and presumed they would retire in the rural areas. The companies set up special programs, such as voluntary savings schemes and transport bonuses, to encourage rural retirement.[9] The policy fit easily into the low-cost labor strategy of the companies, for it shifted the burden of social programs to the rural economy.

STABILIZATION AND THE MINE COMPOUNDS

The threat of a labor shortage in a period of expansion drove the companies back to their pre-Depression labor strategies of ensuring a steady supply of labor at low cost. Rather than return to recruiting, which was both expensive and inefficient, the mines sought to attract labor by less expensive means. To facilitate travel to the mines, the companies petitioned government to provide cheaper and more reliable transport services. They lowered physical standards for recruits and, most important, increased the percentage of stabilized workers. In order to attract such labor, the companies built more housing for married workers, and encouraged miners to bring their families to the mines. Between 1935 and 1939, the proportion of miners accompanied by their families increased by 17.2% at Rhokana, 15.9% at Mufulira, and 1.5% at Roan, where it had always been higher than at the other mines. Since many

Northern Rhodesians preferred living with their families at the mines, the ability to bring their dependents attracted these workers away from southern competitors. Stabilization effectively lured experienced labor at a low cost to the mines.[10]

Longer average periods of employment soon followed. By 1938, 34.7% of Roan's work force of 6,884 men, and 22.2% of Mufulira's work force of 5,024 men, had been employed on the mines for over two years. To further encourage stabilization, management at the Rhodesian Selection Trust mines "informed all native employees that there would be no limit to the number of tickets they could accumulate." RST also agreed to reinstate returnees at their previous wage levels. Although management at Rhokana preferred to limit workers to two-year contracts, by 1938, 26.6% of its work force of 7,030 men had been on the job for over two years.[11] Both mining companies were moving toward more stabilization, albeit at different rates.

The companies cooperated informally to avoid another pre-Depression wage spiral. They established a single wage structure for the mines in the region, and also agreed upon a general policy of footing the transport costs for long leave for workers who had completed 20 tickets.[12] They still assumed, however, that formal cooperation was unnecessary.

As a result, work and compound conditions remained the private preserve of each company. Competition continued as each mine devised its own system to attract labor at minimal cost. Competition for voluntary labor after 1937 once again forced the mines to acknowledge the desires of their black workers, and it was in the area of work and compound conditions that corporate strategy became most flexible. Corporate labor policies were limited by the fact that, as Spearpoint put it, the "natives today are very independent, they know their services are wanted, and that they can pick and choose their masters."[13] Except during the Depression, miners had "voted with their feet" by deserting when conditions displeased them, and compound administrators realized that "better living conditions" would amply repay the Corporation in the increased goodwill of the native employee."[14] However, management in London and Johannesburg pressed to keep labor costs down. By the end of the 1930s, the compound administrators were forced to walk a tightrope between the need for labor and management's insistence upon low-cost labor. As much as possible the mines tried external solutions, such as limiting the flow of labor outside Northern Rhodesia, but as noted above, this policy was only partially successful. Compound conditions became a vital factor in attracting the necessary voluntary labor, and the result was a mixture of appeasement and minimal services.

This contradiction between cost minimization and labor needs was reflected in housing conditions in the mine compounds. Better housing was available for much-needed skilled workers. Roan built a model village consisting of large, double-roomed Kimberley brick houses which were "allocated to old respectable employees of the Companies as a reward for good service." Mufulira also built some better houses for longer service miners, mine police, and tribal elders. Even Rhokana and Nchanga expanded their married housing in 1939 in order to attract experienced miners.[15] But for most miners housing remained overcrowded and inadequate. Building programs at each of the mines tried without much success to keep abreast of the increase in employees. The district commissioner at Nkana complained that "although building seems to be going on continuously, there never seem to be sufficient accommodations."[16] Anglo-American mines were the worst offenders. At Mindolo compound singles' quarters in 1940, workers had less than the legal minimum air space per person. Nchanga in 1937 was overcrowded "to the point of illegality," with housing built for four people housing ten. Though plentiful at Rhodesian Selection Trust, mine housing was still overcrowded. When married miners complained, management at Roan advised workers "to partition their houses with curtains for privacy between children and parents."[17]

The mines once again began to expand welfare and recreational facilities. Before 1937, welfare had not been improved for fear that "the natives will all want to stay in town." Scrivener even believed "welfare work on the Copperbelt is in danger of being over done."[18] The efforts of the United Missions in the Copperbelt (UMCB) to interest mine and government officials in welfare had been coldly received. The missions had found themselves "up against a brick wall in local negotiations," and the mines particularly worried about programs they could not completely control. However, with the re-emergence of a labor shortage, the mines once again turned to welfare and recreation, and turned to the UMCB for help.[19]

The companies instituted special programs for wives and children. The wives of the missionaries residing at each mine, together with two specialists, Dr. Agnes Fraser and Miss Monty Graham-Harrison, set up classes for women. The UMCB ladies saw their role in a more progressive light than management, which preferred to teach women skills to stretch their mates' low wages. Determined that miner wives "see the worthwhileness of the good life," they taught them sewing, hygiene, laundry, handicrafts, cooking, home decorating, and sometimes reading and writing lessons. Their classes were aimed at the "better class of women," as one more attraction to keep skilled married workers on the mines.[20] The mines also set up schools and recreational classes for children in order to satisfy the parental concerns of their married workers. Management realized good facilities for children would hold skilled educated workers, most of whom had high aspirations for their children. The UMCB established primary schools at the mines after 1937, and these schools became an important drawing card for experienced labor.[21]

The UMCB also developed special recreational programs for experienced miners. Under the watchful eye of management, the team set up schools, libraries, lantern-slide shows, debating clubs, and other activities. Reverend Moore established a printing press for vernacular books, and in 1936 he sold about 1,000 books per month. By 1938, four libraries were in operation, and evening classes in English and other subjects drew enthusiastic if sometimes irregular audiences at each of the mines. Lantern-slide lectures run by Moore were quite popular as were debating societies.[22]

Sports programs were expanded to attract and amuse the mass of the mine work force. At Mufulira in 1937 as many as a hundred men came twice a month to David Greig's physical education classes, and even greater numbers played football despite limited facilities. Spearpoint and others established a Central Native Football Committee in 1937 to regulate competition for the Governor's Cup, and by 1939, 80 registered adult teams competed in Copperbelt leagues and competions.[23]

GOVERNMENT WELFARE PROGRAMS ON THE COPPERBELT

As we have seen, the government expanded welfare facilities in the towns. In accordance with the rural orientation of the provincial administration, public programs emphasized the temporary nature of African urban residence. Activities centered on short-term amusements, particularly sports, cinemas, and beer drinking. UMCB Team members set up appropriate activities with newly hired welfare officers. The government established native advisory committees, made up mostly of tribal elders from both government and mine compounds, to work with the township management board canteen committees on welfare programs. This policy underscored the transitory nature of the African urban experience by emphasizing traditional authority. The programs thus provided Africans with adequate but spare services for the duration of their stay in town.[24]

The Colonial Office supported this development. Colonial Office officials had been embarrassed by the interest that the 1935 strike provoked among certain members of the Labor Party and other concerned groups and individuals in Britain,[25] who blamed much of the unrest on the de facto color bar which blocked the ambitions of increasingly articulate and organized African miners. Colonial Office officials feared that amalgamation of Northern Rhodesia and Nyasaland would only aggravate this problem and obstruct the transfer of profits from the copper industry to the metropole. Several reports confirmed these fears. Major Orde Browne's study of Northern Rhodesian labor conditions called the white miners a "sort of human wipsnade including some fine specimens of rogues." The Pim Commission sent out to investigate the financial and economic position of Northern Rhodesia in 1938, criticized the inadequate provisions for Africans. When yet another commission, led by Lord

Bledisloe, rejected the feasibility of amalgamation in the near future, the Colonial Office readily accepted its advice, relieved to be able to maintain a humanitarian position while assisting a key British industry.[26]

In order to control African workers and other potentially disruptive urban dwellers, the Colonial Office suggested improving social services in the urban areas. But it was rather cautious. The Colonial Office's "tendency was to accept the advice of the man on the spot unless there was some positive reason to the contrary. . . . Leaving the initiative to the man on the spot was part of the traditional British attitude towards overseas administration."[27] Consequently, it gave little concrete direction to the Northern Rhodesian government. In this case, however, Colonial Office policy dovetailed with corporate labor strategy and the state's need to maintain order, and was thus readily adopted by government officials.

Both companies supported the expansion in urban government services, but expressed concern that the programs might interfere with industrial discipline. In order to assuage their fears, government officials agreed to respect the authority of the compound managers and left them in complete charge. At the same time, the mines maintained some control over government programs through membership on committees and direct links with Lusaka. Company representatives on local welfare committees and township management boards assured a voice for corporate policy on that level. Difficulties that couldn't be solved locally could generally be resolved by a call to the appropriate officials in Lusaka, and such calls were routine.[28]

Once confident of their control, the mines increasingly relied on government welfare facilities. By 1940, government officials even complained that "there appears to be a growing tendency for the mines to shift their responsibilities for the provision of welfare and recreational expenditures onto canteen funds." Although occasionally lamenting the low percentage of beer hall funds spent in the mine compounds, compound officials basically liked the system.[29] They could hardly criticize an arrangement which underwrote some of the cost of stabilization without threatening corporate policies.

CONTROL OVER A CHANGING WORK FORCE

Disciplinary methods on the mines had to be eased in order to attract and keep labor. As much as possible, Spearpoint fined workers rather than dismissed them.[30] Anglo-American mines made greater use of dismissals and bonus deductions to control troublesome miners, but used less coercive measures when feasible.[31] Both companies relied on the beer halls and recreational programs in the compounds to "give some healthy occupation for . . . [the workers'] leisure hours and train them in good habits and good citizenship and discipline."[32] Despite the increase in stabilization, management at both companies agreed with Scrivener's assessment that the disciplinary system on the mines was quite adequate "to curb the mass tendency [of miners] and [to] foster individualism."[33]

Indeed, both Anglo-American and Rhodesian Selection Trust management underestimated the consequences of stabilization. Despite the clear leadership role of the more experienced miners in the 1935 strike, management dismissed the possibility that further stabilization might lead to collective labor organization. They insisted that the strike was simply an overreaction to a poorly planned tax announcement for, like most colonialists, mine administrators did not perceive Africans as creators of their own history. They blamed desertions and disobedience on the "childlike stubborness" of the miners; Spearpoint even compared his miners to "mischievous school children." Management at both mining companies believed the African "must have some sort of individual development himself. . . . He must have a mind of his own and the power to reason of his own, and until he has got that he cannot be effective as a mass."[34] And any such development was expected to be a long, slow process.

The companies were more preoccupied with the emergence of labor organization among the European mineworkers. A European Mineworkers' Union was established in 1937, and, like its counterparts in South Africa and Southern Rhodesia, it violently opposed corporate efforts to advance African workers into formerly European-dominated jobs. The union had some powerful leaders who were tough negotiators, and their demands for a closed shop and de facto color bar threatened corporate efforts to keep costs to a minimum.[35] African labor looked peaceful by comparison.

Both Rhodesian Selection Trust and Anglo-American management saw no reason to modify compound policies in order to control stabilized African miners. They refused to consider any form of industrial representation, confining the tribal representatives (at the Rhodesian Selection Trust mines) solely to domestic issues. Because of their higher percentage of stabilized workers, Rhodesian Selection Trust mines tried some new tactics aimed at elite workers. Both Roan and Mufulira printed small newspapers which emphasized corporate "good will" towards workers. *Mufulira Compound Magazine*, for example, encouraged worker cooperation, claiming that "it is through work that people are happy, and it is through work that people get what they most wish for."[36] Anglo-American mines, with less stabilization, openly scorned such methods.[37] However, both companies assumed miner retirement in the rural areas, regular long leaves, ethnic division in the work force, and their compound discipline systems would defeat any propensities for collective organization. Government and Colonial Office officials agreed. They were convinced that any problems not solved through regular rotation of the miners could be handled by the police and provincial administration.

AN UNEXPECTED EVENT: THE 1940 STRIKE

This complacency was shattered by a massive African strike on the Copperbelt in March of 1940. It followed directly upon the European Mineworkers' Union strike at Mufulira and Nkana. The first intimations of trouble came on the 23rd of March when Nchanga workers struck for two days protesting a compound assistant's assault on an African woman who accused him of giving her short rations. A witness recalled, "The [Nchanga] strike was to demand more money and better food and to protest the woman being carried in handcuffs from the store after shouting. The men felt very strongly about that. Queen Elizabeth would never be handcuffed and abused like that. Everyone was unanimous about stopping work. We had no trade union, but felt very close. Tribal differences were not important. We were all like one."[38] The strikers returned to work at Nchanga only after management promised to reform the ration system, and to convict the guilty parties.

Other signs of African unrest soon emerged. Notices calling for a strike in the event of a favorable European settlement were posted at Nkana on the 24th, and on the 27th, the European strike was settled. After unsuccessfully petitioning the Chief Secretary for help, the mines announced a temporary war bonus of 2s6d per shift in hopes of calming discontent.[39]

Roan and Nchanga, where no Europeans had struck, accepted the offer. Much to the surprise of both the mine elders and management, however, the African miners at Mufulira and Nkana refused the offer. On the 28th, Mindolo underground workers struck, but Mufulira and Nkana remained at work pending explanations of the offer. On the 29th, Nkana underground and Mufulira went on strike, and by the 30th, almost all workers at Mufulira and Rhokana refused to work. They remained on strike until the tragic attack on Rhokana compound offices which resulted in the killing or wounding of more than 80 workers. This violence broke the strike, and by the 8th the mines were once again running normally.[40]

The strike differed from the 1935 stoppage in several important respects, notably in the nature of the leadership, the organization of the strike, and the clarity and consistency of the demands. These differences suggest the continuing development of worker consciousness among the African miners.

Unlike the 1935 strike, the leaders in 1940 were primarily "experienced middle-aged men." Most were skilled or semi-skilled longer service miners, underground boss boys or capitaōs, rather than the clerks who dominated the 1935 leadership. At Mufulira the strikers chose a committee of 17 workers to represent them, of whom only one was not a supervisor. Most of them had worked on the mine at least two years, and nearly all were underground boss boys. At Nkana, the compound manager rejected as representatives the six boss boys elected by a crowd of strikers. However, Rhokana still had a definite core of strike leaders, again mostly older skilled miners. According to A. Musakanya, "Elliot Bwalya was the main leader of that strike." He was an underground boss boy who both read and spoke English, and was one of the most influential English-speaking Africans at Nkana. Another leader spoke Bemba, Nyanja, Kikabanga ("kitchen Kaffir"), and English.[41]

The strikers rejected black miners associated with management, and ignored elders at both mines who tried to stop the strike. Edward Sampa, a Bemba elder in Nkana, was shouted down by his fellow "tribesmen" and told, "We will take no notice of what you are telling us."[42] The Mufulira elders were so ineffective that when the district officer and compound manager tried to negotiate with them, a crowd of miners collected outside "protesting that these fellows [the elders] were not saying what they wanted them to say and were merely letting them down."[43] The strikers accused the mine police of collaborating against them. The March 24th notice posted at Nkana vilified the police for being "very overbearing towards us." Another notice claimed that "the police—they are like Europeans here at Nkana. We should beat them. We are like slaves because of the police." Nkana strikers attacked the mine police after the Rhokana shooting, claiming "you [police] associate with European mine management. You take information from us to management, you give it to management. That is unfair. And you are well treated, you get everything while we suffer."[44] Similar accusations were made against the compound clerks, particularly Nyasa clerks. Elliot Bwalya told a Nyasa clerk that "we do not want to see educated people, because when you get educated you pretend to be white people, so we do not want to hear from you." As Musakanya recalled, "The clerks were badly hated by the miners. . . . The clerks were well respected by Europeans. So the people think, those people are well respected, they were very much against them."[45] Even more than in 1935, the strikers recognized and condemned collaborators, be they black or white.

This time the organization of the strike was strongly influenced by the previous European incident. The strike leaders had learned from the Europeans that the only way to get more money was to strike. The European miners' behavior during their strike was a constant reference point for African strike leaders. Throughout the strike, the African leaders called for discipline and restraint "just like the Europeans." They warned strikers and their dependents to refrain from violence, demanding "no fighting or argument—let us just go to our homes." Reminding the strikers of European worker solidarity, the African leaders called for similar solidarity among the African workers. They urged compound inhabitants to cooperate and their posters directed people "to let no one say 'I have no food' or 'I have left my work with only 2s6d.' We will all help each other to find food." The strike leaders assured the miners of success as long as everyone followed the European example "just to refuse to work and [to] say what they want."[46]

This strike was more widely supported than the previous one, with all miners firmly agreed upon the need for higher wages. The rapid rise in the cost of living had devalued the earnings of a labor force grown accustomed to a higher standard of living. As Reverend Bedford testified, "New needs have definitely developed here. I mention just a few of them, soap, clothing, furniture, better schools, books, things which were luxuries are now becoming necessities. . . . Certain commodities commonly purchased by the African have increased in cost by 40 to 50 percent. . . . On the other hand, wages have not increased in the same proportion as the rise in the standard of living."[47] The stabilized workers' dependence on wage labor increased their resentment of rising living costs, but even more short-term employees felt the pinch even more. Workers had discussed the need for a wage increase since early August 1939 and, as one of the lower grade miners explained, "They also thought about the 12s 6d—which ordinary labor gets because a person sometimes has children and he cannot give them all their wants, for himself, his children, and his wife." The strike "was not chiefly for one particular class of workers, skilled labor, boss boys, or any ordinary labor, they all had one aim, one heart, because they wanted more money."[48]

In order to appeal to the entire black work force, and to maximize support for the strike, leaders at both mines deliberately coordinated a broadly-based wage demand, stressing the need to improve wages in general. Rhokana originally demanded a wage increase of 5s per day inclusive, or 2s6d a day plus rations. By the 30th, the Mufulira Committee of Seventeen decided upon 10s per day without rations, or 15s per day inclusive. They sent letters and messengers to Nkana, urging them to agree, and thereafter the workers on both mines made the same demand.[49] This figure was meant to open negotiations with the companies, and to provide a rallying point for the miners.

The strike leaders justified their wage demand by placing it within the context of the general prosperity of the mines, the type and amount of work performed by Europeans and Africans, and the material returns for each. They accused the mines of not giving Africans a fair share of the mining profits. They drew attention to the fact that "we perform here the highest types of work, but yet are not well paid. Mufulira mine started about 15 years ago. When the Bwanas came here they had very small houses of grass, and today the whole of Mufulira is as we can see. It has very good buildings. It shows the Africans that this mine is improving, but yet the maximum or the minimum pay of Africans has not been changed."[50] The strikers insisted that they did work that was just as important as the Europeans. In fact, they claimed "they were far more capable of work than a European and that the Europeans who were put over them were incompetent and lazy and abusive."[51] When management rejected this argument, the strikers challenged the companies to let the Africans run the mines alone for a shift, with no Europeans except the surveyors and the electricians. The strike leaders assured management that such a test would prove that African miners deserved higher wages and better compound facilities.[52]

The strike leaders also asked for special concessions for higher grade miners. Reflecting their own occupational positions, they insisted that wages should reflect the different types of work done by African labor. They realized that "there are some people who work with their minds, some work with their hands, different work and the mines should say how much the different classes should get."[53] The strike leaders demanded different starting pay for various grades of work. They complained that "the highest paid African labor did not get the recognition it should," and that since they were married they "should have better houses, and a new scale of higher wages should be introduced."[54] The Mufulira leaders complained that the high death rates from silicosis and related diseases for long-term underground workers entitled them to adequate compensation and pensions.[55] These special demands did not undercut commitment to an overall wage increase, but reflected the concerns of the growing number of higher-grade workers.

This time the strike leaders made even more effective use of the compounds for strike organization than had occurred in 1935. They put up signs in the compound urging people not to worry about food or money, and "to come to an understanding with each other so that the thing should be done." Mass meetings were held on the compound football fields to inform miners about the progress of the strike and instruct them on tactics. When the leaders feared the strike might be broken by force, they convinced the workers to sleep out on the football field together, and by April 3rd a "crowd of between 5,000 and 6,000 slept out in the football field" at Mufulira. Similar events occurred at Nkana. Not only did this express and reinforce solidarity, it also served as strike discipline, for it isolated strike breakers.[56] If a worker chose to sleep in his house at Mufulira, "he was beaten up and he had to go and sleep on the football ground where it was made impossible to go to work." Leaders went about the compound "shouting out in the night and going round the huts at night and passing the word round that anyone who went to work would be punished."[57] Much of the coercion was psychological rather than physical, although a few strike breakers feared for their lives to such an extent that they slept in the bush after work.[58] Thus in this strike, the African workers even more effectively utilized the compound structure to facilitate communication, mobilize collective action, and maintain solidarity.

The organization of the strike reflected its widespread support among the African mineworkers. Neither Mbeni nor Watch Tower had to be used to mobilize the work force. This time, the different ethnic groups helped arrange some meetings. Edward Sampa heard the head of the Bangweulu people tell them "to continue strongly in what they were doing until the Bwanas give us more money."[59] The strike was organized primarily along class and occupational lines, and not ethnic and racial lines. Strike leaders appealed to the work force as a whole, rather than to ethnic groups within it. The result was a strike in which, according to an observer, the workers "displayed a degree of cohesion and solidarity that can only be described as remarkable."[60]

T. F. Sandford, who walked freely among the strikers, "was struck with the great respect they were showing to people in authority. Their relations with the Compound Manager seemed to be excellent, and with the District Commissioner at Mufulira they were on the friendliest terms."[61] At Mufulira, the strike leaders were in firm control. They convinced all the workers to hand in their certificates at once in order to keep the mines from weakening the strike by discharging workers. "The whole thing was carefully arranged by the strikers themselves so that there should be no cooperation anywhere at all with the mine."[62] The organization at Mufulira was so thorough that the workers refused to go back to work until after the Committee of Seventeen told them to. The mines claimed the Seventeen lost their grip at the end, but evidence from the Commission contradicts this. At Nkana, the control of the strike leaders was less obvious, but still largely effective. "A small minority of the Natives at Nkana had established an ascendency over the minds of their fellows," to such an extent that they were able to get a whole crowd to turn away from Sir Stewart Gore-Browne, the African representative in Legislative Council, and the compound manager. In the compounds, visiting Europeans tried unsuccessfully to get information from workers.[63] When meeting with a large group of miners at Nkana on Sunday, Labour Commissioner Howe noticed that "they were much too quiet for Natives in such circumstances," and he "wonder[ed] how it was going to end." Nkana leaders even convinced the strikers to hand in their registration cards when Scrivener threatened to stop rations and pay on April 2nd. Even the day of the shooting, no disturbances occurred until a crowd of strikers faced a pay line for strike breakers. Some looting occurred the following night, but this was limited to attacks on the mine police and non-strikers.[64]

The strike leadership also exhibited considerable negotiating skill. A well-known British labor expert concluded that "on the whole [the leaders'] behavior clearly showed that they are fumbling after the techniques of collective bargaining, and that with suitable guidance they would adopt it with advantage to themselves and their employers alike."[65]

The most remarkable aspect of the strike was the unanimity and solidarity of the strikers in the face of considerable intimidation, both from the physical presence of police troops and the intransigency of management. Nkana management refused to meet with strike leaders or to consider any compromise. This left management trying to negotiate through mass meetings. In frustration it threatened to cut off rations, which only heated tensions.[66] At Mufulira, on the other hand, management spoke with representatives of the strikers, and its moderation, coupled with the compound staff's manipulations, undoubtedly assisted the peaceful conclusion there.

STABILIZATION AND THE STRIKE

The greater effectiveness of the 1940 strike suggests changes had been occurring among the African miners. How can one explain the more coherent set of demands, the well-organized direction, and the wide concensus on tactics to be pursued in 1940? Why were the strike leaders able to organize themselves so much more effectively than just five years before? What had happened to encourage new organizational skills? Why the widespread support and worker solidarity during the strike?

The answers lie in the intensity of mine labor and the growing percentage of stabilized miners on the Copperbelt. For reasons which will be discussed below, the black miners not only perceived their common interests, they also had acquired the skills and information necessary to organize collective labor action.

While the figures on stabilization for this period are on the low side, they are deceptive. Nkana figures are particularly suspect due to a policy of classifying rehired miners as "new" employees. Scrivener's random sampling of 42 Nkana miners in 1938 discovered that 30 of these men had left their homes in the rural areas before 1920, 8 between 1920 and 1925, 3 between 1925 and 1930, and only 1 in 1930.[67] Agnes Fraser, who spent much of her time in the mine compounds, claimed that "I suspect that unwittingly or wittingly the Mines are badly misled on the subject of the temporariness of their employees by the way they move from one camp or company to the other."[68] Arthur Cross also believed "there is a very large number of Africans who have not seen their homes for 10 or 15 years but have moved about in the industrial area during that time and whose wives and families have paid only brief and infrequent visits home."[69]

The encouragement given to married workers increased the tendency towards stabilization. Compound officials facilitated temporary marriages by neglecting to demand legal proof of marriage. Women could live with temporary "husbands" as long as they pleased. Although unattached women could make a living as prostitutes, only registered dependents were permitted to live in the compounds. Most women preferred to live with a man, and since women were in short supply, changing partners in the compounds was easy, even for older women. Many women exploited the situation by going "boldly from man to man, living with each for a few months, and getting what they can out of them." If a woman did not like the treatment she received from her "husband," she could, and often did, find a more generous partner. Women seem to have become a source of competition among men, who were forced to provide a higher standard of living for their wives, or risk losing them.[70]

UMCB classes and missionary schools encouraged women to emulate Europeans. These were particularly popular with "the better class of women," who set the standards in the compounds. By 1940, many women were hanging pictures on the walls, putting up curtains and racks for dishes, and furnishing their houses with beds, tables, and chairs. European clothing became a much-desired mark of status. Many a divorce or desertion centered around complaints of inadequate wardrobes.[71] These new standards increased miners' dependence upon wages. Those workers with the highest wages attracted the most desirable women. Although miners grumbled about women spending all their money on clothes and other goods, most miners continued to compete for their favors.[72]

Other factors pressured married men to remain on the mines. Inter-ethnic couples frequently remained in town because partners could not agree where to live outside the Copperbelt. It became easier to remain at the mines. According to Dr. Audrey Richards, many women preferred town life, and pressured their husbands into staying.[73] Many educated parents stayed at the mines so their children could take advantage of the schools. After the strike, Ernest Muwamba expressed the feelings of these workers when he reported that "the educated people and others who see the value of education also spoke about the pay, that it should be higher than that because they wanted to have their children educated."[74] Parental concern for childrens' education was reflected in the greater stability of the school population. In the UMCB schools, two out of seven Copperbelt school children were there more or less permanently, and over 90% of the 2,500 students had been on the Copperbelt over five years.[75]

As we have seen, these stabilized miners already tended to identify with one another. They also increasingly perceived and resented their collective exploitation. Many of the stabilized miners, particularly those with families, saw themselves as permanent or long-term industrial workers. As one miner testified, "We work for Europeans and we are now used to that life."[76] They no longer accepted poor work and living conditions as temporary inconveniences and demanded to be rewarded solely on the basis of their performance as industrial workers. Such miners valued their labor power in relation to the work of other industrial workers, both black and white.

Daily experiences working in the mines taught African miners how to measure their work against that of other miners. The type of job done and the skill required, as well as the productivity of the worker, became the measure of a man's worth. Many an African miner observed the fact that he did more work than his better-paid European supervisor.[77] After all, skilled African miners frequently performed work similar to that of

Europeans, and they resented the wage differentials. The gap between European and African living standards disturbed the stabilized workers, because it did not reflect the difference between European and African productivity. Stabilized workers were uniquely positioned to perceive this discrepancy. As Field testified, "The more [the clerk] knows the more he believes he is not getting what he should get."[78] Increasing dependence on wages in a period of rising living costs made this discrepancy all the more unbearable. By 1940, most stabilized workers agreed with Julius Chattah's complaint that the money he received "is not good—not for the work I am doing according to my capabilities."[79]

One can legitimately ask why this heightened awareness among the stabilized miners led to general strikes at Roan and Mufulira. Given the shortage of experienced labor, why did not experienced miners return to their pre-Depression strategy of individual mobility in the wage labor market or, at least, confine their labor protests to the privileged sector of the black work force? A number of factors rendered this approach useless. Most important, the unitary wage scale on the Copperbelt limited opportunities to improve wages by changing employers. Miners evidently learned that occupational mobility was best achieved in one's place of employment, where good performance was justly rewarded. Family and community ties built up over long periods of employment also inhibited worker mobility. More than ever, stabilized miners tended to seek improvements within the work context.

The mining companies also closed off the possibility of individual protest by refusing to negotiate separately with stabilized miners for better wages and living conditions. Instead, they continued to minimize differences among the black miners. Although stabilized miners received better wages and housing, the differential existed within a narrow range.[80] In 1941, unskilled labor could make a maximum of 50s per ticket, while skilled underground labor made a maximum of 100s per ticket. Even Special Grade miners rarely made more than £2 per month. Authority at work and in the compounds still ultimately devolved onto Europeans. Skilled workers had some leverage against quick dismissals because of the labor shortage, but this "protection" was easily broken. All of these policies were designed to limit divisions within the black work force in the hope that they would help keep peace.[81]

The stabilized miners began to identify with other black workers. The futility of individual protest forced them to recognize the need for collective labor action. As an early trade union leader recalled, "Even the more educated miners . . . knew the workers must join together to fight, otherwise they would not succeed."[82] During the strike, the strike leaders repeatedly called for solidarity among all miners. They stressed the common interests of black workers, and condemned those who collaborated with management.[83] Strike demands were carefully formulated to reflect the interests of all black miners, suggesting an understanding of both the identity of interests between long- and short-term miners at this time, and the need for collective labor action.

However, the key difference between the 1940 and 1935 strikes was not so much the increased awareness of collective exploitation and the need for collective action, but the ability and determination of the more stabilized miners to do something about it. The stabilized miners were in a position to exploit the opportunities to learn organizational and leadership skills at work and in the compounds. They had both the time and the self-interest to learn skills which might help them improve their status within the industrial hierarchy. The 1940 strike proved that these skills could be put to use in collective labor action as well.

The stabilized, higher-grade miners developed organizational skills while working on the mines. Most of them supervised groups of miners; they gave orders and enforced discipline as part of their daily routine. The dangers of underground work dramatized their authority, which reinforced their importance. Cooperation and obedience to authority were necessary for survival, and by its very nature mine work reinforced both the solidarity of the workers and the leadership of the higher-grade African miners. Not surprisingly, the more skilled workers were highly respected, and often emulated. More than any other workers, they were able to "mould the minds of their less coherent tribesmen in the industrial areas."[84] The occupational hierarchy, therefore, not only taught skilled miners how to organize, but also accustomed less-skilled workers to cooperate with them.

Opportunities to learn leadership and organizational skills existed in the mine compounds as well. The mines misunderstood the UMCB Team's commitment to racial equality and leadership training, and the ability of African miners to use it for their own ends. Management had been reassured by the Team's claim that they only wanted "to supply healthy safety valves for the superfluous energy of this large population, so that instead of using their leisure gambling, gossiping, or fighting, they may be given constructive ways to fuller character and personality."[85] However, management and the Team differed over the meaning of a "fuller character and personality." The Team believed Africans and Europeans were inherently equal, expecting Africans would ultimately enter the industrial world as equal partners with Europeans, albeit in the distant future.[86] Even the most conservative member of the Team, Arthur Cross, advocated "bringing [the African] more into active participation in the conduct of his own affairs." The Team was concerned with the long-range effects of their programs, as well as immediate goals. They saw themselves not only as teachers, but also as participants in two-way conversations. They wanted Africans and Europeans to meet "on the basis of the individual quality and achievement of that person rather than on the basis of his race."[87] To facilitate this, they established "places where the Team and the Africans meet at leisure to chat, discuss, exchange

minds, probe questions arising from current readings and so forth."
Discussions included such controversial topics as trade unions and the
color bar.[88]

The Team wanted to give Africans the chance to develop skills which
would ultimately allow them to participate more fully in the industrial
economy. The UMCB Team geared many of its courses to that need, and
set up specific training courses for those miners with potential leadership
skills. For example, in 1938, Greig and Moore spent three months training future club secretaries for their recreational and social welfare programs. The next year Greig trained African welfare officers to help in the
welfare centers, and ran classes for African football referees. The missionaries trained women leaders as well. The Team established committees of concerned African miners at each of the mines to advise and guide
the recreational and welfare programs. The Nkana African Social and
Welfare Committee helped arrange lectures, choirs, boxing, concerts,
and other activities. Greig reported that the committee "is proving increasingly capable and reliable." A similar group was established at Mufulira in 1938. UMCB members also encouraged bright young men in their
classes to continue their education.[89]

Many of the stabilized miners took advantage of these opportunities.
They had both the time to become involved and the ambition to obtain
skills which would improve their position in the occupational hierarchy. It
was these workers who dominated the UMCB programs. For example,
most captains of compound sports activities were higher-grade miners.[90]
Competition in football and other sports sharpened leadership and organizational skills. Stabilized miners dominated the debating societies, club
activities, and adult education, all of which taught interested participants
parliamentary procedures and oratorial skills which could be used for
organizing large groups. Several informants who later became important
leaders in the African Mineworkers' Union reported receiving crucial
support and encouragement from UMCB members. Mwalwanda at Roan
even said that "Greig is the person who brought me up," and went on to
observe that Greig "had a very great influence among the African
people."[91] Chembe Phiri and Patson Kambafwile, both eventually union
leaders, were strongly influenced by Frank Bedford, the UMCB missionary at Mufulira.[92] Many of the early union organizers worked with the
Team in the mine welfare programs. Godwin Lewanika,[93] Paul Gwamba,
Joseph Mubita, and A. Musakanya are a few notable examples.

Along with specific skills, the Team offered those Africans aspiring
to a permanent urban existence an ideology supporting their right to at
least junior partnership, and potentially equal rights, in urban life. They
emphasized the basic similarities among all men and imparted a belief in
equality. Although material arrangements limited the degree to which
Africans could adopt Europeans standards, no inherent limitations were

implied. These programs assumed Africans should adopt European living standards. The adoption of European sports in particular symbolized
the right and ability of Africans to participate in what had been exclusively European activities. Some Europeans even came regularly to African games.[94] In a subtle way these activities countered the idea that
Africans were merely "tribesmen" and temporary urbanites. Active participation in European culture developed a sense of belonging and per-
manency in the colonial urban environment.

However, it must still be explained why serious strikes did not erupt
at Nchanga and Roan. Both of these mines had stabilized miners, many of
whom became important leaders in the trade union. The same structural
changes which encouraged the development of new attitudes and organizational skills among the longer-term employees at Mufulira and Nkana
occurred at Roan and Nchanga as well. How then can we explain the
absence of major strikes at Roan and Nchanga? They were averted partly
because of quick compromises on the part of management. The two-day
strike at Nchanga revealed both widespread grievances and the ability to
organize a total work stoppage, but these were quickly defused by management's willingness to prosecute the accused officials, investigate conditions, and promise improvements. The failure to strike at Roan is more
difficult to explain. Perhaps the better facilities for stabilized miners made
the 2s6d war bonus more acceptable. Informants suggested that the
memory of the 1935 shooting inhibited the miners.[95] The absence of a
European strike at both Nchanga and Roan was undoubtedly a key factor
as well.

There is little doubt that the European union had a profound effect on the African strike leaders, and the stabilized miners in general.
Because of their junior supervisory positions, these workers consulted
with European supervisors on a daily basis. The elaborate chain of command underground, and the ever-present dangers, forced close cooperation among miners regardless of race. Many of the elite black miners also
understood some English, and despite some efforts by management to
withhold information about the European union, educated African miners easily learned about it.[96] Although European miners opposed the
substitution of cheap African skilled labor, many of them sympathized
with African grievances, particularly complaints about low wages. As one
European miner told the strike commission, "all that is done with the
Native is to exploit him. . . . That does not help him and it ruins us." Some
of the more radical union leaders anticipated eventual collective actions
by African and European workers. They talked with supervisory black
miners about trade unionism, encouraging them to plan for future unionization. As Brian Goodwin recalled, "Many of us wanted a multi-racial
union in the future because we'd have won every strike."[97] Those Europeans opposed to African trade unions still admitted that collective pro-

test was the only effective weapon against management. Thus, whether intentionally or not, the European union stimulated interest in collective labor action.

The rhetoric and action of the European Mineworkers' Union provided leading African miners with tools for opposing management. The European union spelled out an ideology of opposition to management, openly accusing the companies of attempting "at every stage to block us and beat us."[98] The general secretary of the European union at Roan even "characterized the benevolent attitude of Mr. Ayer to his employees as an out of date subterfuge." One European miner publicly accused the mines of controlling the Ndola newspaper "in an attempt to split the workers on numerous occasions." He claimed that management "right from the beginning of the Union here, they have bought our leaders at various stages with the object of smashing the Union."[99] Rhetoric such as this sharpened African consciousness of the opposition between workers and management.

Most importantly, the union proved to black miners that the strike was an effective weapon against management. The successful conclusion of the European strike, without violence, impressed the African miners. Repeatedly throughout the 1940 strike, African strike leaders insisted they were entitled to strike just like the Europeans. As we have seen, the organization of the African strikes was closely based on the European strikes, even to the point of striking at the same mines. This was not merely a coincidence. The African strike leaders deliberately tied their plans to the success or failure of the European strikes by announcing that the black miners would only strike after a European victory.[100] Thus, the European strike provided an important model for the black miners.

The importance of the European Mineworkers' Union does not undercut the crucial role of stabilization in the strikes. Rather, a combination of factors emerges as the most likely explanation. The behavior of the strikers suggests considerable development of worker consciousness among all black miners. At the same time, stabilization produced a group of workers on the mines who sufficiently understood both their identity as workers and the need for collective action to follow the example of the European miners. The nature of the strike leadership and the sophisticated demands support this argument, as does the significantly better organized strike at Mufulira, with its larger proportion of stabilized miners. As an Anglo-American consulting engineer reported, "During the strike it was evident that the leaders or agitators exercised complete control at Mufulira, but at Nkana their control was not so marked." He even suggested that some of the Mufulira strikers come over to help organize the Nkana strike.[101] Thus, the struggle between white miners and capital provided the impetus for the black labor action in 1940, but the ability to carry out that action was the result of a growing worker consciousness among the black miners and the capacity of the more proletarianized miners to channel that development into organized labor protests.

CONCLUSION

Stabilization, not Bemba consciousness, was thus the key determinant of the 1940 strike. Stabilized workers strongly resented the gap between their wages and those of the European daily-paid miners, and in their search for higher wages and better working conditions, they gradually recognized the need for broadly-based labor action. The European Mineworkers' Union, the UMCB and government welfare classes, the compound system, and the structure of production all provided opportunities to learn the organizational skills necessary to carry out such action. While the widespread and enthusiastic support for the strike suggests considerable worker consciousness among both short- and long-term labor, the control of the strike by more experienced stabilized miners points to the critical role of stabilization. To be sure, the links between stabilized miners and the rest of the black work force, and the commitment by stabilized miners to broadly-based collective labor action were still tenuous. But the strike was a turning point in the development of worker consciousness among black miners. The experience of the strike reinforced worker identification and further clarified the conflict between management and workers. The strike forced cooperation among the miners, while the shootings left little doubt about the fundamental conflict between workers and management. At the same time, the failure of the strike underlined the need for new weapons to wring concessions from the mines. In the next decade, the stabilized miners would turn their efforts to this goal.

5

The Struggle for Black Worker Representation

INTRODUCTION

During the 1940s the copper companies continued to depend on stabilization to guarantee a sufficient supply of experienced black labor. Despite the stabilized miners' strike leadership in 1940, management assumed they could control these workers through established discipline systems, by pressuring troublesome individuals, and by providing some job advancement. As in the past, the companies underestimated the impact of industrial labor on the black miners, the widespread commitment to the struggle for better conditions and, most important, the capacity and determination of the stabilized miners, particularly the boss boys, to use skills learned on the mines in defense of their collective interests. Once again corporate labor strategy pushed these miners towards broadly-based collective labor action. Unlike studies which emphasize the role of the European union and the British Labor Party in the 1949 establishment of an African Mineworkers' Union on the Copperbelt, this chapter argues that the introduction of an African union was also the result of deliberate collective action by the stabilized black miners, and that this action reflected important changes in class consciousness and commitment to class action among the mineworkers—changes that would have a profound influence on the African union.

LABOR SUPPLY AND STABILIZATION

When Britain entered WWII, the Northern Rhodesia copper mines expanded production for the war effort. The expansion further strained the tight labor supply by increasing the demand for experienced black labor. As we have seen, the Rhodesian Selection Trust mines already used a high proportion of trained black labor. By this time, Rhokana had come to prefer experienced miners as well, having found that "unskilled workers on the mines were decreasingly efficient," and by 1944, the general manager admitted that "men with no previous experience of mining have very little hope of obtaining work at Nkana."[1]

In order to ensure adequate, steady supplies of experienced but inexpensive labor, both companies continued their policy of stabilization without urbanization. By the early 1940s even Rhokana's management accepted the greater productivity, reliability, and cost-effectiveness of married stabilized labor.[2] Management, particularly upper level management, saw no reason to abandon this policy. After all, they traced the 1940 strike to the European miners.[3]

Both companies thus maintained a "married strength at the highest possible figure." By 1946, the percentage of married workers at the Anglo-American mines almost equalled Rhodesian Selection Trust levels. The average length of service increased as well, although workers at the Anglo-American mines continued to have a higher turnover rate. In 1945, the average length of employment at Nkana was still 18 months, while Rhodesian Selection Trust miners averaged 35 months. In 1944, the number of employees who had worked over 2½ years was 25% at Rhokana, 26.6% at Nchanga, 37% at Roan, and 34.9% at Mufulira.[4] These figures are probably low for Anglo-American due to their book-keeping methods. For example, at the same time that Scrivener reported a re-engagement rate of 16%, a government investigator (Lynn Saffery) found that 80% of his 1,017 informants had had two engagements at Nkana, and 16% had had three engagements. Saffery and Godfrey Wilson put stabilization rates on the Copperbelt at a much higher level than official figures.[5] Their conclusions are buttressed by a labor department report from Mufulira which concluded that "the total number [of miners] with mining experience past five years must be large."[6]

Table 5. **Percentage of Married African Mine Employees, 1942–1946**

Mine	1942	1943	1944	1945	1946
Mufulira:					
No. employed	8,144	8,498	6,927	6,574	6,455
% married	59.26	65.78	58.83	55.00	59.00
Nchanga:					
No. employed	2,281	3,242	2,907	3,054	3,227
% married	59.67	44.11	44.10	43.88	45.29
Nkana:					
No. employed	10,091	10,624	9,621	9,896	9,226
% married	36.77	32.61	36.85	39.51	45.53
Roan Antelope:					
No. employed	11,625	12,168	9,559	8,858	9,338
% married	46.98	50.90	48.08	53.99	52.11
Totals:					
No. employed	36,928	39,157	32,769	31,680	30,999
% married	49.61	47.78	46.88	48.45	50.69

Source: Northern Rhodesia Department of Mines, *Annual Report*, 1946, p. 32.

LABOR CONTROL AND STABILIZATION

Despite their belief that the 1940 strike had been caused by the Europeans, the compound managers were disturbed by the behavior of the more skilled, stabilized black miners during the strike. They recognized the dissatisfaction among these miners, and feared more resistence unless some concessions were made. As Spearpoint pointed out in a memo on native labor policy, "It is from the higher grade natives that we may expect labor troubles; they are the people who measure their wages against those of the Europeans, and it is mainly this class which we will have to satisfy if we hope to keep free of industrial upheavals." Scrivener and Field came to similar conclusions.[7]

The compound managers advocated special treatment for the higher grade miners. They asked for "a bold recognition of the facts and an overhaul of the existing wage classification. . . . Meanwhile careful attention should be paid to the quicker advancement of skilled boys to their maxima." Field and Scrivener took the bold step of proposing some form of representation for experienced miners. Field went even further, suggesting that these miners "should be housed and fed in a separate Compound, thus creating a class who will defend their own rights against natives not in this class."[8]

The general managers and company directors overruled these suggestions, insisting that current labor strategy sufficed. They opposed further wage increases after the Forster Commission award (which reflected the still uncertain future of the copper industry, and pressures from a Colonial Office bent on securing a reliable low-cost supply of copper during the war). Instead, they set up a new wage structure which widened the wage gap between experienced and unskilled black labor. A three-tiered grade structure was created: grade A, most skilled; grade B, semiskilled; and grade C, unskilled. A special grade was established for the most educated clerks, but little else was done. While the companies agreed to follow the *Forster Report* recommendations (made by the Forster Commission which investigated the 1940 strike) for improving landscaping, rations, and recreational facilities, they rejected the need to improve housing.[9] As late as 1946, at a joint conference in Johannesburg, managers from both companies concluded that "the provision of a better type of housing for allocation to boss boys is not necessary, and the provision of larger houses for employees with many children should be avoided for as long as possible."[10] They dismissed the need for pensions, bonus payments, and improved worker compensation.

If the companies saw little reason to ingratiate themselves with the stabilized employees through material rewards, they were much concerned about securing the compounds. With this in mind, all mines agreed to follow the Forster Commission's recommendation to adopt Roan's system of tribal representatives. By 1941, 105 such representatives existed on the Copperbelt. Although company administrators admitted that the representatives "have a limited value and such as they do possess is reduced by the fact that they have little or no real status or authority," they believed that "it is in our interests to make a success of the existing tribal representatives and prevent labor matters getting into the hands of the more irresponsible elements." Management declared all compound conditions and general grievances the sole prerogative of the tribal representatives, insisting they were the legitimate representatives of the miners.[11] Channeling discussions of work and living conditions for the mass of the work force through these men emphasized the mines' refusal to accept Africans as permanent industrial workers.[12]

During the war years, the mines also invoked special moral and legal mechanisms to minimize worker protest. Absenteeism and desertion dropped dramatically after the establishment of the Emergency Powers in 1942, which gave the government the power to stop strikes and to jail recalcitrant workers.[13] Propaganda for the war effort impressed the miners. Leading Africans in the compounds organized war support groups to raise money, stressing the need for industrial peace to "save the King." Groups such as the Nkana-Kitwe War Fund Committee were very popular, and the miners took the war effort seriously. In 1943, for example, the Nkana-Kitwe War Fund collected £1,640 from the black miners, a large sum given the level of African wages.[14]

COOPERATION BETWEEN THE COMPANIES: THE CHAMBER OF MINES

In order to increase their control over labor and other matters of common interest, the companies established a Chamber of Mines in 1941. Several factors influenced this decision: the possibility of future strikes, fear of uncontrolled competition for labor, and the desire to influence government policy, particularly the new labor department. Based in Kitwe, the Chamber became a forum for hammering out a uniform labor strategy for the Copperbelt.

The Chamber standardized employment conditions in order to reduce the market bargaining power of black labor. A ceiling was set on the percentage of married employees as well as on the quality and quantity of married housing. Wage grades, bonuses, clothing issues, and allowances were standardized as well.[15] The system standardized working conditions on the Copperbelt mines, thus reducing the rewards for changing employers and hopefully maintaining a cheap and stable work force at each mine.

The mines also recognized the advantage of presenting a united front to the Northern Rhodesian government. The Chamber coordinated relations with government officials and became the companies' voice. The secretary of the Chamber maintained almost daily contact with

Lusaka, and the chamber served as the meeting point for government and mine officials on the Copperbelt. As one might expect, Chamber representatives frequently participated in official meetings at Lusaka.[16]

The companies pressured the new labor department through the Chamber. The department had been established by the Colonial Office against the wishes of the provincial administration, and was part of a world-wide effort to establish labor departments throughout the British empire. Although it was planned before 1940, the strike precipitated its creation.[17] Management worried that labor officers might be "tainted" with progressive ideas about African trade unions and other matters, and that visits from labor officers would encourage the more articulate African miners to express their grievances and ultimately organize unions.[18] As one of the earliest labor officers discovered, "There is considerable suspicion that we are constantly trying, without full authority from Government, to rush ahead for some obscure ends of our own." In order to forestall this eventuality, the Chamber pressured government officials to limit the activities of the labor officers, hoping to establish "a feeling that the Labor Department is bound in its actions by the goodwill of the Chamber."[19]

Since the provincial administration had opposed the creation of a labor department, the companies easily controlled the new agency. Many of the provincial administrators worried that idealistic labor officers would disturb the delicate balance between settler and mining interests worked out by the colonial state. To ensure smooth relations between the department and the administration, early appointees were seconded from the provincial administration. The department deliberately hired men "who had an easy manner, . . . who would fit in and be useful."[20] Under pressure from administration and mine officials, the department agreed that problems raised by individual workers, or groups of workers, would be directed to the compound manager. Questions of policy would not be discussed with Africans, nor would labor officers become intermediaries between workers and the mines.[21] This reassured the administration, but the companies still mistrusted the new department. For its part, the Chamber maintained close relations with Lusaka in order to protect its autonomy.

The companies, both individually and through the Chamber, also maintained regular contact with the Colonial Office in an effort to influence policy in their favor. During the war, this was easily achieved. Britain needed copper, and anything interfering with copper production was immediately suspect. As Harold Macmillan bluntly informed Creech Jones in Parliament, "For the period of the war I want copper and a great deal of it." In response to Creech Jones's questions about black labor conditions on the Copperbelt, Macmillan admitted that although small improvements could be made, basically the best the Colonial Office felt it could do for the African at this time was "to aim at a little unobtrusive infiltration [into better jobs and wages] without saying too much."[22] More dramatic improvements might threaten industrial peace, something the British government would not accept in wartime.

MAINTAINING CORPORATE AUTHORITY IN THE COMPOUNDS

Management at both mines carefully monitored outside influences on their black mineworkers as well. Company representatives protected corporate interests on the township management boards by establishing the principle of non-interference in industrial matters. Reassured by their congruity of purpose, the mines gradually allowed the township management boards to control more of the welfare services for their workers. This dependence upon the townships lowered welfare costs so that in 1945 Rhokana only spent £164 on welfare, in contrast to Roan, which hired its own welfare officers and spent £1,270.[23] By the end of the war, both companies questioned the need to provide welfare services at all. Although realizing that "welfare work has a close bearing on the general tone of compound life," and that "anything which will keep [the black miner] engaged in his spare time will no doubt tend to restrain any vicious proclivities which he may possess," management saw no reason to increase their share of amenities "unless some useful results will eventuate for such action."[24] As long as the township management boards respected corporate authority, the companies welcomed their services.

But the companies' management strictly controlled the activities of the UMCB Team, which was suspect because of its connections with liberal British opinion, and its financial independence. This suspicion was further aggravated by two Team members, Moore and Bedford, who criticized the companies at the Forster Commission. The mines reacted to these statements by refusing the 1940 UMCB offer to direct all mine welfare programs. The companies limited UMCB activities to education, libraries, and programs for women and youth. Those missionaries who threatened mine policies were pushed off the Copperbelt.[25] Arthur Cross, the Team leader, was informed that "it would be helpful if the Societies' representatives would confer with the Mine Management before making statements, the accuracy of which may be in doubt, or which may deal with controversial matters affecting the Company's and their relations with the Natives."[26] Management made it clear that the Team could work on the mines only if their activities remained within corporate constraints.

The companies also used their influence to challenge, and often remove, Europeans who interfered with labor relations. Corporate power quickly came down against those who challenged the status quo. One of the first victims was the outspoken UMCB missionary, R. J. B. Moore. The mines convinced District Officer A. T. Williams to reject Moore as headmaster of the new Kitwe school. Moore discovered to his chagrin that "it seems that anyone who knows too much about these mining compounds is a marked man. Godfrey Wilson . . . has just written saying he had had to resign for this same reason, coupled with conscientious objections."[27] Despite the Team leaders' regard for him personally and for his ability and the quality of his work, Moore was transferred out of the Copperbelt the next year.[28]

Similarly, the Chamber quickly challenged Labor Officer William Saffery's critical report of conditions on the mines. Despite some compound manager support, the Chamber's critique, which was widely circulated, questioned both Saffery's knowledge of the nation and his use of statistics. It accused him of using a standard of living table "designed to maintain a person, or persons, in health, comfort, entertainment, social life, and in some degree, luxury." The Chamber disagreed strongly with his assessment of mine housing, rejected his claim of widespread malnutrition in the mine compounds, and refused to accept his conclusion that miners could not live on their present income.[29] Having countered the report, the mines moved to suppress it, and had their way. The labor department agreed to withhold the report from circulation on the pretext that it was merely an inter-departmental preliminary study. Requests for copies from outside Northern Rhodesia were refused. Saffery was carefully kept away from the Copperbelt, and soon turned to South Africa.[30]

In 1945 the companies reacted to government social welfare officer Archibald Elwell in a similar manner. In 1944, Elwell had been sent to Northern Rhodesia by the Colonial Office as the first official government social welfare officer. Posted in Kitwe, he soon aroused the suspicions of the European community by befriending the Africans. In a memorandum on "The Development of African Social Welfare Services in the Urban Areas of the Copperbelt," Elwell advocated extensive reorganization and expansion of Copperbelt welfare services, an expenditure of about £50,000 per annum for ten years, and the creation of African Welfare Sub-Committees which "should feel free to discuss any subject they may so desire, political or otherwise."[31] Both the mines and the government balked at these proposals. The mines claimed Elwell's suggestions would increase "the population of undesirable people in town and . . . foster detribalization at a time when it may still be possible to retard such an unwanted feature in African social life." Matters came to a head in January 1946, when Elwell accepted the Kitwe African Society's invitation to speak on trade union organization. The mines immediately accused him of seditious behavior, demanded his removal, and the general manager at Rhokana barred him from the mine compounds. The Kitwe Management Board's Native Affairs Advisory Committee dismissed him from the committee, and asked "that he disassociate himself from all Welfare activities in this area." The Secretary of the Kitwe African Society, Joseph Achiume, was removed by the district commissioner, and by 14 February 1946, Elwell had been reassigned to Livingstone in disgrace, his welfare proposals tabled indefinitely.[32]

INDUSTRIAL PEACE DURING THE WAR

During the war years the mines successfully maintained labor peace. No collective labor protest marred relations with black labor. Most black miners went quietly about their work on the mines, more intent on keeping their jobs than anything else. Memories of earlier strikes, with their shooting and killing, dampened support for labor protest.[33] The Emergency Powers established in 1942 made strikes illegal; appeals to African patriotism undoubtedly helped as well. After 1944, cutbacks in the black labor force due to lowered production also increased anxiety over job security. As a result, absenteeism and desertion fell to new levels, and by 1946 the desertion rate at Rhokana was only 13.46 per 1,000 miners.[34]

The tribal representatives remained within company guidelines, rarely questioning the authority of the compound manager. While passing on small complaints about rations, housing, and general compound conditions to the compound managers, the representatives concentrated on buttressing their own authority. They were concerned with maintaining orderly and stable compounds, where traditional authority was respected. As much as possible, they tried to solve domestic disputes in the compounds along traditional lines.[35] They railed against the urban native court assessors for usurping their prerogatives on domestic matters, and treated the boss boys' committees as rival organizations.[36] This was precisely the role management had in mind for them.

Those workers most apt to organize collectively, namely the more skilled stabilized miners, became enmeshed in efforts to improve their position through special committees. As the compound managers had predicted, these miners agitated for some kind of representation soon after the 1940 strike. The supervisory workers, or boss boys, pressed labor officers to help them set up representative bodies to defend their interests. The labor officer at Mufulira, P. J. Law, found the boss boys "a very forceful body. . . . Most of them were experienced long-term miners, often having served 10 to 15 years. They were quite restive. They didn't like the tribal representative system. They thought they should have a say."[37] The underground boss boys at Mufulira even elected a committee of fifteen and asked for an office before the mines agreed to establish boss boys' committees. At Luanshya and Nkana, the boss boys also pushed for representation, although Nchanga was slower to get involved. The boss boys at all the mines demanded direct negotiation with management over wages, work, and living conditions. They dismissed tribal representatives as the instruments of management, and insisted upon independent organization. As one of the labor officers observed: "The boss boys are tending to hang together more as boss boys than as Africans. They seem to regard themselves as quite apart from the ordinary worker. What they want to do is to bring up points in connection with their own condition apart from the ordinary workers."[38]

These arguments convinced the labor officers, and they advised the mines to permit some form of representation for the boss boys. Warning management that "the boss boys and clerk classes exert a very considerable influence over the masses and they are quite capable of inciting the masses to excesses to further their own intereses," the Nkana labor officer, William Stubbs, informed the Chamber of Mines that "if some concession is not made to the boss boy class a more unreasonable demand may be expected before long." He suggested forming associations to represent the boss boys and no one else. At the same time, he promised to "keep in the closest touch with the development [of these boss boys' committees] with a view to obtaining to the greatest degree the confidence of the boss boys and to guiding any association of them along sane and moderate lines, while not neglecting to advise them how best they can further their own interests."[39]

With the help of some compound administrators, the labor officers won a reluctant Chamber over to their plan. Both Field and Scrivener supported the boss boys' committees. Although opposed to African trade unions, both agreed that special provisions had to be made for more skilled labor.[40] The Chamber worried that the proposed Trade Unions Conciliation and Trade Disputes Ordinance of 1942 might allow the committees to register as trade unions. In that event, they foresaw neither government nor themselves having any further control over the committees. This fear was alleviated when opponents tabled the Ordinance in the Legislative Council. The governor reassured management that the boss boys would not be permitted to form a union. Their fears somewhat assuaged, the Chamber decided to accept boss boys' committees as the "reasonable answer to the present situation."[41]

Management carefully monitored the committees in order to limit their impact on the rest of the work force. Although favoring the committees, the compound managers worried that they might become springboards to a broader interest in trade unions. To avoid this, the compound managers attended committee meetings, kept a watchful eye on the proceedings, and made certain "there would be no artificial 'shoving' [towards trade unions] on the part of the Labor Officer."[42] In alliance with the governor and other provincial administrators, the Chamber kept the labor commissioner under tight wraps. It even demanded that a lecture précis be given to the compound manager in advance and that the lecture be subject to compound manager approval. The commissioner himself opposed this, but bowed to government pressure and directed the labor officers to cooperate. He reluctantly ordered an end to actions which might encourage trade unions.[43] This reassured the companies and, at least for the moment, maintained the social order so necessary to the colonial state.

STABILIZATION AND THE STRUGGLE FOR BLACK WORKER REPRESENTATION

The absence of serious black labor protest during the war lulled the companies into complacency. With the boss boys' committees securely under control, management assumed their present system would contain black protest for the foreseeable future. Yet, by 1946 the more skilled black miners set up junior branches of the European Mineworkers' Union, and three years later formed an African Mineworkers' Union. How can we explain this dramatic turn of events?

Most studies have invoked the intervention of the European union and the British Labor Party. Berger asserts that an African union was established because of "the ever-present tension between the Government and the white Mineworkers' Union" rather than as a response to black worker unrest. She dismisses the role of the more skilled miners, insisting that the worker committees formed in the early 1940s "had not shown signs of turning into a mass organization." Other authors stress the role of the British Labor Party, which came to power in 1946.[44] British politics and the formation of the European union clearly helped inspire the African Mineworkers' Union, but initiatives by the stabilized black miners were equally important. These initiatives were primarily the result of experiences in the work place in the particular historical circumstances of the period.

The scarcity of experienced black labor enabled both boss boys and clerks to continue pressing for at least minimal improvements in their conditions of work. These miners felt entitled to special consideration from management. As one of them told the Forster Commission, "There were two classes of Natives, the younger ones and the older ones, and the older ones [i.e., experienced ones] should receive preferential treatment."[45] Such higher-grade miners were increasingly aware of the need for some form of organization to protect their interests. Some of them joined the African welfare societies which resurged on the Copperbelt. Encouraged and guided by the UMCB, these societies attracted the most educated Africans from both the mines and the government townships. Their members were disillusioned with the government-dominated Urban Advisory Councils, and in 1942 set out to replace the Native Welfare Advisory Committees without government or company interference. The societies were ostensibly concerned with recreation and social welfare, but discussions inevitably strayed to such topics as advancement, the color bar, and trade unions. For example, in 1944 the Luanshya African Welfare and Recreation Society devoted "considerable time . . . to the question of the large-scale dismissal of African mine employees."[46] Elwell's speech to the Kitwe African Society drew a large and attentive audience, and members as a rule raised contentious issues with visiting lecturers. Meetings were large, well organized, and conducted in English. The use of English emphasized the educated status of members and their capacity to negotiate directly with Europeans. Members hoped this approach would bring a sympathetic response from government officials and, consequently, improvements for Africans in both political and economic life.[47]

Most higher-grade miners perceived the futility of individual protest, and thus the need for organization at the work place.[48] They wanted improvements within the industrial context, and yet in 1940 had seen European strikers win important concessions, while Africans made minimal gains. The Europeans had a union and the Africans did not. The lesson was clear; African miners would have to establish some form of collective labor organization. As one informant recalled, "We could see that the Europeans got good pay because they had a union. We had no representation. That's why African pay was so low. We knew we must get some representation to get more pay."[49]

As we have seen, the first rumbling of worker representation was from the boss boys who had established committees at each mine. Enthusiasm abounded; early meetings showed great promise. Agendas were drawn up, attendance was high, and discussions were spirited. The first meetings drew 200 boss boys at Nkana and 120 at Mufulira. At Roan and Nchanga, a labor officer's idea for a "suggestion book" was accepted with alacrity. All the committees beseeched labor officers to teach them proper procedures for running meetings and voicing grievances.[50]

Reflecting their limited consciousness, the boss boys' committees initially demanded special treatment solely for themselves. They petitioned for separate and better housing, and for permission to return to their previous house after long leave in order to reap the benefits of earlier improvements and to maintain neighborhood ties. They asked for rations two or three times a week instead of every day, with pick-up in special lines.[51] Complaints about working conditions focused on the special concerns of boss boys and other supervisory workers. The Mufulira Boss Boys' Committee demanded special facilities at the mine skips, special badges for longer-service men, and preference over Europeans for leaving the mine at the end of the day. They wanted a change house, dry clothes, and a hot drink after work, the same as the European miners. All the committees denounced the meager compensation payments and inadequate medical care. They also demanded that silicotics be given light work instead of being dismissed.[52]

At this point the committees showed no sign of becoming mass organizations. In fact, they willingly cooperated with both labor officers and management to obtain improvements for themselves, and expressed little concern for fellow miners. Such behavior may be seen as a pragmatic solution to a colonial industrial environment; it also reflected the boss boys' identification with each other, as well as the restricted scope of that commitment itself. Their interest in collective bargaining and trade unions still precluded a wider interpretation of collective labor action.[53]

At the same time, these complaints also revealed the boss boys' deep commitment to industrial labor, and their determination to fight for recognition as a legitimate section of the industrial work force. The issues raised by their committees may appear petty, but it must be recognized that these were the grievances of a stabilized labor force. They signalled the end of a purely migrant labor force; the boss boys were fighting for a permanent position in the industrial work force. They rejected the validity of the dual wage structure, asked for equal treatment with white miners doing similar work, and demanded to know "why there was such a difference in the treatment of the Native and the European . . . as both the European and the Native worked under the same conditions." They refused to accept managerial abuse and arbitrariness. Thus, even while speaking for themselves, the boss boys were transforming the role of mine labor.[54] They let management know that some black miners no longer would accept temporary, second-class status on the mines.

It was this commitment to industrial labor that eventually forced many of the boss boys to broaden both their consciousness and their base of collective action. As we have seen, management sabotaged the committees from the very beginning by limiting their subject matter and frequently ignoring requests.[55] By 1944, however, many boss boys had become disillusioned and attendance at meetings dwindled accordingly. At Luanshya the labor officer reported that the Roan boss boys were "disheartened by the lack of ability to get anything done." Stubbs had a similar experience at Mufulira. He blamed the disinterest "largely [on] boredom and the absence of any real incentive; the committee had expected something more exciting than more meetings on tribal representative lines."[56]

The rising cost of living aggravated boss boy frustrations as well. In 1943 Saffery reported that the average-sized family on the mines could not live off the wages of the male head of household.[57] The situation worsened in the next few years, with the prices of commodities representative of African cash expenditure nearly doubling between 1938 and 1947.[58] This was particularly hard on the stabilized miners who depended largely on their wages. This decline in real wages was all the more bitter when compared with the rewards given to European miners. As one labor officer recalled, the comparison between European and African living standards "was a thorn in the side of the African mineworker. It went quite deep."[59] This was particularly true for the more skilled miners, who realized they were perfectly capable of doing many European jobs, and felt they had "grown up" and "should be allowed to advance into positions of Mine Captains, Shift Bosses and Miners." This situation even led Saffery to predict "serious upheaval" if it was not remedied.[60]

Since cautious attempts at self-improvement failed, the boss boys began to recognize the need for bolder measures. The committees thus broadened the scope of their demands to the point that the labor officers complained that "they seldom bring up matters which concerned only themselves as a class."[61] They pressed for advancement for both skilled and unskilled workers, and demanded better housing, higher wages, better education, adequate compensation, and pensions for the entire black work force.[62] They insisted that just as "the Europeans need money for food, clothes, education, or business, fare, pleasure and the like; the African needs these as well, if he or she is to live the real life and life indeed."[63] The committees paired these demands with calls for regular joint meetings with all similar associations on the Copperbelt.[64]

THE SEARCH FOR NEW WEAPONS

By the end of the war, the boss boys perceived the futility of cooperating with management. They were ready to try new methods to reach their goals.[65] As Labor Officer Richard Luyt recalled: "The interested [boss boys] . . . became frustratedly and impatiently aware that if they had to work with the boss boys' committees the majority were going to be a drag around their head. They began to find that they had better look elsewhere."[66]

This frustration was shared by many other miners. The more stabilized miners, for example, had expected rewards for their patience and cooperation during the war, but were embittered when improvements failed to come and the rising cost of living cut deeper into earnings. Economic difficulties increased as war veterans flooded the job market. Incidents such as Elwell's dismissal raised suspicions about the government's concern for African welfare.[67] Leading Africans complained vociferously to Gore-Browne, so much so that he felt compelled to warn Legislative Council in 1945 that "the African is very conscious today of grievances." A year later he repeated this warning and predicted dire consequences if something was not done. The district commissioner in Luanshya reported "feelings of frustration, if not actual exploitation, among both the intelligentsia and many of the less-skilled workers."[68] Similar situations existed at Mufulira and Nkana.[69]

At the end of the war, clerks at several of the mines organized associations. The Roan Clerks' Association, formed in 1945, held three meetings over a six-month period, but suffered internal divisions and then desertions as rumors of an African trade union spread. Leaders of the association did help organize a boycott in Luanshya in 1946, which both provided leadership experience and emphasized the greater potential of broadly-based collective action.[70]

Increasingly, the boss boys, the clerks and other concerned miners advocated some form of broadly-based worker organization. Labor department classes in worker cooperation, organizational procedures, and the proper presentation of grievances had taught boss boys and some clerks skills which could be transferred to a broader representational base. These lessons undoubtedly helped bring about African trade unionism. Both Stubbs and Law recalled frequent questions about collective bargaining and unions from higher grade miners at this time, and UMCB records indicate a growing interest in these subjects.[71] During his brief stay in 1945, Elwell influenced a number of leading miners as well, providing both information and encouragement about collective action.[72] Probably the greatest influence, once again, came from the example of the European miners. As the labor department bluntly reported in 1946, "There is a demand among the more advanced and intelligent African workers for trade unions; . . . there can be little doubt that it is due to an awareness that Europeans have formed trade unions for the purpose of collective bargaining and they feel it is only by this means that they can be given an opportunity of improving their wages and working conditions."[73]

A number of incidents outside the mines also reaffirmed the ability of Africans to organize themselves. The massive railway workers' strike in 1945 proved that Africans could effectively organize a widespread strike and sustain collective action in an orderly manner. The strike also revealed the possibility for multi-racial cooperation among workers, when the European railway workers not only supported African demands, but also loaned money to their black workmates.[74]

The next year, the Luanshya boycott showed Africans could organize effective collective action on an urban-wide basis. The 14-week boycott against the stores in the 2nd Class Trading Area of Luanshya protested the rising cost of living and poor treatment meted out to African customers. Directed by a "Boycott Control Committee" composed of members of the Urban Advisory Council, the Luanshya African Welfare Society and mine employees, the boycott was virtually complete and apart from isolated cases went off without incident. The purpose was to force an official investigation and to "raise Africans' wages in relation to the prices which the African has to pay for commodities."[75] The miners did not strike during the boycott, but the Roan Boss Boys' Committee threatened a work stoppage if the government did not appoint a study commission. The clerks' association supported the boss boys in a show of solidarity.[76] As Gore-Browne had predicted, Africans increasingly recognized their potential economic power, and seemed more determined than ever to exercise it.[77]

During this period of union resurgence, the Europeans also launched a campaign to establish a multi-racial union on the copper mines. This had long been a cherished plan of union leaders Brian Goodwin and Frank Maybank, who had been trying to convince the union to establish African branches since 1942. Both men believed that Africans would ultimately move up into more skilled positions, and they wanted to ensure it was done on the basis of equal pay for equal work. Both Goodwin and Maybank spoke primarily for white labor, but had the foresight to recognize the potential of multi-racial unionism. The government's deportation of Maybank in 1943 halted their efforts but in 1945, while in London trying to get Maybank back into Northern Rhodesia, Goodwin learned from Sir Walter Tryne (C.O.) that the Colonial Office was about to send a trade union advisor to the Copperbelt. Goodwin concluded that "knowing how the Colonial Office administrators' minds worked, it was going to be years from now and he was going to organize it mainly as a tribal elder system." Upon his return, Goodwin informed the union council that the government was going to organize African miners "whether we liked it or not."[78] He and Maybank (now back from exile) campaigned to incorporate the Africans into the European union, and soon won their point. In 1946 the union not only voted to delete clause 42, which reserved certain jobs by color, but also affirmed equal pay for equal work and promised to fight for trade schools to train African artisans. For the present, they offered black miners better living conditions and better pay.[79]

A group of black miners, most of them boss boys, accepted the European union's offer, and started setting up African branches at Rhokana and Roan. According to Brian Goodwin, these were soon "ticking away quite nicely;" they had a good chance of attracting African members.[80]

Most scholars have either ignored this unlikely alliance or blamed it on the machinations of self-interested European miners.[81] However, this overlooks very real changes that had been going on among the stabilized black miners. As we have seen, although these miners increasingly identified with the rest of the black miners as they came to realize the futility of exclusive unionism, they were gloomy about the prospects for an African trade union in the near future, knowing full well that "anyone who mentioned union in the African context before Mr. Comrie came was aiming for to get into trouble." As Pascale Sokota recalled, "Mr. Elwell got into trouble. . . . He happened to mention the word trade union, and that was enough to get him into trouble."[82] Consequently, many of the more ardent advocates of trade unionism concluded that a multi-racial union was the only viable prospect for African worker organization at the time. The boss boys, moreover, associated on a daily basis with European miners, often on quite good terms. They could see they had more in common with the European miners than with management, and many avidly supported equal pay for equal work.[83] While never naively willing to accept the European leaders' promises, and always somewhat suspicious of European good intentions, some of the higher-grade African miners could see they would be better off fighting management as part of a multi-racial union. As Stubbs revealed: "The Africans mistrusted the Europeans . . . but they were no fools. They were prepared to learn from anybody who would teach them."[84] And the lesson was clear: a permanent work organization with the Europeans was preferable to no organization at all.

GOVERNMENT AND COMPANY REACTIONS

Until the European union began organizing the African miners, the Colonial Office and the Northern Rhodesian government assumed African unionization was a specter of the distant future. In 1945, the new British Labor Government did little to alter Colonial Office policy towards African trade unions. Party stalwarts advocated gradual development of worker representation, with the emphasis on gradual. In fact, in 1946 Andrew Bevan, a Colonial Office advisor on labor affairs assigned to Northern Rhodesia, reported that "the African in Northern Rhodesia is not yet ready for industrial self-government and that for some time to come he will need help and guidance in the settlement of his affairs." The labor commissioner in Northern Rhodesia was in "complete agreement with Mr. Bevan's memorandum," claiming that "it will be difficult for some time to obtain true representation of the workers except on a tribal basis." Legislative Council members echoed this opinion, with Gore-Browne the only dissenting voice.[85]

Only when European union leaders and African miners began organizing joint meetings did government and mine officials become alarmed. The leading African miners had already proven their capacity for collective action in 1940 and in the Luanshya boycott. Officials realized a multi-racial union was a distinct possibility in spite of the tradition of racial conflict on the Copperbelt. The recent cooperation between European and African railway workers further underscored this possibility, and by April of 1946, the labor commissioner was urging the chief secretary to support African trade unions. "If we do not adopt this course," he warned, "I am sure we shall have trouble with irresponsible Unions."[86] In June, Gore-Brown and Welensky came out in favor of African trade unions, and when Governor Waddington, Gore-Browne, and Welensky went to London for a constitutional conference on Northern Rhodesia, they advised the Colonial Office to support some form of industrial organization for African miners. Otherwise, they warned, the European Mineworkers' Union would incorporate African miners into their union.[87] Despite opposition from the mining companies, the colonial state and settler capital insisted that state-dominated African unionism was necessary to maintain social order and the reproduction of the system, and they acted accordingly.

British officials responded favorably to these arguments. Labour Party leaders had long been suspicious of the white miners in Northern Rhodesia, and were easily persuaded of the dangers of a multi-racial union. Britain needed copper to rebuild after the war, and the government looked with disfavor on anything which threatened production. The new Secretary of State for the colonies, Arthur Creech Jones, was a well-known advocate of the African miners. He supported the Northern Rhodesian delegation, and in October of 1946 the Colonial Office sent a trade union specialist, William Comrie, to the Northern Rhodesian Labor Department for the express purpose of organizing African trade unions.[88]

In Northern Rhodesia, Governor Waddington opened the new session of the Legislative Council with a formal commitment to African trade unions, and most legislative members were in full accord. Still convinced that European and African antipathy would block a multi-racial union, the copper companies worried that the cure would be worse than the disease. They complained that "nothing [could be] more harmful to the Territory than forcing trade unionism on the African in his unprepared state of development."[89] However, this time Colonial Office policy and the colonial state prevailed, and Comrie arrived on the Copperbelt. An African Mineworkers' Union had unexpectedly become a reality.

CONCLUSION

The mining companies failed to perceive the inherent contradictions of stabilization without urbanization. Along with the colonial government, the companies assumed they could contain the consequences of stabilization by avoiding a permanent black urban work force. Consequently, when the boss boys, and later the clerks, managed to establish committees to advance their own interests, management refused to cooperate. This decision had unexpected consequences. By frustrating boss boy and clerk attempts to gain a narrow victory, the companies inadvertently pushed the miners towards a broader conceptualization of worker identity and a heightened awareness of the opposition between management and workers—an awareness capable of transcending racial divisions. Having perceived the futility of an elite solution, these miners increasingly recognized the need for a broadly-based organization to advance worker interests. Economic conditions after the war in turn pushed these miners towards collective action. Caught between falling real wages and rising expectations after the war, the more proletarian miners searched with new vigor for weapons with which to confront capital. Some of the boss boys and clerks joined the European union, an action which ultimately precipitated the African Mineworker's Union.

Thus, contrary to Berger's assertion that "African workers had shown little evidence of a wish to organize themselves independently,"[90] it is clear that corporate labor policies increased both worker cohesion and commitment to broadly-based organization. When the war ended and opportunities for collective action increased, these changes facilitated the creation of an African Mineworker's Union in the coppper industry.

6

The Unionization
of Black Labor, 1947–1953

INTRODUCTION

After a fitful start, the African Mineworkers' Union (AMWU) expanded dramatically. By 1953, it had to its credit a large membership, a successful three-week strike, and a veto of the tribal representatives. During these years, it entered into a long period of ambivalent relations with the African nationalist movement as well. The contradiction between union solidarity and political neutrality has led scholars to question the degree of class consciousness among the black miners. Most studies assume the unitary nature of the mines and mine compounds created an industrial parochialism which obscured both working-class indentity and the need for class-based political action to protect worker interests.[1] There is evidence, however, that the stabilized miners used the union to develop both worker consciousness and commitment to trade unionism among the African copper miners. Furthermore, the more highly skilled miners began to recognize that workers should join political parties to fight for class goals. Though constrained by corporate and state antagonism to union political activity, these miners urged Union support for the emerging nationalist party on the grounds that their plight would not improve until Africans controlled the government.

COMPANY OPPOSITION TO THE UNION

The companies were less sanguine than government in their assessment of African trade unions. Management regarded trade unions "as a real menace,"and initially hoped to forestall full unionization.[2] At the Johannesburg Conference in December 1946, both companies "stressed the dangers and difficulties attending the implementation of the Government policy and [decided] to slow it down as much as possible."[3] The companies urged the labor department to introduce collective bargaining techniques through the works committees, which had replaced the boss boys' committees and the clerks' associations in 1946. The committees had

114

about 15 members, representing different departments. Most members had been in a boss boys' committee or clerks' association; a number were tribal representatives.[4] The Chamber tried to convince Comrie to meet with the works committees, and to gradually teach them trade union principles.[5] The mines hoped this would divert miner interest in trade unions, and neutralize Comrie's presence on the Copperbelt.

However, the higher-grade black miners and the European Mineworkers' Union opposed such a policy. Goodwin and Maybank continued arranging meetings with interested African miners to establish African branches of the European union. They circulated pamphlets on trade unionism in the compounds, and held regular meetings outside the compounds. The African branches continued meeting at Nkana and Luanshya. By the time Comrie arrived in 1947, it was clear that trade unions, with or without European workers, were going to be established.[6]

Government and Colonial Office officials pressed the companies to support an African union, fearing African branches of the European union might be established at any time. They worried about the potential bargaining power of a multi-racial union, and the possibility that it might threaten future copper revenues, and consequently the transfer of surplus to the metropole. Government officials, and some legislative council members, believed a government-monitored African union would be easier to control.[7] They also warned that subversive radical influences from South African socialists might have unpleasant consequences. Placing the need for social order above the short-range desires of the mines, the government rejected Chamber arguments for worker committees, and bluntly informed the companies that "it was not for the Government, nor the Chamber, to lay down how the African Union should conduct themselves."[8] The labor commissioner insisted that "the advice of the Trade Union officer must be available to any African, individuals, or groups, who ask for it."[9]

These threats, along with continued efforts by the European union, finally persuaded the companies to abandon their opposition. Management reluctantly conceded the inevitability of some kind of African trade union, and suddenly Comrie found "management's attitude leaves nothing to be desired. The change is almost embarrassing."[10]

The companies then joined forces with the labor department to stop the European union by warning the black miners to ignore European union leaders. Working through the tribal representatives and the works committees, the officers played on the long history of abuse and suspicion between the races. The alliance between white and black miners was too fragile to withstand such pressure. Black miners were easily persuaded that "the European miners had sweet tongues, but didn't mean what they say."[11] On a more pragmatic level, Katilungu opined that African interests would suffer in a multi-racial union dominated by whites. He and Namitengo did not rule out the possibility of eventual amalgamation between the two unions, but for the time being, the Africans decided to form their own union.[12] Goodwin reported that "when I went back to hold a normal branch meeting [at Nkana] I was snubbed. A similar thing happened at Luanshya, where I had formed two branches also. . . . Once the African union was organized by Comrie, we [the European union] couldn't even get close to it. We couldn't even liaison with it because of the influence from the colonial administration. . . . Scrivener did a lot to keep us away. He got regulations supported by management that you had to get written permission if you wanted to enter the compound. All this was against us."[13] Those Africans who continued to support the Europeans were soon shouted down by their fellow workers, and a few were even dismissed.

Despite this cooperation, the companies still opposed rapid unionization among the miners. Management saw Comrie as a dangerous radical, bent on stirring up unreasonable demands among the black miners. In meetings with government and labor department officials, management questioned whether "unionism was really wanted or understood by Africans," and demanded that "unions not be pushed forward artificially."[14] The companies tried in every way they could to slow down the pace of unionization. Sometimes the compound managers refused Comrie and his followers a place to hold meetings in the compounds. Company spies attended meetings, and the companies sent their often highly inflammatory and inaccurate reports to Lusaka. The Chamber also opposed the establishment of a full-time union secretary and a closed shop.[15]

While sometimes irked by management resistance, government and labor department officials shared its misgivings about African unions. They especially worried that an idealistic Colonial Office might give too much power to African labor. Increasingly influential settler voices in the legislative council railed against misplaced Colonial Office paternalism. Sympathetic government officials, while supporting African trade unions, clearly looked to contain African labor action, and government officials pressed Labor Commissioner William Stubbs to keep Comrie under control, something Stubbs fully agreed with. As a result, Stubbs informed Comrie pointblank that "while it was his job to explain what trade unions were, the longer it took him to form one the better that I would be pleased."[16] Law was stationed at Nkana as senior labor officer, "to keep a friendly eye on Comrie." This was particularly necessary from the administration's point of view because Comrie had to work through an interpreter. "The administration was worried about him [Comrie] talking to interpreters and what the interpreters might say." An early report that an interpreter for Comrie was translating "strike" as "fight" only increased government anxiety.[17]

Under this pressure from government and company officials, Comrie agreed to proceed slowly, but steadily, towards an African union. For his part Comrie preferred this course because of some earlier experiences in Germany, where he felt he had pushed unions prematurely.[18] As a result, the labor department ruled that "if workers wished to organize, the department of labor would make available to them people who would help them in the techniques, the practices, of organizing, and help them with an understanding of the legislation over all labor matters. We taught them some of the basics of economics so they didn't make ridiculous demands, and showed them how to read a simple balance sheet."[19] Comrie met regularly with his early followers, and drilled them in trade union principles. But there was no sense of urgency once the threat of a multi-racial union subsided.[20]

STABILIZATION AND THE UNION

Initially, the ability and determination of the black miners to establish a strong trade union movement remained in question. While interested, most African miners had remained aloof from the attempt to form a multi-racial union, and for some good reasons. There was no tradition of trade unionism among the mineworkers, only the history of two bloody strikes, and many workers identified collective industrial protest with shootings and death. For the unskilled short-term worker, unions remained very much in question. They "wanted to know what benefits would come from the trade union."[21] One person later recalled, "A lot of people were afraid to join the union because they thought if they quarreled with the companies they would be sacked."[22] Some of the tribal representatives opposed a union, fearing the loss of their own prestige, and discouraged union membership.[23]

However, despite the cautious attitude of company and government officials and the initial reluctance of many black miners, within a few years the union had developed a large committed membership, organized a successful Copperbelt-wide strike, and voted the tribal representatives out of power in the mine compounds. How can we account for this development? Stabilization emerges as the necessary but not sufficient ingredient. The growing determination of all black miners to fight for higher wages, some support from government officials and the rise in copper prices with the 1949 devaluation of sterling certainly argued for unionism. At the same time, the stabilized more skilled miners provided both the leadership and support so crucial for the union's rapid expansion.

After the war, the companies continued to rely on stabilization in order to provide the labor necessary for an increasingly copper-hungry world. By 1950, over 2,000 black miners on the Copperbelt had completed 120 months or more in the employment of the mining companies.[24] At Roan, in 1951, out of a total of 8,426 workers, 4,586 had worked two years or longer, and 2,321 had over four years' employment.[25] Clyde Mitchell's 1951–52 survey of Roan discovered that 42.3% of the miners were uncertain when they would return home (go home when wealthy, etc.), and 23.4% saw themselves as semi-permanent or permanent town dwellers.[26] Anglo-American figures were less complete, but still revealed increased stabilization. In 1951, Mitchell collected data from Nchanga which indicated that 49.2% of Nchanga's African work force (5,649 men) had worked longer than a year on the mine, and that 19.8% of the work force had been employed longer than two years. The percentage of married workers among the higher grade miners rose correspondingly. At Nchanga, for example, miners employed longer than a year generally did more skilled labor, and a higher percentage were married as well.[27] By March 1948, 60.6% of Mufulira's workers and 56% of Roan's workers were married. Anglo-American lagged behind with 44% at Nchanga and 49.3% at Rhokana, but by September 1952, these figures had risen to 61% and 46.2% respectively. Soon after that, the Chamber of Mines set a maximum of 60% married labor at each mine.[28] Thus, by the late 1940s, at least 50% of the black miners on the Copperbelt could no longer be classified as migrant laborers, in that they had long established communal and occupational ties in the industrial area.

Table 6. **Percentage of Married African Mine Employees, 1948–1952**

Mine	1948	1949	1950	1951	1952
Mufulira:					
No. employed	7,526	7,734	8,769	8,548	8,893
% married	56.40	58.30	61.42	62.13	62.84
Nchanga:					
No. employed	4,155	4,559	5,449	5,826	5,907
% married	44.32	45.78	52.89	58.27	55.27
Nkana:					
No. employed	10,052	10,227	10,837	11,295	10,862
% married	51.13	44.56	45.50	45.47	51.33
Roan Antelope:					
No. employed	10,782	11,136	11,275	10,359	10,074
% married	54.40	49.40	53.75	58.50	63.65
Totals:					
No. employed	35,841	36,429	39,456	39,545	30,311
% married	52.06	50.52	53.18	54.92	57.75

Source: Northern Rhodesia Department of Mines, *Annual Report*, 1952, p. 25.

As we have seen, by the end of the war many of the stabilized miners accepted the need for some form of broadly-based collective labor organization. The same factors which encouraged this attitude continued to operate after the war. The rising cost of living, dependence upon wage labor, and expectations of lengthy residence at the mines pressed against low African wages, while experiences at work and in the compounds heightened awareness of worker identification and opposition to management. Individual and elite protests had proven unsuccessful, and many of the stabilized miners began to see trade unions as the only weapon for advancement. As Mwendapole recalled, "It wasn't difficult to point out to these miners that when they got organized you will be able to improve this or remove that."[29]

It was from among the most skilled stabilized miners that Comrie found his most committed followers. He met many of them at a meeting of Scrivener's "Brain Trust," an interracial group of Europeans and Africans in existence since 1947 that discussed matters of mutual interest. Much to his surprise, Comrie "found extraordinary similarity between the more experienced African worker in the Mines and Europeans of various races in industry elsewhere."[30] He was "impressed by the very intelligent standard of the questions and, above all, by the amazing frankness of the speakers." He felt that "there is a minority . . . who are definitely well advanced and who hold very definite views on the position of the African generally."[31] He chose ten trusted men to help proselytize among the miners. They were chosen by their established reputation on the mines and became known as "the disciples." Most of them had been out of the rural areas for over ten years, had more education than the average miner, and worked in group 6 or higher. Of the ten, two were Lozi, two Nyasa, one Coloured, and four Bemba. Most were either clerks or boss boys.[32]

The disciples and other early converts preached unionism within the compounds. All were well known and respected, and many were active in compound organizations such as welfare programs and church groups. As the strike leaders had done in 1940, the union leaders mobilized followers through contacts in compound organizations as well as family and friends, and networks. They even asked sympathetic tribal elders to lobby for attendance at union meetings. Indeed, some early union supporters were tribal representatives, such as Herbert Gwanda at Roan. As in the past, however, the stabilized higher-grade miners played the key role. They had the most to gain from a union, and the greatest commitment to worker representation. They led the union movement.[33]

News of union meetings spread quickly through the compounds. Meetings soon became major social events, drawing large audiences. One informant recalled, "It was the union in those days, you know. And if union people called a meeting, you can even see men and women and children listening to the union men talking."[34]

Comrie's support, together with the prestige of the early union leaders, reassured doubting miners. The meetings "made people feel happier and more hopeful."[35] The experience of common problems in the compounds wove ties of sympathy between privileged and lower-grade miners, and made residents more receptive to union advocates. Work experiences helped too. Miners of all grades could see that on their own they had not been able to raise wages or alter corporate labor policies. All agreed on the need for higher wages, greater job security, and improvements in work and living conditions. They listened intently to the trade union organizers' assertions that only a union could bring these desired improvements. This argument carried a great deal of weight with miners on all grade levels, and support for the union began to build at each of the mines. As one miner told Epstein, "I joined in 1949 because all the people I trusted and knew to be wise were the ones who were encouraging others to join—especially my tribesmen who were educated."[36]

THE ESTABLISHMENT OF THE UNION

The first success for Comrie's followers came at Nkana, where a union branch was formed in February 1948. A few prominent supervisory miners resisted, preferring to follow Goodwin and Maybank, but Comrie's arguments and the long history of abuse and racialism by European miners tipped the scales. The miners decided to establish their own union under Comrie's guidance. Executive Committee elections were keenly contested. Lawrence Katilungu,[37] Simon Kaluwa, and Philip Simwanza won the positions of president, secretary, and treasurer, respectively. Except for Kaluwa, the candidates were either mine clerks or hospital orderlies. The prominence of stabilized higher-grade workers in the union movement reflected the politicizing effects of stabilization. While Katilungu's underground experience and connections with Bemba royalty undoubtedly broadened his appeal, it was his experience as an industrial worker and his negotiating skills that sealed his election.[38]

The Nkana Committee members worked long and hard, touring the Copperbelt in efforts to arouse support. Comrie came with them. "Many of the meetings [were] history lectures in which Comrie explained the history of the trade union in Britain, and of the growth of the Labour Party and how it succeeded. . . . It was a slow business stretching over the months with regular visits to each of the towns."[39] The task was not an easy one. Compound managers were hostile and refused to provide meeting rooms, which held down attendance. The *African Miner* speaks of these men as "the first inspired, who did not mind when and how they slept, nor what and how they ate, wherever they went.[40]

Gradually branches started at each mine. By May 1948, Mufulira's had 300 members and an Executive Committee. A union branch formed more slowly at Roan, where some of the leading black miners continued working towards a multi-racial union.[41] The higher degree of skill and longer association with European workers at Roan probably increased African receptivity to these overtures, a situation which Comrie found "most irritating." Many distrusted the "Nyanja-cum-clerical element," who comprised the majority of those interested in starting a union. The boycott also preoccupied many leading miners during 1947. However, by

June 1948, a few keen members of the works committee and 150 Africans decided to form a union. Nchanga finally established a branch in late 1948. By that time, all four mines had branches, with a total membership of 5,000.[42]

In March 1949, the four branches united to form the African Mineworkers' Union. By that time, there were 3,200 paid members at Mufulira, 1,800 at Roan, 2,180 at Nchanga, and over 5,000 at Nkana. Although ultimate authority was vested in an annual conference of delegates from all branches, executive power rested with the executive council elected by the annual conference. The council consisted of about 21 members, who met at least four times a year. The supreme council—an inner core composed of the president, secretary, and treasurer—directed the union's business with the consent of the executive council and the annual conference. The union president chaired executive council meetings and had a casting vote in meetings of the supreme council and conference. The general secretary, while subordinate to the president, had vast discretionary powers as well, which allowed him to build up personal followings along patron-client lines. A delegates' conference, held at Nkana in March 1949,[43] elected Lawrence Katilungu, president, Simon Kaluwa, general secretary, and Philip Simwanza general treasurer. Robinson Puta was elected vice president, Jameson Chapoloko, deputy general secretary, and J. R. Namitengo, vice treasurer.[44]

The companies signed a Recognition Agreement with the union in which they acknowledged the African Mineworkers' Union as the sole organization representing African interests on the mines. Individual union branches had their negotiating rights curtailed, and the union was formally recognized as the spokesmen for all the miners in the copper industry.[45]

The mines also agreed to a new manning structure, and a general wage increase in 1949. The grade divisions increased from three to eight, with grade 1 being unskilled. These divisions created greater opportunities for occupational mobility and a wider range of wage levels. Scales increased in each group as well, particularly among the higher groups. This settlement rewarded all miners, while reassuring the stabilized miners that their interests would be protected.[46]

CORPORATE EFFORTS TO CONTAIN THE AFRICAN MINEWORKERS' UNION

Despite the signing of the Recognition Agreement and the favorable wage settlement, the companies worried that the fledging union would begin to make "unreasonable" demands. In order to avoid this, they contrived to contain union activities. The companies renewed efforts to advance more skilled black miners into formerly white-dominated jobs on the assumption that advancement and not trade unionism was the real goal of the stabilized higher-grade miners.[47] Management at both mines hoped new job opportunities would divert these miners from union activities. Since these miners were both the most ardent union members and the most experienced organizers, diverting them had the potential of inhibiting the union movement. The companies also stood to gain by the substitution of cheaper black labor, which they were more anxious to achieve now that an African trade union threatened to raise black labor costs.

An abortive conference in 1947 among the European Mineworkers' Union, the government, and the mine bogged down over the European union's insistence that Africans doing formerly European jobs receive equal pay. Without that condition, European union leaders claimed advancement was merely a cover for cheap labor substitution. Both government and company officials balked, claiming that African labor was not yet capable of equal performance on the job. Management insisted that the principle of African progression "resolved itself into one of sociological or public policy," and therefore was a matter for government. The companies wanted a public declaration by the government supporting the principle of African progression, and an eventual legislative solution.[48]

The companies pressed the Colonial Office for a commission to study the issue in hopes that its recommendation favoring African advancement would supply the rationale for legislation. In 1948, the Colonial Office set up a commission, headed by Andrew Dalgleish, a veteran British trade-unionist, member of the Forster Commission in 1940, and participant in the 1947 talks. His willingness to accept advancement without equal pay during the abortive three-party talks had aroused the wrath of the European union. As a result, the Europeans refused to cooperate with the commission, but it went ahead and, after careful evaluation, recommended that 54 categories of work not performed by Africans could be opened up either immediately or after a period of training.[49]

However, political changes in Northern Rhodesia undermined the possibility that these recommendations would be adopted by the legislature. The European community had been greatly strengthened in 1945 when a majority of 13 to 9 was granted to elected versus nominated Legislative Council members. Three years later, official and elected members were given ten seats each, and four seats were added for nominated unofficial members representing African interests, two of whom were Africans.[50] Also in 1948, the Council developed a convention whereby the consent of four unofficial members was given the same weight as the advice of all eleven. These changes greatly increased settler power, particularly that of the white miners. Increasingly government had to compromise with the European community in its daily affairs. As a result, when the Dalgleish report provoked an outcry in the Legislative Council, especially from labor leaders Brian Goodwin and Roy Welensky, the governor tabled the report until a more auspicious moment.[51]

The moment failed to come as Europeans in Northern Rhodesia were swept up in a move to establish a Central African Federation out of the two Rhodesias and Nyasaland. Self-rule had long been a dream of the settler community, but their previous attempts had been rejected. However, when Welensky and a few other settler politicans raised the possibility of Federation, the Colonial Office responded more favorably.[52] The mines supported Federation as well. As the federal issue rose to the fore, the mines became less willing to risk white miner anger over the advancement issue. Dalgleish recommended a three-party conference meet in August 1948 (chaired by Attorney-General Edgar Unsworth), but it soon foundered on the equal pay issue. After unsuccessful attempts to mediate disputes, the government withdrew its support, declaring that it would wait for new developments, particularly changes brought on by Federation.[53]

Although advancement fell victim to politics, the companies found other methods to frustrate the union. They lobbied for separate unions at each mine, arguing that "it is quite wrong at this stage for the Africans to organize on a Copperbelt basis and that for a long time to come each mine should have its separate Union which would negotiate only with the Management of that mine."[54] When that failed, the companies resorted to general uncooperativeness. They also failed to install a phone in the head offices for the union, and refused to allow automatic deductions of union dues from the payroll until 1951. The general manager insisted that the African personnel managers act as intermediaries between union leaders and themselves, and rejected special privileges for the Union's Executive Committee on the ground that they "would give the Executive Committee an undue sense of their own importance."[55]

In order to better handle union complaints, the companies reorganized the compound administration in 1949. They renamed the mine compounds mine African townships, the compound administration became the African personnel department, and the compound manager became the African personnel manager. The African personnel department now paralleled the European departments at each mine. The department heads advised European miners to handle African employees "very differently from the past." Complaints against black workers were to convey "the bare facts only, no suggestions."[56] Management hoped this procedure would minimize union accusations of victimization and other abuses.

The mines also strengthened the mine police. A limited number of police were given the power to arrest miners in the compounds "for affray, theft, and house breaking, not for illegal brewing." This was a temporary measure until the Northern Rhodesian police could take over, reflecting management's continued belief "that [mine] police have to be kept under constant supervision, otherwise they make more trouble than one would have without them."[57] In an effort to counter police unreliability, and to ensure alternate sources of information, the companies sent hired informers to trade union meetings and other compound activities. Both union leaders and labor officers "were watched the whole time."[58]

The mines also increased the status and authority of the tribal representatives in an effort to divide the work force along ethnic lines and undercut union influence. Management insisted that compound conditions, and in fact anything not relating to industrial matters, remain the preserve of the tribal representatives, which pitted union against tribal leaders. As Field put it, "Any setback the union may receive will strengthen the tribal representatives."[59] Many representatives opposed the union, fearing loss of their authority and willingly cooperated with the mines.

Most important, the companies pressed government labor officials to maintain control over the union. They complained to the government that African personnel managers were losing "much of their ability to command respect and obedience among the African labor force." The companies even sent highly inaccurate reports to government officials which contributed to "this feeling growing up in Lusaka that something terrible was happening in the Copperbelt." In addition, they pressured labor officers and the provincial administration into persuading union leaders to be "reasonable and limit their demands."[60]

The governor and the provincial administration supported management's efforts to control the union. The governor even personally reprimanded Roan's branch chairman, Alfred Mwalwanda, for "rude behavior."[61] Government officials willingly joined the mines in an effort to moderate labor department support for the union. The labor commissioner thus directed all his subordinates "to instill in the minds of representatives of African Trade Unions that truculent and offensive behavior can only harm their cause." Even Comrie was ordered "to assist in the development of good industrial relations between employers and employees."[62] The more idealistic labor officers' concern for African labor was circumscribed by the state. The colonial government and the settlers wanted African unions to contain African labor rather than to protect it. As in so many other parts of Africa, labor officers increasingly became mediators between management and labor rather than advocates of labor.

THE UNION AND COLLECTIVE LABOR ACTION

Still union leaders pressed for improvements. Working within the guidelines set by the Recognition Agreement, branch leaders met regularly with African personnel managers to discuss such issues as alleged victimization, unfair discharges, assaults, work, and compound conditions. The supreme council negotiated with the Chamber over issues affecting the mines as a whole, although sometimes Katilungu intervened when local discussions reached an impasse. Between 1949 and 1953, the union engaged in over thirty separate disputes, and organized more than twelve strikes, one of which was industry-wide.[63]

Table 7. African Trade Union Strength

Mine	Total African Employees	African Trade Union Members	% of Total
Mufulira	9,043	7,908	87.45%
Nchanga	5,886	4,239	72.02%
Rhokana	11,509	6,533	56.76%
Roan	10,373	8,037	77.48%

Source: RCM/CSD/202.5, no. 3, NRCM, Memo on the AMWU, 11 November 1952.

Union membership increased dramatically. In 1949 about 19,000 miners out of a total work force of 36,972 belonged to the union, and in three years membership rose to 25,000, or over 80% of the black mine work force.[64] While the greatest number of trade union members were in Groups 1 and 2, the higher-grade longer-service miners had the highest percentage of union membership (see Table 8). At Nchanga, for example, 67.3% of African miners making more than 150 shillings per ticket belonged to the union, as opposed to 30.7% of those making between 25 and 49 shillings per ticket.[65]

Table 8. Nchanga Employees Contributing and Not Contributing to Trade Union Funds through Paysheets, 1951

Group	Non-Contributing	Contributing	Total	% Contributing
0		1	1	100.0
1	2,174	1,126	3,300	34.2
2	189	144	333	43.2
3	303	246	549	44.8
4	399	467	866	53.9
5	168	205	373	55.0
6	52	73	125	58.4
7	11	21	32	65.6
8	21	40	61	65.6
Special	1	8	9	88.9
Totals	3,318	2,331	5,649	41.5

Source: J. Clyde Mitchell, Data from Nchanga Consolidated Mines Staff Records, 30 April 1951. Table 10.

Table 9. **Nchanga Trade Union Contributors by Length of Service, 1951**

Length of Service in Months	Total Employees	% Contributing
Under 12	2,870	34.3
12–23	1,662	42.7
24–35	730	54.5
36–47	204	58.8
48–59	87	66.7
60–71	34	61.7
72–83	24	58.3
84 and Over	38	71.1
Total	5,649	41.2

Source: J. Clyde Mitchell, Nchanga Staff Records Survey, 30 April 1951. Table 28.

In 1952 the union proved that it could organize Copperbelt-wide strike action. The 1952 strike revealed both increased solidarity among the workers and improved organizational skills among union leaders. Fully 79% of union members voted to strike when the union called a strike ballot after wage negotiations with the Chamber broke down early in the fall of 1952.[66] Despite disputes within the leadership over the proper political stance for the union, union leaders and union members closed rank behind Katilungu in support for the strike. The union set to work organizing a strike plan through committees at each mine. Strict rules were imposed. "They were not to move in large numbers, not to listen to any rumors, as much as possible to keep in the house or go into the bush for hunting; to use the time as much as possible in gardening, to keep away from beerhalls and from drunkeness. In case of any wild rumors, the section leaders were to be consulted." Section committees set up picket lines. A meeting called on October 19 at one of the Rhokana mine welfare fields drew the largest crowd ever on the Copperbelt. Union leaders addressed the crowd, and Katilungu told the audience, "This meeting is a symbol of labor unity on the Copperbelt. . . . It represents the culmination of long and difficult struggle by the Africans." He asked everyone to "respect the spirit of this struggle," and told the crowd "I have put my finger on the mouth of the gun which killed our brothers. I promise you one thing, no rifle will be shot at anyone if you follow my orders."[67]

The strike proceeded as planned, and for three long weeks the union maintained strict discipline. Almost no one was to be seen, F. M. N. Heath, the District Commissioner at Luanshya, noticed that African picket men were on guard at the entrance of the Mine Townships,

but there were no passers-by to attract attention. As you drove past the rows of huts where the strikers lived there was hardly a sign of life. Not even the children, who normally would be playing in the yards and along the roadsides, were to be seen. There was no one moving about. The Mine Officers were deserted. . . . Throughout the day the atmosphere remained unchanged as if human activity had ceased. . . . There was no excitement and no crowds gathered at street-corners. No one seemed interested in the mine lying silent across the valley.

The strike continued in this manner for nearly a month. Miners and their wives cultivated their gardens for food, and occasional public meetings provided instructions and moral support.[68]

When the companies finally agreed to arbitration, the African union accepted an offer from the European Mineworkers' Union to bring out Ronald Williams, legal advisor to the British National Union of Mineworkers to help with the talks. Under Maybank's direction, the European union supported African demands, and worked closely with the African union and Ronald Williams to bring about a favorable settlement.[69] The African union, in turn, supported the European union's position on equal pay for equal work, (something they had also privately negotiated with the union in 1950).[70] The African union not only organized its workers in collective labor action, it also proved itself capable of recognizing interests in common with Europeans.

Later in 1953, the union once again proved its capacity to mobilize the mineworkers by organizing a campaign to abolish the tribal representatives in the mine compounds. This came in the wake of the companies' plan to expand the number of representatives by creating a Copperbelt Tribal Council. Most of the representatives welcomed the idea, hoping it would stop the highly resented incursions on their authority by court assessors, trade union officials, and political leaders.[71] On 11 December 1952, the council held an inaugural meeting at Wusikili. The African personnel managers informed members that the mine committees would receive funds for compound welfare, and that they would "have district responsibility as a sort of Town Council and . . . [the mines expected] them to engage more and more in the welfare of the people living in the Townships."[72] The Council was to act as a workers' representative for all problems outside the work place. This threatened union authority, and the union leaders reacted immediately. They called meetings in every mine township to denounce the tribal representatives as traitors to the union and federal stooges. Branch officials asked miners to pressure tribal representatives to return their gowns, and to stop cooperating with the companies. At Nchanga, violence nearly broke out when Robinson Puta, secretary of the Nchanga union branch, threatened recalcitrant representatives. Union leaders demanded the abolition of the tribal representatives, and asked the Chamber to put the issue to a vote. Reluctantly, the companies agreed to a secret ballot in March 1953. The union leaders expected the same cooperation they had received during the recent strike, and they judged correctly. The miners rejected the representatives by a resounding vote: 84.1% of the labor force voted, and 96.9% voted against retention.[73]

THE UNION AND AFRICAN NATIONALIST POLITICS

During this same period, African nationalism was growing in Northern Rhodesia in response to the European bid for federation. Africans in Northern Rhodesia feared that Southern Rhodesia would dominate the Federation. They knew Southern Rhodesia well, and had no desire to see its institutions adopted in their own country. In resistance to federation, the 1948 annual meeting of the Federation of African Societies transformed itself into a political body, the Northern Rhodesian Congress. In 1951 the congress was renamed the Northern Rhodesian African Congress, and Harry Nkumbula was elected president.[74]

Many unionists joined the party. In 1952, Congress set up a Supreme Action Council to plan and, if necessary, to order a total withdrawal of labor in order to cripple the colonial government. Both the president and the secretary of the African Mineworkers' Union held seats on the council and endorsed its aims.[75]

Some of the leaders of the African Mineworkers' Union organized closer cooperation between workers and Congress through the Trade Union Congress (TUC). Formed in 1951 under Comrie's guidance, the Congress had fallen into disuse under Katilungu's leadership. Capitalizing on this neglect, the Puta/Chapoloko faction of the union turned the TUC into a forum for anti-Federation propaganda. Both Robinson Puta and Jameson Chapoloko opposed the separation of political and industrial issues. They called on African workers to unite against the colonial state in a movement for national liberation. The TUC maintained a political subcommittee which included a number of prominent branch leaders from the AMWU. It formulated plans for rallying worker support behind the nationalist movement.[76] Chapoloko even spoke of a Federation-wide TUC. While dubious about Southern Rhodesia, Chapoloko "hoped they would get such an organization going within two years, with Nkumbula as President. Thus uniting under Congress they would be able to gain a stranglehold on the economy."[77]

Despite both the structural and ideological congruence between the African Mineworkers' Union and Congress, union leaders were divided on the question of political involvement. The more militant among them preferred close cooperation between the union and Congress, while Katilungu and the moderates were more circumspect. Katilungu stopped the Supreme Action Council's call for a political strike in February 1952 because it would interfere with an industrial dispute then in progress on the mines. He refused to cooperate with Puta and Chapoloko's plan to call

Table 10. **Trade Union Congress Officers and Political
Action Subcommittees, 1952**

Executive Officers, August 1952		
Office	Name	Union
President	Dixon Konkola	Railway Workers
Vice-President	Robinson Puta	Mineworkers' Union
General Secretary	Matthew Nkoloma	Mineworkers' Union
Executive Member	Jameson Chapoloko	Mineworkers' Union
Executive Member	Justin Chimba	Unknown
Political Action Subcommittee, 1952		
Chairman	Dixon Konkola	Railway Workers
Secretary	Matthew Nkoloma	Mineworkers' Union
Member	Paul Kalichini	Industrial Workers
Member	Jonathan Mubanga	Municipal Workers
Member	Chanda	Railway Workers
Member	Matthew Mwendapole	Mineworkers' Union
Member	Jameson Kamitengo	Mineworkers' Union
Member	Jameson Chapoloko	Mineworkers' Union
Member	Gordon Chindele	Mineworkers' Union

Source: Bates, *Unions*, p. 127.

a strike at Nkana protesting the deportation of Simon Zukas, a European involved in the ANC and an advocate of worker political involvement. When management dismissed Chapoloko and others involved in the strike, Katilungu did not protest. Later in March 1953, Katilungu withdrew the union's support for Congress' two days of national prayer to protest British support for federation. Katilungu claimed participation in the strike would bring massive dismissals and threaten the union. He believed the union's job was to fight for a better position for African miners, and so refused to countenance political action which might endanger worker interests.[78]

THE UNION, CONSCIOUSNESS, AND CLASS ACTION

This contrast between the African union's aggressive pursuit of collective labor action in the industrial sphere, and its ambivalent relations with Congress, has long puzzled scholars. Most Copperbelt studies have accepted Epstein's hypothesis that the distinctive, unitary nature of mine work and the mine compounds produced a parochial group consciousness which encouraged commitment to trade unionism, but obscured class identity at the workplace and in the political arena. Berger even questions the existence of group solidarity among the miners and stresses the divisions within the union. Henderson is more aware of the miners' role in the development of nationalist politics, but also questions the degree of class consciousness or even trade union consciousness among the miners.[79]

Such scholars not only underestimate the consciousness of the stabilized black miners, they also underestimate their commitment to forming a broadly-based worker organization and the ability to bring along fellow miners in this effort. In addition, they devalue miner belief in nationalist politics.

As we have seen, the early union leaders were stabilized miners, most of whom already supported worker solidarity and collective labor action. Comrie's lessons on trade unionism further clarified this perception. As Mwendapole recalled, "Comrie taught us that we must organize ourselves, that when we got organized we could improve this or remove that."[80] A number of Comrie's early followers recalled being deeply affected by his lectures, particularly his insistence on the need for worker solidarity.[81] The very structure of the work force, moreover, forced the stabilized miners to identify with the work force as a whole. Although a larger percentage of the higher groups belonged to the union, there were more lower group members. At Roan, for example, 46% of Groups 6 through Special Group (6% of the work force) were union members, while 19% of Groups 1 through 4 (85% of the work force) belonged to the union. However, Groups 1 through 3 held 60% of the union membership.[82] The numerical preponderance of less-skilled miners kept the union leaders from adopting an exclusivist orientation and all but forced them to stress solidarity regardless of ethnic or occupational identities.

In order to broaden its appeal, the union deliberately addressed problems which affected both lower- and higher-grade miners. After winning an initial wage increase in 1949, the union turned its attention to housing and compound conditions. Branch officials held regular interviews with the African personnel managers to discuss specific complaints. In 1949, for example, the Roan union branch asked for roofs over the latrines and showers, for wash slabs in the washing blocks, sluices in latrine floors, and doors for kitchens. The Supreme Council requested better housing and increased rations for everyone, as well as electric lights in compound housing. Wage demands always included advances for all grades. The union also demanded special improvements for higher-grade miners, such as special shades and gauze for better housing, an inclusive wage covering the cost of food, and improvements in special and improved-type housing.[83] Thus, as much as possible, the demands aimed to increase the union's popularity with the entire work force.

The trade union leaders taught trade union principles and built commitment to the union through monthly public meetings. These meetings attracted large crowds; attendance ran as high as 8,000 or more. Fanny Musumbulwa recalled that "if union people called a meeting, you can even see men and women and children listening to the union men talking."[84] The local Executive Committee ran the meetings, but rank and file participation in discussions was encouraged. Workers were reassured that "the changa-changa cannot discharge you for staying in the Union," and in general were encouraged to believe that only the union could bring them more improvements.[85] Unity was also stressed. As one leader put it:

> The union emphasized all people were workers, as one tribe. People felt very strongly about that. We had trade union leaders from different tribes. This broke up the tribal divisions. For example if someone said I'm from Ngoni, I'm from this and that, but when these leaders came to speak at the meeting, it doesn't matter whether they are Bemba, Ngoni, for they all went to hear the trade union meeting, it was for the trade union not for Bemba, not for Ngoni, or any other tribe, but it was for everybody, and when the changes came they came for everyone.[86]

At both the large monthly meetings and in the daily bustle of the branch office, union leaders denounced ethnic and occupational divisions, insisting that "there must be brotherly feelings and true fellowship in every Trade Union."[87] These "lessons" helped to overcome ethnic and occupational differences and bred the capacity for class identity.

Union leaders also emphasized the stability of the black work force, the unequal rewards given to black and white labor on the mines, and the need to organize effective action to reduce these inequalities. As far as Katilungu was concerned, "Labor in the Copperbelt was stable." He framed union demands on the assumption that African miners were full and permanent members of the industrial work force. This position legitimized union demands, for if African miners were fully committed industrial laborers, the union could legitimately claim the same rights and needs as European labor. The gap in remuneration between black and white labor, said the leaders, should reflect occupational differences rather than color. They also pointed to the readily visible differences in the living standards of black labor as proof for their argument. This in fact became a constant theme. For example, in 1951 Katilungu argued that "the Europeans employed on the mine were supplied with furniture and electric light, therefore it was not thought too much for the Africans to ask for electric lights in all houses." A year earlier, the union demanded a profit-sharing scheme for African miners identical to that enjoyed by European miners.[88]

Table 11. **Mineworkers' Average Monthly Wages, 1952**

	African	European
Surface	83s	£89.0s
Underground	101s7d	£101.0s

Source: Notes on the Conciliation Proceedings with the African Mineworkers' Union 1–6 October 1952. CISB, Economic and Statistics Bulletin, August 1952.

The process of negotiating with the companies further sharpened worker perceptions. Management's frequent refusals to accede to union demands clarified, and even dramatized, the class cleavages. The frequent deflection or outright refusal of union demands, support for the tribal representatives, the refusal to grant a closed shop, and the last-minute compromise on a profit-sharing scheme, together with frequent minor irritations, magnified awareness of management's hostility. Katilungu expressed this when he complained that "the Union leaders . . . were surprised when they heard the Chairman continually say 'no' to their requests."[89] With each unsuccessful negotiation, both union leaders and members grew more aware of the antagonism between workers and management.

Miners increasingly turned to branch officials for help with their problems. Matthew Mwendapole, a branch official at Nchanga, recalled that "there were always a lot of people in the office, all complaining about different things. I would go to morning council, and then I would stay there all day till 10 o'clock in the evening. People would come through complaining about this and complaining about that."[90] Even unsuccessful negotiations failed to stop the union's growth, for most miners perceived the futility of alternative forms of labor protest. They believed that the union was a weapon which would make management realize that "we are not people to play with."[91] Union leaders promised future successes if the workers remained solidly behind the union. Clearly this promise was enough, for by 1951 almost all miners were pro-union. As Mwendapole recalled, "Once the miners grasped the whole thing, that the Trade Union was the only tool, the only instrument of change, they became very committed to it."[92]

Commitment to the union and willingness to act collectively was undoubtedly encouraged by historical circumstances as well. The labor department quieted fears of company reprisals. Both the 1952 strike and the vote against the tribal representatives occurred during the government and Colonial Office campaign to "sell" Africans on the advantages of Federation. Consequently, government officials refused to support drastic measures to break the 1952 strike, the union's ability to maintain control over the strikers and the threat of cooperation between white and black miners left the companies no real alternative to arbitration.[93] In this atmosphere, the mines could do little to affect the tribunal appointed by the Colonial Office. Indeed, despite testimony by the companies against a wage increase, the tribunal awarded a substantial across-the-board wage increase.[94] According to informants, this award and the successful veto of the tribal representatives proved union effectiveness, and increased support for the union.[95]

Thus, by 1953 most miners recognized their identity of interests in opposition to management, and were prepared to act collectively to secure their group interests. Although daily social interaction in the mine compounds generally followed ethnic and occupational lines, these divisions did not inhibit worker solidarity during industrial conflict. In fact, during the 1952 strike the black miners proved themselves capable of transcending racial divisions by their alliance with white mine labor. This has been explained as mere middle-class aspirations, but such a view ignores the nature of the white miners on the Copperbelt, their long traditions of militant worker organization, and the capacity for white and black miners to understand their common status as workers. Such interracial cooperation is further proof of the degree to which consciousness of class position, commitment to class action, and willingness to form worker organizations was entrenched among the black miners by the early 1950s.

STABILIZATION AND POLITICAL CONSCIOUSNESS AMONG THE BLACK MINERS

What of the political consciousness of the black miners? We have seen that as wage labor on the Copperbelt became a permanent condition of life, class consciousness and commitment to class action developed as well. Following the approach used by Perrings and Gutkind,[96] one would predict the eventual recognition by these miners of the need to pursue class ends through political action. However, as already noted, the African Mineworkers' Union refused to cooperate with the nationalist efforts. This apparent lack of interest in the nationalist movement has led scholars to question the existence of miner populist or a political consciousness. Indeed, the Copperbelt case has been used to attack the assumption of an inevitable link between political action and organized labor in Africa.[97]

A closer look at the evidence suggests a different interpretation. True enough, management and the state were prepared to thwart union actions, despite conciliatory efforts surrounding the Federation campaign. Government officials might refuse to interfere in industrial disputes, but they had no qualms about stopping an alliance between the union and Congress. Labor officers and company officials insisted that the union must remain outside politics, and threatened dire consequences to worker advancement if this advice was not followed. Comrie made this one of his basic trade union principles, but his vision did not go unchallenged.

Katilungu's behavior while President of the Union indicates as much. His involvement in the African National Congress (ANC), his growing suspicions of a corporate-state alliance, and his participation in the planning of Congress's national prayer days indicate considerable commitment to political action by the union. According to an informant, he withdrew from the two-day protest only after his followers had been threatened with dismissal. The companies had already fired workers at Nkana for a political strike over the Zukas affair, and Katilungu realized this was not an idle threat.[98] In 1953, at the union's annual conference, Katilungu warned the delegates that "he had heard at Caux that the government wanted to restrict the activities of the African trade unions. They only wanted an opportunity to show that they were deviating from the constitution." He believed an unofficial strike supporting ANC might provide that excuse.[99] When faced with a choice between massive disruption on the mines and possible loss of employment for miners in an economy offering few alternatives, Katilungu's decision to keep the union outside politics is understandable as a pragmatic solution to limited options, rather than proof of a lack of political consciousness.

The evidence from oral interviews and other sources reveals considerable commitment to the nationalist cause among miners.[100] There was widespread support for Congress among the miners during this period. As we have seen, many trade union leaders were active in both ANC and the Trade Union Congress. A leader of the trade union and Congress at Chibuluma recalled that "the trade union in 1951 was more a political party than a trade union. That is why the government did not like it."[101] Miners figured prominently in Congress, and used methods pioneered by the union to build political parties. The union "made people like the importance of meetings. We called big meetings. This was before the Congress came into being. People got used to meetings so when these things about the government were talked over, they went too."[102] As one informant stated, the trade union "was the mother of the political parties. She had only to guide it as children."[103]

Most miners supported the nationalist movement for the same reasons as other Africans. They believed popular self-rule would bring a better life for all Northern Rhodesians. They feared Southern Rhodesia would be the hegemonic force in the Federation, and had no desire to see its institutions prevail in their nation.[104]

The limitations on miner political consciousness stemmed in part from the ambiguous connection between management and the state. Since the establishment of the African Mineworker's Union in 1949, the government, or at least the labor department, had appeared to be impartial, if not openly favorable, to the cause of the miners. In 1953, for example, the Guillebaud Tribunal settled a strike in their favor, largely to mollify African discontent over the Federation issue. While outright coercion by government officials emphasized the special relationship between government and the companies, the alliance between government and management was still far from clear.[105] Even those miners who agreed with Simon Zukas that "a trade union must act politically in defense of its members" did not recognize the potential contradictions between the goals of the African union and the nationalist movement. Congress promised to improve the relative position of Africans and white men, and to stop the color bar, both fundamental tenets of the union.[106] The militants had no more revolutionary vision of society in mind at this point.[107] They simply advocated using the union's organizational powers to support political causes in the belief that the African miners would gain from African political advancement. They recognized the need for worker political action, but did not yet differentiate between nationalist and class politics.

CONCLUSION

This chapter has shown how the stabilized miners used the African Mineworkers' Union to strengthen class consciousness and unionism among the black mine work force. At the same time, we have seen the limitations placed on the union by the government and the companies— limitations which forced politically conscious miners to shun union involvement in nationalist politics. This case reinforces the need to separate consciousness from behavior, and to study the development of both within a specific historical context.

7

The Neutralization
of Labor Protest, 1953–1964

INTRODUCTION

During the Federal period the mines followed new strategies to control black labor. In alliance with the state, the companies relied upon a combination of force and corporate paternalism to limit both industrial and political action by the African Mineworkers' Union. The union became less and less active in national politics. This widened the chasm between the union and the African nationalist movement, and has been seen by scholars as further proof of miner parochialism.[1]

There was no real divergence between unionism and nationalism. Indeed, the struggle against the mining companies and the state increased both worker and political consciousness among the black miners, despite severe limitations placed on the expression of that consciousness. Furthermore, the growing alliance between mining capital and the newly triumphant African nationalist party, UNIP, gradually revealed the emerging class structure in Zambia, and the conflict of interest between the mineworkers and the dominant class fractions, whether black or white. The expression of this opposition, while varying with economic and political circumstances, continues to challenge Zambia ruling class dominance to this day.

AFRICAN ADVANCEMENT

In 1953, increasingly expensive black labor and rising production costs threatened the high profit margins of the copper companies.[2] The need for trained black labor eliminated a return to cheap black labor, and the growing militancy of the African union raised the specter of future wage demands and labor unrest. The companies could see only one solution: African advancement. Management firmly believed that the advancement of skilled black miners into European jobs would reduce costs by replacing more expensive white labor and mollify the most militant members of the African union, who were generally more skilled

136

and eligible for advancement. Thus advancement would both permit a restructuring of the work force that lowered labor costs,[3] and would enlarge the number of supervisory black miners. Ronald Prain, director of RST, and to a lesser extent, Oppenheimer, believed the creation of a black group of supervisory miners would reduce class tensions and promote the development of an African middle class willing to support the Federation and its promise of multi-racial partnership.[4]

With the Federation safely established, and both Federal and Northern Rhodesian governments highly dependent upon copper revenues, the companies hoped to obtain support for their plans despite opposition from the white miners.[5] Both firms had moved their headquarters to Salisbury by 1954 in order to more easily cultivate closer ties with Federal officials.[6] They also counted on the growing support among liberal whites and Northern Rhodesian government officials for the establishment of a black middle class.[7]

The companies calculated well. While neither Federal nor Northern Rhodesian officials could openly support the companies' struggle against the European miners, they agreed to ignore the controversy by declaring it solely an industrial matter.[8] The Legislative Council passed a resolution in 1954 to the effect that "every lawful inhabitant of Northern Rhodesia had the right to progress according to his character, qualifications, training, ability, and industry, without distinction of race, colour, or creed." The senior provincial commissioner even promised the Chamber that government would protect advancees if the mines formally recognized an association of higher-grade miners.[9]

When copper was released from British controls in April 1953, and consequently from British pressure to maintain production, the last stumbling block to African advancement was removed. Within ten days the first meeting to discuss advancement was held with the European union.[10] The battle for advancement continued in February 1954 with four-way talks between the companies, the European union, the European salaried staff association (MOSSA), and the African union. The companies wanted to discuss the possibilities for fragmenting certain European jobs—i.e., dividing a job into several parts, with a black miner performing each fragment at wages appropriate to the existing African wage scale and standard of living. When the talks foundered in July over the issues of job division and equal pay, the government appointed a commission of inquiry under Sir John Forster, who had led the probe of the 1940 strike. Under pressure from the companies, the commission recommended advancement be started on the basis of a dual wage structure and the fragmentation of designated European jobs. With this endorsement, and support from American Metal Company,[11] the companies demanded renegotiation of the European union's recognition agreement. After months of bitter bargaining the European union finally agreed in January 1954 to transfer twenty-four categories of European jobs to African workers. These could be fragmented. Other European jobs in Schedule A, however, remained on the European wage scale, and the union agreed to accept such workers into its ranks. The union did try to retain a veto over transfers, but Rhodesian Selection Trust bitterly resisted. At the last minute, on September 27, the veto was dropped and the Anglo-American and Rhodesian Selection Trust mines negotiated a common agreement with the European union.[12] Having won the first battle against white labor, the mining companies proclaimed a triumph for "partnership" between the races and the future of the Federation.

STABILIZATION AND CORPORATE LABOR STRATEGY

This victory, and the increasingly technical nature of copper production, resulted in growing stabilization of black mine labor. The number of black miners in the three lowest grade categories (1–3) fell from 74% in 1953 to 60% in 1960, whereas semiskilled black miners rose from 25% in 1948 to 31% in 1959; skilled workers (Grades 8–13) increased from 1% to 4% of the work force during those years. The mining companies encouraged trained black labor to live at the mines with their families for even longer periods. Married housing increased, and the percentage of married miners increased from 60% in 1951 to 87% in 1960.[13] Labor turnover on all the Copperbelt mines fell to 27% in 1956, and to a mere 9.3% in 1962, not much higher than the rate for European labor.[14]

Stabilization left the companies with the problem of managing a fully industrialized and unionized African labor force still dissatisfied with the differential between European and African labor conditions. The companies failed to divide workers along ethnic lines, and lived in fear that miner politics would interfere with production.[15] Management also anticipated demands for higher wages and better living conditions after the successful Guillebaud Arbitration.[16] Behind these issues lurked the ever-present possibility of a multi-racial mineworkers' union. Management, therefore, needed to formulate a strategy to insulate black miners from political influences, separate them from European miners, and minimize the power of the African union.

In search of such a strategy, the mines turned to established experts on African labor. In 1949 Ernest Oppenheimer hired J. D. Rheinnalt Jones as Advisor on Native Affairs for Anglo-American. Formerly president of the South African Race Relations Institute, Rheinnalt Jones was a world-renowned expert on African life, and an ardent exponent of the "Human Relations" movement pioneered by American managerial expert, Elton Mayo. Jones, like Mayo, emphasized the need for "counteracting, redirecting, and channeling the working class's new-found organizational ability." Stressing the need for harmony and esprit de corps among the workers, Rheinnalt Jones assured management that worker loyalty could be won from the union through corporate paternalism. A number of South African industrialists had already moved in this direction, and some of them formed the South African Institute of Personnel Management (later the National Institute for Personnel Research) to adapt these ideas to South African conditions.[17] The institute gave Rheinnalt Jones's advice wide currency.

Jones visited the Copperbelt in 1949, and again in 1952. In view of the general labor shortage, the need for experienced labor, and the strength of the African Mineworkers' Union, he saw no alternative to improving facilities in the mine compounds. "The companies are doing all they can for their welfare," he said. He recommended a highly publicized extension of welfare activities and housing in the compounds, and assured the companies that increased worker satisfaction and loyalty would more than repay the initial costs.[18] Rheinnalt Jones was especially keen on special housing and job advancement for the African clerks. He predicted this would minimize discontent, and that "if a strong body of African clerks is built up and given appropriate authority, they will acquire a sense of responsibility towards management and comprise valuable emissaries for passing on information and countering 'loose talk' and adverse propaganda. They will ally themselves with management and function as a 'go between' with the mass of African workers. . . . To my mind there is no doubt that development on these lines would act as a valuable aid to industrial relations."[19]

Prain of Rhodesian Selection Trust favored a more paternalistic labor strategy as well. Deeply influenced by the liberal ideas current among American and European managers, Prain believed stabilization and advancement would only work if African wages and living conditions improved. In 1951 he publicized a five-year plan for the improvement of African living conditions on the mines on the grounds that "enlightened management today recognizes that it is not sufficient merely to have employees; it must have employees who are contented and happy and likely to stay, and such employees need conditions of remuneration and health which will induce them to stay until the time of their retirement. This may involve investing the shareholders' money in hospitals, good housing, recreational facilities and in providing not only good wages and other financial conditions while the employee works, but also the assurance of a pension at the end of it." Prain insisted that the initial costs must be set against "the goodwill and industrial relations value of this recommended policy."[20]

By 1953, upper-level management at both companies pursued a paternalistic labor policy on the Copperbelt as the best method to further their control. Prain and Oppenheimer confidently predicted this "enlightened self interest" would soon be repaid in increased productivity.[21]

CORPORATE PATERNALISM

Initially, the general managers and African personnel managers (formerly compound managers) on the Copperbelt opposed these changes. As late as July 1952, the executive committee of the Chamber stated unequivocally "that there was no intention of any change in the accepted scheme for African welfare." And in August 1952, the African personnel committee of the Chamber rejected most of Rheinnalt Jones's suggestions.[22]

However, direction from above prevailed, and experts were brought in from outside the Copperbelt to oversee the changes. These new men visited the mines and wrote up recommendations for improvements. Eric Bromwich, who became Chief of Study at RST in 1954, investigated housing, compound conditions, and industrial disputes. Rheinnalt Jones continued as chief advisor at Anglo-American. At all of the mines by 1954 "there were indications that the African Personnel Management were being pushed aside by Management. Labor Control, Job Study, etc., were being set up but entirely separated from the African Personnel Department."[23] Increasingly, the older personnel officers were reduced to location superintendents while the new staff organized and manned the new programs.

In a dramatic change of policy, the experts deliberately encouraged both social and organizational divisions between the higher-grade miners and the rest of the work force. They believed the African trade union would be less trouble if some of the leading trade unionists could be forced into a supervisory union like the European salaried staff association.[24]

In the past, both companies had deliberately minimized differences within the mine compounds for fear of "creating too wide class distinctions." When the union began, management hoped that the higher-grade miners in the union would act as a moderating influence by turning the union into an organization for themselves.[25] Efforts to divide the work force had always been made along ethnic rather than occupational lines.

However, African advancement, Federal support for a black middle class, and increasing disenchantment with the union leaders led to a change of policy. Corporate officials now worried that the union leaders had "obtained a wholly undesirable ascendancy over the mass of African workers," and were "usurping the traditional position of tribal chiefs."[26] Since most trade union leaders were higher-grade workers, a separate union for them might isolate a large percentage of the leadership. Management hoped this would have "the effect of balancing the extremist in the present union."[27]

After the completion of the first advancement negotiations, the companies began encouraging advanced workers to form a supervisory union. They had a receptive audience among some African clerks who had petitioned for a senior African union.[28] They had become increasingly alienated from union leadership, and were resentful of it. The companies had subtly encouraged the idea at first and then openly supported it.[29] A small number of interested miners soon set up the Mines African Salaried Staff Association (MASA). Most of them were long-term mine employees and many were clerks in the compound office. Many were Lozi or Nyasa, who felt their close association with Europeans and their ethnic identity blocked them from the union leadership.[30] By October 1954 MASA had 56 members at Mufulira, 120 at Nchanga, 105 at Rhokana, and 107 at Roan. This was out of a potential membership of 1,100 at Mufulira, 750 at Nchanga, 1,311 at Rhokana, and 1,606 at Roan.[31]

The new compound programs reinforced occupational divisions as well. Improvements focused on higher-grade workers, since maintaining equivalent conditions no longer mattered. For example, although housing improved dramatically for all workers, the mines put their greatest effort into housing for higher-grade workers. Between 1956 and 1964, the mines built 17,500 houses at a capital expenditure of over £11 million,[32] and by 1960, all the mines had improved housing for most workers. In 1957 the special type of house built in 1953, with three rooms, kitchen, a spacious store-room, ceilings, and electric lights, was upgraded further. At Mufulira, for example, the best houses now had stoves, built-in shelves, larger rooms, steel windows, sinks, and lavatories, and lights. The mines grouped these houses together in order to encourage neighborhood ties among higher-grade workers and sharpen divisions within the work force along occupational lines.[33]

Welfare programs and staff were reorganized and expanded to fit the new labor strategy. The mines hired trained welfare officers. David Greig and Dick Howie transferred from the Luanshya and Kitwe Township Boards to Rhokana and Roan respectively. The African staff at the mines worked as welfare assistants, sports organizers, case workers, carpenters, clerks, and librarians, as well as manual laborers. Mine staff gradually took over most womens' work, leaving UMCB missionaries in the schools and some of the womens' programs.[34]

Welfare work was intended to promote loyalty to the companies, and to undermine political and trade union activities among the miners. The companies ordered welfare personnel to stay out of political and union activities to safeguard their role as company spokesmen. They were instructed to cultivate leading Africans in order "to obtain information as to what the African is thinking, especially in-so-far as Trade Union and political trends are concerned."[35] They tried to divert miners away from politics and towards social and economic advancement. Activities which developed political leanings were discontinued. Leadership training in clubs and other group activities fostered moderate thinking, in an effort to discourage political extremism. The clubs looked to "develop and train leaders . . . [to] be moderate in outlook, i.e., see the other man's point of view."[36] Wherever possible, welfare personnel were to engage miners in conversations designed to counter malicious rumors about the companies. During industrial conflicts, welfare personnel were expected to help management by diverting employees with amusements and other activities.[37]

With the establishment of a predominantly stabilized work force, welfare programs increasingly focused on the problems of adjustment to prolonged urban living. At all times the goal was to contribute to Africans' "induction into urban life." Case workers counseled miners and their dependents with their personal problems. Classes for women continued to stress skills which augmented the miners' salaries and facilitated adjustment to urban life. Self-improvement programs expanded as well, particularly the libraries and reading rooms.[38]

Special schools prepared sons of mine employees for future employment on the mines. The first of these youth training schemes began at Rhokana in 1953 under the leadership of David Greig. The Luansimba Training Scheme, as it was called, concentrated on "reclaiming and educating potential 'dead-end kids'," and it was so successful that similar schemes were set up at each of the other mines. They served the double purpose of occupying youth in the mine townships, and indoctrinating future recruits into the values and behavior patterns of industrial labor. These schools attracted miners, who welcomed the opportunity to guarantee their childrens' future employment.[39]

These programs were accompanied by well-organized propaganda efforts reinforcing the benevolent image of the companies. Each mine started a newsletter explaining the mine and the world from the companies' perspective. In 1953, Roan had an eight-page monthly, *The Roan Antelope*, to report on township events. "Its tone was personal, friendly, designed to spread a feeling of good will between management and workers and to encourage employees to take advantage of the many welfare activities." The paper was in English and Bemba, and in 1953–54, 53% of the mine township read it. In 1956, Rhokana also sponsored a newspaper specializing in township news, *Luntandaya*, which was selling 3,668 copies per month by December. *Luntandaya* printed letters, and soon became a popular means for expressing opinion. Both papers countered trade union and political propaganda, and cast the firms in the best light.[40]

To further reinforce loyalty, as well as protect miners from undesirable political influences, the companies deliberately limited mine compound facilities to legal residents and their registered guests. The mines feared improved compound conditions would attract "hangers on," lower the standard of living of the mineworkers, and possibly bring in subversive political ideas. They called for government regulation of the flow of Africans into the Copperbelt, and public officials, sympathetic though they were, could not do much other than agree to step up prosecutions of loafers. Regular raids by mine police, as well as an elaborate registration system at each mine, discouraged illegal visitors.[41] These efforts, too, isolated the miners from other Africans, and emphasized the special privileges awarded mine employees.

THE STRUGGLE TO MAINTAIN THE UNION

The companies hoped their new labor strategy would fend off confrontation with black labor. They were quite ready, however, to use stronger methods to enforce change as well.

As events turned out, more forceful methods were necessary. Union leaders reacted strongly to the threatened secession of the supervisory level miners. They called meetings and asked friends and families to coax association members back into the fold. Union leaders accused the breakaways of trying to destroy the union. Staff association members were compared to *makopa*, or dead fish, a name soon spread throughout the Copperbelt. Those who refused to join the union were denigrated as "fools because even they will also be discharged one day. They are blind because they cannot realize that the Union is here to safeguard the freedom of future generations." Anyone not entirely with the union was declared an enemy.[42]

Most of the miners responded to this call for unity. Throughout 1954 relations between some of the supervisory miners, particularly clerks, and the rest of the work force steadily deteriorated. In February of that year, the joint push for equal pay by the European and African unions had raised the hopes of higher-grade miners for dramatic pay increases. Potential advancees who spoke recklessly of buying cars and living like Europeans heated tensions and raised the prospect of desertions.[43]

The crisis brought a change in union leadership as well. The unity between lower- and higher-grade miners, particularly potential advancees, was shaken. Less-skilled miners feared that leaders in line for advancement would refuse to risk industrial conflict for their own job security. Some miners even dropped out of the union. Most reacted by voting for more militant leadership in the 1954 branch elections, unseating leaders in line for advancement. Men with well-known records of political activism and involvement in the Trade Union Congress, like Robinson Puta at Nchanga and Sylvester Nkoma at Roan, were elected.[44]

This victory suggests that the struggle against management was politicizing the black miners. Epstein discovered that the new branch leaders were partially elected for their reputation as ruthless negotiators,[45] but it seems reasonable to assume that the victories reflected some support for political activism. This hypothesis is further strengthened by the continuing support for the African National Congress among miners, despite its decline soon after Federation. In fact, when Luanshya Africans established a Congress branch in late 1953, they solicited the assistance of Puta and Chapoloko.[46] Miner militancy was growing.

THE 1955 STRIKE

The union leadership gradually closed ranks to save the union. Katilungu agreed to demand a 10s8d per shift across-the-board wage increase set up by Puta and Nkoma. This was to be for union members only, in an effort to stop miners from joining MASA or just leaving the union. While this demand was primarily designed to strengthen the appeal of the union, it had a political aspect as well since the 10s8d increase would qualify many African miners for the vote under current Northern Rhodesian franchise laws.[47] The architects of the increase, Puta and Chapoloko, realized that this was a political as well as an industrial statement. Katilungu's agreement, knowing full well it would be unacceptable to the companies, reveals a growing unity of purpose among the union leaders. In a branch meeting at Roan, Katilungu even supported the militants' call for a long strike in defense of the union.[48]

During the next two months, miner support for militant union leaders grew steadily. When the companies rejected these demands, the workers almost unanimously voted for a strike action. In January 1955, all but 4,115 of the 34,000 African miners stopped work, and a bitter two-month struggle began.[49] The union leaders adhered strictly to classical trade union regulations. Picketers marched, daily meetings solved problems; support systems supplied food and other necessities; and all essential services to the mines continued. When the companies threatened to dismiss all workers in late January, the strikers and their families "formed processions in the streets carrying branches of trees, waving cloths and singing, marched through the streets up to 10 A.M and converged at a public meeting where their leaders addressed them. These processions were organized as a demonstration of mass support for the strike and for the workers' solidarity." Efforts to intimidate workers through loudspeakers operating from vans in the township failed miserably, and attempts to import strike breakers backfired. Many of the 2,000 "scab workers" brought in by management joined the strike. The unity and determination of the work force held fast.[50]

By February, both government and company officials were thoroughly exasperated with the union. Government officials agreed with the companies that "the power of the Union must be broken, new leaders found and a new means of negotiating with the Africans set up."[51] Neither Federal nor Northern Rhodesian treasuries could afford the loss in revenue. Now that African opinion no longer had to be conciliated in order to establish Federation, government officials willingly used state power to control the union.

The companies went a step further and schemed to dismantle the union. They suggested a return to wage councils or some other form of worker representation, for as far as they were concerned, "trade union-ism for Africans has been tried, and has failed. It was artificially created and is rotten to the core. . . . The leaders are at best, lacking in intelligence and experience, and the mass of the workers is but little removed from primitive savagery."[52]

Only the timely intervention of Ronald Williams, legal advisor of the National Union of Mineworkers (U.K.), kept the companies and govern-ment from destroying the union. Williams, who had presented the Afri-can case to the Guillebaud Tribunal, was supported by the European Mineworkers' Union, perhaps in hopes that continued talks about amal-gamation with the African Mineworkers' Union might succeed.[53] Williams threatened adverse publicity if the companies continued hiring scab labor, and prevailed upon the African union to drop its wage demand provided the strikers were rehired. After considering an effort to bluff Williams, the head offices relented. They instructed the local general managers "to re-engage the strikers at their previous rates of pay, and to ignore the strike discharges as far as pensions and leave rights, dependent on uninterrupted service were concerned." Miners who had been re-placed by new recruits were placed in a labor pool, with the promise that they would be reabsorbed into the work force within two months.[54]

The settlement did not alter management's hostility to the union or its determination to strengthen the staff association. In no mood for compromise, they declined to discuss dismissals even in cases of alleged victimization, and inaugurated a labor rationalization scheme which im-peded reabsorption of the labor pool. As a result, a number of union activists in the labor pool were kept at manual labor, and some workers were not reinstated at all.[55] In June 1955, the companies offered all supervisory and staff category miners the option of transfering to monthly pay at an increase of 14% per year,[56] and four months later, the African union reluctantly agreed to recognize MASA. They came to regret this decision when the companies announced the MASA members held 62 of the 75 newly advanced jobs, with another two for the Mines African Police Association.[57]

The union vigorously renewed its campaign against MASA. It can-celled the October 1955 agreement to recognize the association, and at meetings throughout the Copperbelt union leaders ridiculed staff min-ers, accusing them of being "the child of the mining companies." They warned members that the companies were out to destroy the union, and called for unity in the struggle to save it. They reminded members that "the companies established the Staff Association so those people with the top jobs would not join the industrial union."[58] "[The companies] are taking away the ones with education, the ones who understood things, the ones close to records, the ones who understood production problems, and you have the trade union in the hands of people who are not so good, the uneducated people."[59] Union leaders instructed members, whenever they saw a staff miner, to "shout at him and laugh at him and call him a *makopa.*"[60] Miners were to boycott any activities organized by staff members, and to pressure friends or relatives who had joined the association to return.

The miners quickly responded to the call for unity. Wherever MASA members and their families went, hostile compound inhabitants followed, jeering and singing insulting songs. One informant recalled getting stoned occasionally, and seeing children shouting insults at the children of staff members.[61] Union members refused to use African interpreters in the compound offices, and boycotted welfare and feeding stations, all run primarily by staff members. Occasional violence broke out. Feelings ran so high that when three union men were jailed for intimidating staff miners, 400 to 500 fellow workers went to the Boma and insisted upon being jailed also. A riot squad had to disperse them.[62] One participant recalled: "The miners themselves decided that if men were taken out of the union to form another splinter then they would have nothing to do with these scabs. You wouldn't even talk to a man; you'd have nothing to do with them." Hostility reached a point where "it was only a very bold man who could go up and greet a man on monthly contract."[63]

Many potential staff members refused to accept staff status out of loyalty to the union. A few staff members even returned to the union because of social pressures. An Ngoni clerk told Epstein that he rejoined the union "because I found that the Association did very little for the ordinary members. In fact it does nothing at all. . . . Another thing that is bad is that all people hate you as soon as they hear you are a member, even women. My wife used to quarrel with me for not attending Union public meetings. She forced me to attend because all her friends were laughing at her, and saying that her husband was an informer."[64] By May 1954, only 279 miners out of a potential membership of 4,160 belonged to MASA, and by March 1955, only 469 out of 3,535 eligible miners had joined the association. Lameck Chisanga reported that the staff association was not really functioning at this time and that many of the miners who joined refused to participate because of loyalty to the union. Indeed, in the spring of 1956, MASA leaders still complained about their small membership.[65]

Thus, rather than destroying the union, the struggle to protect the union appeared to be strengthening it. Except for a small number of advancees, the black miners stood firmly by their oganization. Bates attributes their solidarity to the homogenizing effect of the mine compounds and the pervasive pattern of racial stratification on the mines.[66] Such conditions doubtless made a difference, but the fact remains that miner solidarity transcended racial divisions. Worker unity, not racial unity, was the clarion of the fight against MASA. The miners

Table 12. **Workers' Response to Staff Association**

Workers' Response	No. of Workers		
	Rhokana	*Nchanga*	*Mufulira*
Eligible for Staff Association, Dec. 1955	803	528	574
Refuse to take staff positions as of Aug. 1956	311	75	151
Accept cut in pay rather than become staff	228	—	85

Source: Verbatim Testimony, Branigan Commission, 24–25 October 1956, and 1 November 1956.
Note: Roan figures not available.

clearly understood this. They saw the attack on the union as an attack on their collective interests as workers. If anything, the struggle to protect the union deepened worker consciousness.

The struggle for the union increased political consciousness among the miners as well. As Chisata recalled, "People [the miners] began to realize that no matter how much we fight for our rights we cannot succeed entirely if we don't change the government set up."[67] Before the 1955 strike, government officials had appeared reasonably impartial in industrial disputes. Indeed, in the early years union leaders had looked to government labor officers for aid and assistance against the companies. The 1955 strike destroyed that illusion. The police protection for company propaganda vans as they toured the compounds during the strike, government support for the staff association, and the realization that only Ronald Williams' intervention prevented a government attempt to weaken the union, clarified the alliance between the state and the companies. Indignities suffered by miners in the labor pools after the strike further exacerbated miner resentment against both company and government officials. More and more miners began to understand that industrial action availed little if not joined with political activity to secure class interests. One informant affirmed that "some miners even began to feel more anti-government than anti-mine, believing the biggest enemy was the government."[68]

In 1955, militant union leaders further consolidated their hold on the Trade Union Congress. Dixon Konkola, President of the Northern Rhodesian Railway African Worker's Trade Union and an active African National Congress organizer in 1952–53, wrested the presidency of the Trade Union Congress away from Katilungu. He created a sub-committee of nine, headed by himself and Nkoloma, to deal with political matters. These leaders maintained connections with the World Federation of Trade Unions (WFTU).[69] They publicly announced their support for joint action by Congress and African unions. Konkola openly condemned the staff association, and called for political and industrial action against the association.[70]

Congress became increasingly involved in the union's fight against MASA. This comes as no surprise since the leadership of both organizations continued to overlap. By 1956, twenty out of a total of fifty-nine branch officials of the African union were officers in Congress and thirty-two were full members. African National Congress leaders occasionally made political speeches at union meetings and union leaders did the same at Congress meetings.[71] Congress saw the staff association as part of the hated Federal plan for an African middle class, and its assault on the staff association fit neatly with the general nationalist rhetoric: the economic objectives of the union and nationalist goals coincided. Union and party leaders could readily join forces in their condemnation of the Federation. Katilungu even began speaking of Nkumbula as Northern Rhodesia's national leader.[72] On 11 June 1956 Katilungu attended an African National Congress meeting in Lusaka where Nkumbula accused the companies of trying to break the union. On June 23, African National Congress and the African Mineworkers' Union held a public meeting to discuss trade union issues, and Congress supported the union's demands on both the leg-guard issue and the termination of the staff association.[73]

THE ROLLING STRIKES AND THE STATE OF EMERGENCY

The growing tension between the union and the companies came to a head in the summer of 1956 with the infamous rolling strikes. Throughout the spring the union had tried unsuccessfully to rescind its 1955 recognition of MASA. Instead of cooperating with the union, the Chamber announced in June that all employees eligible for the association must go on monthly pay and leave the union by July 1. Miners who refused to cooperate faced demotion or discharge. The union reacted swiftly, organizing a series of strikes, which culminated in a series of "rolling strikes" at the end of the summer.

These strikes were organized by the supreme council on July 30. Each mine shut down for three days: first a big mine, then a small mine, and so forth. The series began at Roan on August 2, followed by Broken Hill on August 9, and through it all, the union demanded the termination of the 1955 agreement and the dissolution of MASA. When the strikes ended, the union banned overtime as a protest against monthly pay, and on 3 September informed the companies that miners would not work on Saturdays, nor would they wear leg-guards or present identification discs when going underground. (Leg-guards were disliked because they wore out clothes and Europeans did not have to wear them.) The mining companies refused to permit unprotected workers underground, thus continuing the work stoppage.[74]

The strikes were well organized and solidly supported. Strikers stopped going to the welfare centers to express their hostility to staff miners. Small groups of friends pooled savings to help one another, garden produce was bartered to obtain necessities, and union leaders drew up plans to feed everyone if rations were withdrawn.[75] Frequent meetings in the compounds facilitated organization. Union leaders used songs and slogans to spread the influence of the union. According to a prominent leader, "Two or three of these songs sung and repeated at general meetings were enough to consolidate workers' opinions."[76] Occasional open-air mass meetings supplemented local communication. Disciplined orderly behavior predominated, with the union leaders clearly in control.

The 1956 strike has been seen correctly as an industrial dispute. Some scholars, however, have played down its political aspects. They assert that the strike, coupled with the Branigan Commission's rejection of Congress's control over the union, and later apolitical behavior of the miners, indicate worker disinterest in political affairs.[77] The issue, however, is not the degree of Congress' control over the union, but the degree to which the miners had come to accept political action in pursuit of class interests. Viewed this way, there is evidence of a growing willingness by the union to use political action in the struggle against management. After all, the nationalist leaders publicly supported the strike effort, and Congress and union leaders were in close touch throughout. The union framed accusations against the staff association in nationalist as well as industrial terms in their call for an end to MASA and the Federation.[78]

Company and government officials themselves did not doubt the political dimension of the strikes. They believed "the rolling strikes were the first stirrings against the Federal solution of a black middle class . . . and a rejection of the class of blacks who wanted Federation."[79]

Having failed at negotiations the companies turned to the Northern Rhodesian government. By August, both company and government officials were ready to purge the union of its leaders on the assumption that they were responsible for its militancy and political connections. On 10 September 1956, a state of emergency was declared; officials arrested thirty-two union leaders, declared martial law, and sent contingents of Northern Rhodesian police into the townships. Within a few more days, police arrested fifty-five miners, forty-five of whom were union officials, who were "rusticated" with their families to the rural areas, and banned from the Copperbelt.[80] The companies and the government hoped this would bring the union under control.

A commission under the chairmanship of Patrick Branigan investigated the strike. Unlike the Guillebaud Tribunal, the commission did not concern itself with conciliating African opinion over federation. The commission ignored African National Congress testimony that "negotiations have failed mostly due to the uncompromising attitude of the employer and the I-am-not-concerned reaction of the Government." The commission rejected the companies' claim of African National Congress involvement, and chastized the companies for misjudging African feelings about MASA, but agreed with the companies that changes were needed in union structure and negotiating procedures in order to minimize future disturbances.[81]

Buttressed by these recommendations, government officials decided to weaken the union and return to earlier forms of worker representation.[82] Meanwhile, Katilungu, who had been out of the country during most of August and early September, returned to Northern Rhodesia in the midst of the controversy. Faced with the threat of dismantlement, Katilungu had no choice but to cooperate with government and company demands, and agreed to fewer full-time paid officials and supreme council members. (The presidency and general-secretaryship were combined.) He also conceded to arbitrate the wage demands, and drop the demand for dues check-off. Katilungu advised branch committees to cooperate with township advisory committees, withdrew the request for shop stewards, and directed members "to stop calling monthly-paid employees such names as 'informers' or 'makopa.'" He advised miners that "the union has no enmity against the staff association." In addition he accepted a moratorium on wage claims, and consented to turn his attention to improving the general work and living conditions of the work force, while assuring the companies that "the union would also campaign among its own members to improve their manner of living and to keep their houses and gardens clean and in good order."[83]

The union also promised to stay out of politics. In 1957, some of the younger more politicized union leaders tried to maintain both political and union offices,[84] but management and the labor department opposed this. In 1958, the companies offered to collect union subscriptions in return for a promise that the union would use neither its funds nor its organizational structures for political purposes. Again, Katilungu agreed. He resigned from the Constitution Party, and the one Congress official elected to a union post promptly quit his political position. One year later, the companies imposed even more stringent conditions against political activism in the mine townships.[85]

THE CREATION OF A LABOR ENCLAVE

Thus, after the rolling strikes, the black mineworkers appear to have accepted the futility of aggressive trade union and political action. They turned inward and concentrated on maintaining and enjoying their relatively privileged economic status. As we have seen, most studies of the copper miners in this period have taken this behavior as evidence of an absence of both trade union and political consciousness. This is erroneous.

In the first place, the behavior of the miners and the union must be examined in the context of both the industrial environment and the larger political economy of the period. After the rolling strikes the union was like a "weak kitten."[86] Katilungu had promised the miners that "when production comes to normal and general life is decently maintained, then we are going to find new ways of approaching on all problems and grievances as a whole."[87] However, little came of these promises. The union could not stop company dismissals, nor could it even secure a small wage increase to restore confidence in its own leadership. The state of emergency struck fear in the hearts of unionists and put the union in a very poor bargaining position. Membership dropped precipitously.[88]

Furthermore, the events of 1955 and 1956 had destroyed an illusion miners might have had about gaining government help against management. The lesson was clear—management could and would ally with the state in order to maintain industrial peace on their terms. The labor department's acceptance of continuing dismissals of strike activists only served to emphasize this fact. The government had come down clearly on the side of the companies, and the miners knew it. Overt union activism was a quick way to lose one's job, which dampened whatever enthusiasm for labor protest existed after the rolling strikes.[89]

The nature of the mine compounds also increased vulnerability to managerial discipline. The very factors which facilitated the development of worker solidarity and collective action also permitted management to weed out "trouble-makers" in the compounds. The visibility of the workers, and the presence of all black miners within the compounds, enabled management to keep a close watch over its work force. Compound officials and their aides, the mine police, maintained close surveillance of the compounds. Company spies reported meetings and other possible "irregularities."[90] Direct confrontation with management became correspondingly more difficult.

This was nowhere more evident than the political sphere. The companies discouraged political meetings in the mine compounds, and Rhokana even banned the Congress district secretary from the mine township. District level ANC meetings and Congressional youth leagues were forbidden, and transgressors were fired. For example, Nkana's (Rhokana) leading Congress supporter, Chiyendi, was discharged in February 1958 for seditious statements about the Queen and propaganda against the missionaries. A number of Congress leaders at Rhokana were deliberately allowed to become redundant,[91] and then be dismissed. Miners had to get permits for political meetings, and when meetings were held, speakers were guarded, wary of the inevitable informers in the audience. As one informant recalled, "You could find yourself in an awkward position, you could land yourself in trouble." Caution became the price of survival.[92]

At the same time, rewards for cooperation increased. The companies offered to help build up union membership if the union eschewed nationalist politics. Compound welfare programs were expanded once

again as was case work. Case workers counseled miners and their dependents with their personal problems, and classes for women and children
continued to stress skills which helped adjustment to urban life. Self-
improvement facilities, such as libraries and reading rooms, multiplied.
Carefully orchestrated propaganda repeatedly reminded the mineworkers and their families how lucky they were to have such a high
standard of living. Management warned miners that this prosperity depended upon their cooperation and productivity.[93]

The companies also tried to divert worker energies into the mine
communities, rather than national politics or union activities. Area committees were set up in the mine townships to "harness the political social
aspirations of the African community to community development projects." They were designed "to give people a greater interest and pride in
the running of Township affairs as well as fostering the idea of voluntary
welfare work in the community." Welfare services aimed to divert miners
from more controversial organizations.[94]

Special privileges for staff miners and mine police reinforced divisions within the work force. Living in staff housing sections became a
badge of supervisory status, and exclusive clubs sheltered staff members
from the mockery of union miners. Special classes for wives of advancing
Africans taught these women more "middle class" living habits.[95] All such
programs isolated supervisory miners and reinforced their dependence
upon management.

These changes took place in a period of increasing rationalization of
the mine work force, and of unemployment in the economy at large. The
mines found it difficult to maintain profits with the fall in copper prices in
1957. The high cost of both black and white labor forced management to
further rationalize production, and wherever possible, men were re-
placed with machines. From February 1957 to September 1958, Nkana's
labor force was reduced by 25%, Roan's by 16.5%, Mufulira's by 20%, and
Nchanga's by 11%. Turnover on the mines decreased correspondingly,
falling to 20% in 1958. Competition for employment on the mines grew.
The practice of hiring employees' children only aggravated matters. By
1960, Nchanga reported over 1,000 job applicants per week for only 20 to
30 positions, and similar figures were reported at the other mines.[96] Such
conditions reinforced corporate propaganda about the lucky mine employee. Once again market factors favored the employers.

It was in this environment of decreasing economic opportunities,
increasing dependence upon wage labor, and more stringent corporate
discipline, that the behavior of the black miners must be examined. By the
late 1950s, most miners were fully proletarianized and depended on
wages and pensions for their long-term security. Many had lost or severely loosened the ties with their rural homelands. The unemployment
threatened these workers severely. Underground miners could not find
comparable work outside the mines, making them even more vulnerable

to the possibility of dismissal. As in the Depression years, the miners responded to job insecurity by increasing their cooperation with the employers, but this time the companies offered the miners the opportunity to become permanent industrial workers. The firms were willing to pay for a smaller more skilled and stable work force.[97] Absenteeism, always a good indicator of employee commitment, continued to fall throughout the 1950s, reaching levels below those of British coal workers and the U.K as a whole. For most miners, the rewards of cooperation simply outweighed the possible gains of collective action. The rewards of mine employment were tangible, and in a tight wage labor market, they overrode larger considerations for most workers. Harry Franklin sensed this when investigating African absenteeism in 1960. He concluded that the widening gap in living standards of mine employees and other Africans, and the difficulties securing mine employment, made the mine workers "value their job very considerably."[98]

This refusal to jeopardize employment security limited the behavior of both staff and union mineworkers, forcing a conservative isolationism and economistic strategy on the work force. The mines were too powerful, and the rewards for cooperation too great, to allow any other course of action. Consequently, both union and staff members accepted small but steady improvements negotiated within the industrial structure, rather than the dramatic protests of the past. The miners became increasingly absorbed in maintaining the "good life" in the mine townships. The union was expected to protect living standards, not extract new concessions. Political activity in the compounds assumed less importance than films, football games, and other sports and dances which drew large crowds. Men and women jammed the beer halls, consuming large quantities of beer. Elite miners socialized together in their clubs. Both staff and daily-paid miners concentrated on maximizing the material advantages of mine employment. Some leading miners even asked government and the mines to "take action against loafers and unemployed persons living in the mine compounds at the expense of their friends and relatives." As long as some economic progress could be seen, the miners willingly limited their demands. They accepted small increments in their standard of living in return for industrial peace.[99] Considering the options available at the time, their behavior is understandable.

CLASS CONSCIOUSNESS IN A LABOR ENCLAVE

The question arises whether this economistic behavior reflected a change in class consciousness among the black miners as well. Certainly in the case of the supervisory miners, management did everything it could to encourage a feeling of being "separate and superior from the rest of the workers." Some of these miners did align themselves with the Federation, even joining the multi-racial United Federal Party and running for political office. This alienated the rest of the miners, bringing all supervisory workers into question as "informers." Sandford Chiwila recalled "a lot of strong feeling about this." He claimed that "some of the elite were still concerned about the average worker, but found it difficult being accepted by the workers."[100] This hostility isolated the staff miners increasing their dependence upon managerial favor,[101] and their need to cooperate with management. Thus, a vicious circle developed which pushed staff miners to behave as a "labor aristocracy."

However, there is evidence that for most miners the class consciousness developed before 1955 remained intact. Most, for example, rejected the middle-class orientation of staff members. More to the point, after an initial setback, union membership revived. By 1958, about 15,000 miners belonged to the union, and by 1963 membership had risen to over 30,000. Kambafwile, who helped revive the Mufulira branch after 1957, reported that the willingness to limit worker demands did not diminish commitment to collective action.[102]

The union once again transcended racial and occupational divisions in the mine work force. The African and European unions joined forces against the Honeyman proposals (intended to muzzle the European union), and in 1961 the European union supported the African demand for a unitary wage scale.[103] The staff and daily-paid black miners resented the gap between European and African wages, and in 1961 they formed a Liaison Committee to pressure the companies into abolishing it. Only strong opposition from management and a 10% salary increase convinced MASA to settle separately with the companies. In the subsequent strike, the union demanded MASA's abolition, not because of feelings of irrevocable differences, but because staff members could not be relied on as allies in industrial disputes. The union wanted advancement for all rather than the few, a unitary wage scale, and reincorporation of the advancees into the union.[104] These demands revealed a continuing desire to unify the work force, and a perception of the common interests of staff and daily-paid miners despite management's opposition.

Within the constraints set by management, most miners and their dependents also continued to support the nationalist political parties. In 1958 miners flocked to the more radical Zambian African National Congress (ZANC), and later, its successor, the United National Independence Party (UNIP).[105] As the tempo of political conflict increased, so did political activity in the mine townships. Mine inhabitants obtained permission to hold political meetings, and the rallies drew large crowds despite competition from corporate welfare activities and the pressure of company spies. Speakers were understandably cautious, but rebelliousness surfaced occasionally. For example, one informant reported sneaking an African nationalist leader into the opening ceremony of a mine welfare hall, where he stood up and shouted "ZANC," much to the consternation of mine officials.[106] In the turbulent years before independence, competition between ANC and UNIP created havoc in the townships. Women and youths joined political brigades in support of their parties, and opposition between UNIP and ANC, exacerbated by the fact that most staff miners belonged to ANC, was rife, and sometimes flashed into violence. In Mufulira a club manager only escaped serious injury from an ANC youth group by locking himself in the pantry until rescued.[107] Unrest reached such a point that the Whelan Commission was set up to investigate the situation.

Miner commitment to UNIP and the nationalists affected the union as well. The growing collaboration between Nkumbula and a number of English organizations and companies harmed ANC's legitimacy for most Northern Rhodesians, and Katilungu's growing involvement in ANC during 1959 proved unpopular. Hostility towards Katilungu increased when he accepted the Federal government's invitation to serve on the hated Monckton Commission.[108] The miners accused Katilungu of neglecting the union for politics. Several informants claimed this was the primary reason for his downfall. Mwendapole believed "Katilungu had become unpopular, especially his part in the Monckton Commission. He took part in the Monckton Commission totally against the opinion of the people of the country."[109] Also, after Katilungu's dismissal, most union leaders with ANC sympathies were purged from the union. The next union president, John Chisata, was an avid UNIP supporter. He brought the union back into the TUC, and in 1962 even agreed, although reluctantly, to an unsatisfactory settlement with the mines in order to facilitate UNIP's chances in the upcoming election.[110]

Still there were persistent strains between the union and UNIP. Chisata clearly disliked calling off the 1962 strike for political reasons, and he warned Kaunda that further UNIP interference in the union would not be tolerated. Despite his cooperation with the pro-UNIP faction of the TUC, Chisata continued to stress the political independence of the AMWU.[111] His refusal to cooperate with UNIP angered party officials, who accused union leaders of being "opportunists with no national interests at heart."[112] Accusations of this kind only aggravated the situation.

In 1963 relations between UNIP and the union deteriorated further when the party openly supported a staff association plan to establish a single new union for the black miners, the United Mineworkers' Union (UMU). As the Federation crumbled, and the mining companies, particularly RST, moved closer to Kaunda, the staff miners realized they could no longer count on protection as the "middle-class buffer group" of the Federal government. Some other form of protection had to be found. A number of the staff association leaders had long cherished the hope of establishing a single union, and they persuaded the membership to establish the UMU in close alliance with UNIP and the United Trade Union Congress (UTUC). UNIP leaders decided to support the new union in the hope that it would be more amenable to party direction than the present

union, and allowed the United Mineworkers' Union to use party plat-
forms throughout the Copperbelt. The new union leaders adopted the
party's method of door to door canvassing and held rallies at which
leaders called for worker unity, claiming that "we are not like the African
Mineworkers' Union. We want those underground to join with the educated levels so that we can fight together. It is practically impossible today
to challenge the companies and win alone."[113] Some miners found the
union attractive because of UNIP support against management after
Northern Rhodesia's independence.[114]

The African Mineworkers' Union broke with the UTUC once again,
and launched a vitriolic campaign against the United Mineworkers' Union. The African Mineworkers' Union fought against the new union not
because it opposed a single union, which it did not, but because it opposed
a union which could be controlled by politicians. The AMWU leaders
spread through the Copperbelt urging a boycott of the UMU. "Only
fools," they claimed, "could now support leaders who had proved so
treacherous in the past." As if to prove their dedication to the entire work
force, the AMWU agreed to a new manning structure and local wage scale
in return for a general wage increase.[115] The companies helped the
AMWU also, for despite growing cooperation with UNIP, management
preferred a union free from party politics. They agreed to make membership transfers from the African Mineworkers' Union to the United
Mineworkers' Union a complicated and very public procedure. Each
dissident had to wait in highly visible queues, and publicly declare his
desire for cancellation. The companies also refused to recognize the
UMU as a legitimate employee organization. Gradually these efforts paid
off, and in June of 1964, the UMU disbanded, and a new Mines Local
Staff Association was formed.[116]

Relations between the African union and UNIP continued to deteriorate after independence. Both staff and daily-paid miners resented
the local wage structure which the mines had pushed through during the
1964 crisis over the UMU. The new agreement tied wages of local employees (Zambians) to the local economy, rather than the European wage
scale, thus destroying the unitary wage scale so painfully worked out in
1961. It limited the wage ceiling for black miners, and even lowered the
wages of some higher-grade miners. In 1966 miner dissatisfaction finally
exploded in a strike. Staff and daily-paid miners joined forces, demanding a return to the unitary wage scale. Undaunted by nationalist rhetoric,
the strikers accused the Zambian government of colluding with management in order to oppress the workers.[117] Once again the miners were able
to transcend racial divisions, and to identify themselves and their opposition in class terms.

How can we explain this discord? Having argued for the commitment of the black miners to the nationalist cause despite corporate restric-

tions on political behavior, we cannot attribute the hostility between union and UNIP leaders to the absence of populist political consciousness among the miners. Instead, the answer lies in the nature of miner political consciousness. Participation in industrial labor created a sense of identity among the copper miners, an awareness of the alliance between the state and management, and recognition of the need to engage in political activity in order to protect worker interests. Union leaders and the mineworkers expected political action to create conditions that would secure their class interests. The miners believed they played a critical role in the economy, and were entitled to adequate rewards. As Mwalwanda recalled, "The miners looked forward to when this would be their own government. The government are the people, especially working people are the government, because when you don't have working men you cannot have a government.[118] When UNIP leaders tried to use the union for national goals, they were sharply rebuffed. From the point of view of the nationalists, union leaders were simply being selfish and uncooperative. UNIP leaders accused the miners of being "a committed bunch who, if left alone would cripple the economy of the country to nothingness."[119]

The contradiction between the class-based political goals of the union and the national concerns of UNIP deepened after 1962, when the newly elected nationalist ministers faced the problem of establishing a black government. The demands of the African miners conflicted with the new government's need for copper revenues and its program for rural development. To promote these policies, government opposed wage increases, and the UNIP-dominated TUC pressured the miners not to strike. This aggravated the miners, who increasingly felt they had lost out since independence and that UNIP had abandoned them in favor of the companies.[120] The political alliance which had originally offered a better life for African workers along with that of all Africans now appeared little better than the colonial regime. It was this commitment to political action for the benefit of workers that caused the rift between UNIP and the union, and the possibility of its resurgence has continued to fuel the tension between the union and the party.

CONCLUSION

We have seen that the mines finally recognized the need to adapt their labor strategy to the realities of their stabilized well-organized black labor force. The resulting arrangements were particularly effective because of both limited economic opportunities outside the mines and the alliance between the mining companies and the state. The resulting divisions within the work force, the failure of the union to engage in embryonic nationalist politics, and the acceptance of limited gains within the industrial context showed that management's strategy did modify worker behavior to some extent. Still, the occasional cooperation among both European and African staff and daily-paid miners revealed the persistance of class consciousness among workers. Their understanding of the need for class-based political action also endured, despite constraints on political behavior.

CONCLUSION

Participation in the copper industry of Northern Rhodesia during the colonial period forged new attitudes and behavior among the black copper miners based on shared experiences in the production process. But participation in wage labor was not the sole determinant of worker consciousness or action.

Perrings suggests that objective class interests largely determine the degree to which workers develop class consciousness and a commitment to collective labor action in pursuit of class goals; workers more dependent on wage labor are therefore more conscious of their class interests and more committed to action protecting those interests.[1] The Copperbelt is a good place to test this assumption, because a combination of market forces, industrial needs, and corporate strategy resulted in the early stabilization of a section of the work force. These miners developed forms of consciousness and action which can be partially understood by class position. They exhibited a growing identity among themselves, and an understanding of their differences with management. Their growing dependence on wage labor intensified the need to improve the returns for their labor. Increasingly, they organized strikes, worker committees, and eventually unionization. By the 1950s and early 1960s, the more stabilized miners were committed trade unionists. They recognized their common interests with other miners and the need to organize collective action against management. Many of them also recognized the fundamental identity of interests among black and white workers in the copper industry, and condemned those blacks allied to management. Thus, throughout this period the more proletarianized black miners acted upon economic rather than racially or ethnically defined categories within industry.

These miners also perceived both the emerging class structure in Zambia and the need to organize politically. Their struggles to protect the union during the mid-1950s further exposed the alliance between management and the state, and encouraged them to organize against the state

159

as well. Between 1954 and 1957, Congress and the union joined forces against federation. A number of leading trade unionists held high posts in Congress and the TUC, and actively supported plans to organize collective labor action for political purposes. This commitment to the nationalist cause continued after the state of emergency in 1957, despite less political action. Contrary to the assumptions of Bates and others,[2] later conflicts between the union and UNIP reflected not a lack of political awareness, but rather the high degree of political class consciousness among the largely stabilized African mine work force.

On the surface, the data appear to support Perring's hypothesis. There are, however, a number of problems with it. The less proletarianized workers on the copper mines readily joined labor action during the colonial period. They participated in the 1935 and 1940 strikes. Within a few years of its establishment, most of them supported the union, and later its fight against MASA, the Federation, and UNIP. The evidence suggests that working and living conditions on the mines intensified the impact of wage labor on all the black miners. Daily interaction among the miners, corporate efforts to minimize ethnic and occupational differences, and the common subjugation to corporate authority facilitated identification among both stabilized and less stabilized miners before 1953. At the same time, the visible gap between European and African material rewards, the example of the European union, and the experience of collective labor protest heightened awareness of opposition between management and the black miners. Thus, the combination of living and working on the copper mines, and the struggle to improve working conditions, transformed worker consciousness among the black miners in a manner which a narrow structural approach cannot explain.

The behavior of the more proletarianized workers varied as well. In the early years, the more skilled miners moved between mines rather than organize collective action to improve their work conditions. After leading two major strikes, these miners abandoned broadly-based labor action in the 1940s and concentrated on improving their own conditions through boss boys' committees and clerks associations. Although these same workers later led the drive for unionization, in 1953 a section of the most proletarianized miners broke from the union and formed the staff association. Many of these men supported either ANC or multi-racial parties, while the union supported UNIP. Then in the early 1960s, MASA collaborated with UNIP to establish the UMU, while UNIP-union relations deteriorated dramatically. Yet, staff and daily-paid miners organized a massive strike in 1966, accusing UNIP and the companies of collaborating against them.

Some authors have tried to explain this behavior by recourse to the labor aristocracy thesis, which assumes that the privileged position of the more skilled sections of the black work force led to a narrow trade union consciousness, and little political consciousness.[3] We have seen, however, that the black copper miners exhibited contradictory behavior—while at some points they pulled away from politics, at others they rejected the class basis of the new Zambian government, and supported worker action for political ends. This vacillation has continued, with relative quiescence during the mid-1970s contrasting with more recent strikes against UNIP.

Clearly, class membership alone has limited predictive value for understanding the behavior of the black miners on the Copperbelt. Rather than behave as labor aristocrats in a consistent fashion, these miners changed tactics to facilitate their struggle with capital. While experiences in the production process, both in the mines and the compounds, encouraged the development of class consciousness and commitment to class action among more proletarianized miners in the Copperbelt case, the form of action taken by these miners depended on the real, or perceived, options available to them.

Such options were strongly influenced by a number of factors. Labor protest needed effective leadership and widespread support, but labor had to have some leverage over management as well. The labor supply and skill structure of the labor force affected labor's bargaining power. A shortage strengthened labor's position, while a surplus weakened it. This did not always apply equally to labor as experienced workers were generally harder to replace and therefore sometimes enjoyed the upper hand, which could push occupational groups within a work force towards different forms of labor action.

Corporate labor policies also affected the form worker struggles took. Such policies were shaped by the technical needs of copper production, the labor supply, established labor policies and the position of the industry in the world market. As we have seen, the need for reliable semi-skilled black labor during a labor shortage very early pushed the mines to stabilize a section of the black labor force. The still uncertain future of the mines, and a miscalculation of the stabilized miners' consciousness and organizational abilities, led management to treat all African workers alike, with important consequences for the development of class consciousness and action. Not until the value of sterling dropped and profits soared in the 1950s could the companies afford to challenge the white miners, increase the percentage of black skilled labor, and separate that labor from the rest of the black work force, thereby reducing the effectiveness of the union.

Of course, corporate policies were most effective when backed by the colonial state. Capital wanted to maximize profits, while both black and white labor wanted to maximize wages. The obvious solution for capital— outright coercion of the work force by the state—was impossible, for the state had to maintain some semblance of concern for the citizenry, particularly the white miners. As a result, the Northern Rhodesian government rejected mining capital's desire for African advancement in order to protect white labor. The state also established a labor department and eventually encouraged African trade unions. While created to control African labor, and therefore to guarantee the transfer of surplus to the metropole, the labor department did legitimize organized labor action and taught workers, however unintentionally, skills which were used in both industrial and political action. But when the Federation reduced the political influence of the white miners, its future became tied ever more closely to the prosperity of the mining companies, and the settler state now faced a common problem: how to permit African advancement without endangering the class structure. To accomplish this, they used both the carrot and the stick—rewards to those Africans who cooperated and punishment to those who rebelled. As we have seen, union and staff miners soon recognized their vulnerability to these pressures, and adjusted their behavior accordingly.

Although the impact of state and corporate policies varied with specific circumstances, they seem to have affected class action more readily than class consciousness. Corporate and state policies designed to cripple worker unity were less successful than those aimed at modifying the form of class action taken by the mine work force. For example, while corporate policies during the Federal period split the work force along occupational lines and forced both supervisory and daily-paid miners into more economistic behavior, these modifications were a "reasonable" response to the power of the companies, the collaboration of the state, and the political economy of Northern Rhodesia at the time. They did not reflect a decreased awareness of class divisions and class opposition, but rather a modification of the perceptions of how best to protect class interests. The withdrawal of the union from politics at this time, moreover, reflected the vulnerability of the union to corporate pressures after the state of emergency, rather than less commitment to political action. This case suggests the greater malleability of class action by historical factors, with class consciousness being more fundamentally tied to the production process and the industrial environment. Thus, the Copperbelt data not only illustrate the value of class analysis in the African colonial context, but also reveals the differential impact of historical factors on class consciousness and class action.

This conclusion has broader implications for African labor history. First, it demonstrates the limitations of a purely structural approach to the study of migrant labor. While the structural class position of migrant labor is clearly an essential component for any analysis, it cannot by itself explain worker consciousness or behavior. It leaves little room for other influences, particularly the impact of living and working on the mines, corporate and state labor strategy, the tradition of class struggle, and human ingenuity—all important ingredients in the development of class consciousness and class action. The Copperbelt data reinforce the need for a more historic approach that recognizes the importance of structure without lapsing into structural determinism.[4]

Similar implications emerge for the analysis of fully industrialized workers in Africa. As we have seen, scholars have explained economistic tendencies among both black and white workers exclusively in terms of differences in their income and access to power. Such workers have been labelled labor aristocrats, and even, in the case of South African white labor, petty bourgeoisie.[5] This paradigm assumes that the material advantages accruing to more-skilled workers in the African context separates them from less-skilled workers. In the case of South Africa, the structural position of white labor supposedly places them outside the working class. The Copperbelt data cast some doubt on the utility of this approach. During the colonial period, elite black miners acted in a variety of ways. White labor collaborated with black labor at various points, despite the widely resented differential in their material rewards. Class position alone cannot explain this.

The Copperbelt case also argues for analyzing worker consciousness and behavior separately as well as together. This is particularly important in the highly repressive societies of colonial and independent Africa. As some scholars have begun to observe, behavior in such societies often fails to fully reflect consciousness. For example, van Onselen discovered that Southern Rhodesian miners expressed their discontent through absenteeism and desertions, rather than strikes. In contrast, Jim Silver found that violent strikes among Ghanaian gold miners did not reflect revolutionary class consciousness. Attitudinal surveys by Lubeck, Sandbrook, and Arn have produced similar insights.[6] Further systematic efforts in this direction are needed, both to allow a more accurate assessment of industrial labor, and to discourage the facile dismissal of worker economism so common in African labor studies.

More specifically, the Copperbelt case raises some important comparative issues in South African labor history. As we have seen, the labor strategies adopted by the Anglo-American mines in Northern Rhodesia differed dramatically from those in South Africa. Economic factors alone cannot explain the differences. The answer lies more in the overall political-economy of the societies in question. For various reasons, white miners in Northern Rhodesia never developed the political clout of their South African counterparts, and found themselves unable to legislate a protected position in the economy in the manner achieved by South African white labor. These differences emphasize the unique nature of the South African experience, and should caution against uncritically extending the South African model of racially structured capitalism[7] to other parts of Southern Africa.

Finally, this study also establishes the need to reevaluate scholarship on the copper miners, particularly the relationship between miners and national politics. The explanation of political apathy is no longer acceptable. Earlier literature emphasizing the key role played by the miners in the nationalist movement now seems more credible.[8] But this must be placed in the context of rising class consciousness among the miners, as well as the situational constraints on miner behavior. Such an approach would further clarify the development of political consciousness among the miners, and lead to a more accurate assessment of the miners' role in Zambian politics, both in the past and the future.

APPENDICES

Appendix A

Married Employees in the Mines (In %)

Year	a Rhokana	b Nchanga	c Mufulira	d Roan
1929	—	—	—	28.4
1930	—	—	—	—
1931	—	—	—	26.0
1932	18.9	—	—	37.3
1933	27.2	—	32.0	43.4
1934	28.0	—	28.1	42.9
1935	27.0	—	38.9	57.0
1936	38.9	—	44.9	65.1
1937	41.7	48.1	51.6	61.9
1938	42.6	46.5	47.8	59.9
1939	44.2	43.1	54.8	58.5
1940	39.8	53.8	61.6	53.3
1941	46.1	58.1	59.7	54.5
1942	42.0	47.5	59.3	44.9
1943	—	—	—	—
1944	—	—	—	—
1945	39.51	43.88	55.0	53.99
1946	42.79	46.08	—	52.36
1947	46.12	46.81	60.17	53.07
1948	48.36	45.84	59.58	53.61
1949	45.05	43.55	61.57	49.77
1950	45.41	47.07	61.42	52.03
1951	45.98	55.70	65.73	59.64
1952	51.33	55.00	66.30	63.65
1953	52.73	57.00	64.00	67.02
1954	57.50	58.00	66.00	68.80
1955	62.94	68.80	70.00	73.65
1956	69.40	65.70	73.00	75.99
1957	76.90	71.40	72.00	77.90
1958	74.10	69.00	75.00	82.00
1959	73.70	75.00	82.00	79.30
1960	71.40	76.00	73.00	79.60
1961	82.00	87.00	71.00	82.10
1962	77.70	82.50	85.00	86.90

Sources: Column d (1929), RCM/CSD/W(2)HA 64, Sir W. Simpson, Report on Conditions at Roan Antelope, 1930; Columns a–d (1931–36), *The Pim Report*, p. 44; Columns a–d (1937–41), RCM/CSD/ KHB 41, NRCM, Memorandum (on the Saffery Report), 26 April 1944; Columns a–d (1942), The Saffery Report, p. 51; Columns a–d (1945–62), Department of Labor, *Annual Reports*, 1953–62.

Appendix B

Labor Turnover at Roan Antelope, 1938–60

Year ending 30th June	% Turnover
1938	83.1
1943	73.5
1947	77.0
1948	61.6
1949	62.0
1950	43.6
1951	41.5
1952	40.5
1953	31.5
1954	36.0
1955	24.5
1956	16.6
1957	17.7
1958	19.8
1959	19.6
1960	22.3

Source: "Africans at Roan Antelope," mimeograph, Luanshya, May 1961, p. 11.
Note: Voluntary absenteeism figures are low, 1.3% underground and 0.1% on the surface. This compares with rates of 2.0% and 0.4% in 1957, and more than 10% in 1941.

Appendix C

Average Length of Service at Roan Antelope, 1930–60

Year	Average Length of Service in Years
1930	0.4
1931	0.5
1932	0.7
1933	1.1
1934	1.2
1935	1.3
1936	1.3
1937	1.4
1938	1.6
1958	6.6
1959	6.7
1960	7.5

Source: "Africans at Roan Antelope," mimeograph, Luanshya, May 1961, p. 9.
Note: The average age of employees is 35½ years.

Appendix D

Copper Production and Value, 1932–1964

Year	1 Average yearly price	2 Long tons copper (× 1,000)	3 Copper Sales (£m)	4 African employees	5 European employees
1932	26	68	—	5,572	893
1933	32	104	—	7,190	1,026
1934	39	138	—	13,808	1,729
1935	40	144	—	13,224	1,758
1936	44	142	—	11,957	1,575
1937	61	148	—	17,926	(2,037)
1938	46	213	8.9	20,358	(2,296)
1939	51	212	9.5	20,924	2,609
1940	64	263	12.7	24,382	2,971
1941	62	228	10.5	27,270	3,098
1942	62	247	11.3	30,425	3,306
1943	62	251	11.6	32,805	3,566
1944	62	221	10.3	30,470	3,445
1945	62	194	11.2	28,304	3,272
1946	77	183	12.3	27,832	3,426
1947	131	192	20.4	29,166	3,681
1948	134	213	25.8	30,932	3,958
1949	133	259	31.2	33,061	4,293
1950	179	277	43.4	34,814	4,604
1951	221	309	62.2	35,432	5,184
1952	260	313	72.4	36,668	5,504
1953	256	363	90.0	36,147	5,879
1954	249	378	91.2	37,193	6,294
1955	352	343	114.2	35,190	6,566
1956	329	383	116.2	37,533	7,065
1957	219	417	89.4	38,763	7,304
1958	198	375	75.3	32,824	6,739
1959	238	417	115.4	35,014	7,259
1960	246	559	132.6	36,806	7,528
1961	230	560	119.4	39,036	7,641
1962	234	539	119.4	37,681	7,780
1963	234	568	127.8	36,948	7,676
1964	352	633	164.3	38,097	7,455

(*continued*)

Sources: Column 1—L. H. Gann, *A History of Northern Rhodesia*, p. 329 (1932–40); *The Economist* (1941–45); *Northern Rhodesia Chamber of Mines Year Book 1956*, p. 60, and *Copperbelt of Zambia Mining Industry Year Book 1964*, p. 44 (1945–64).
Column 2—W. J. Barber, *The Economy of British Central Africa*, p. 127 (1932–58); *Mines Department Reports*, 1959–64.
Column 3—*Northern Rhodesian Economic and Statistical Bulletins*, 1938–54; *Northern Rhodesia Chamber of Mines Year Books*, 1956–63; *Copperbelt of Zambia Mining Industry Year Book*, 1964. Figures for the value of copper exports in S. H. Frankel, *Capital Investment in Africa* (p. 254) give an indication of the rate of expansion in the 1930s. The value of exports in 1932, a year after production began, was over £2 million, and had risen to almost £4 million in 1936.
Columns 4 and 5—Paper prepared by the Chamber of Mines for submission to the Forster Board of Enquiry, 6 September 1954 (1932–40); *Branigan Commission Report*, 1956, p. 5 (1941–55); *Brown Commission Report*, 1966, p. 160 (1956–64). Figures for European employees in 1937 and 1938 are estimates.
Note: Columns are Average yearly electrolytic copper price (London Metal Exchange) in £ per long ton; Northern Rhodesian electrolytic and blister copper production in long tons (2,240 lb. per ton); Gross value of copper sales; and Average numbers of Africans and Europeans employed in the industry.

Appendix E

NRCM African wage structure, 1941
(In shillings per ticket)

Period of Service (in months)	Underground grades			Surface grades		
	C	B	A	C	B	A
0 to 6	15.0	25.0	40.0	25.0	40.0	50.0
6 to 12	17.5	27.5	42.5	27.5	42.5	52.5
12 to 18	20.0	30.0	45.0	30.0	45.0	55.0
18 to 24	22.5	32.5	47.5	32.5	47.5	57.5
24 to 30	25.0	35.0	50.0	35.0	50.0	60.0
30 to 36	27.5	37.5	52.5	37.5	52.5	62.5
36 to 42	30.0	40.0	55.0	40.0	55.0	65.0
42 to 48	[max.]	42.5	57.5	42.5	57.5	67.5
48 to 54		45.0	60.0	45.0	60.0	70.0
54 to 60		47.5	65.0	47.5	62.5	75.0
60 to 66		50.0	70.0	50.0	65.0	80.0
66 to 72		[max.]	75.0	[max.]	67.5	85.0
72 to 78			80.0		70.0	90.0
78 to 84			[max.]		[max.]	95.0
84 to 90						100.0
90 to 96						[max.]

Source: RCM/CSD/Box 11A:NRCM, Minutes of the first meeting of the African Wages Sub-Committee, 28 January 1941.

Appendix F

**Basic Rates of Wages of African Mine Workers
before and after the Guillebaud Award
(In s/d per ticket)**

Surface		Surface	
Before *the Award*	*After* *the Award*	*Before* *the Award*	*After* *the Award*
Group 1:		Group 4 *contd.*:	
45/–	80/–	87/6	127/6
47/6	82/6	90/–	130/–
50/–	85/–	Group 5:	
52/6	87/6	172/6	217/6
55/–	90/–	175/–	220/–
57/6	92/6	177/6	222/6
60/–	95/–	180/–	225/–
62/6	97/6	182/6	227/6
65/–	100/–	187/6	232/6
76/6	102/6	192/6	237/6
Group 2:		Group 6:	
52/6	87/6	190/–	235/–
55/–	90/–	195/–	240/–
57/6	92/6	200/–	245/–
60/–	95/–	205/–	250/–
62/6	97/6	210/–	255/–
65/–	100/–	215/–	260/–
67/6	102/6	217/6	262/6
70/–	105/–		
Group 3:		Group 7:	
62/6	97/6	222/6	272/6
65/–	100/–	227/6	277/6
67/6	102/6	232/6	282/6
70/–	105/–	237/6	287/6
72/6	107/6	247/6	297/6
75/–	110/–	257/6	307/6
77/6	112/6	267/6	317/6
Group 4:		270/–	320/–
75/–	115/–	Special Group:	
77/6	117/–	290/–	340/–
80/–	120/–	300/–	350/–
82/6	122/6	310/–	360/–
85/–	125/–	320/–	370/–
			(continued)

Basic Rates of Wages of African Mine Workers continued

Underground		Undergound	
Before the Award	*After the Award*	*Before the Award*	*After the Award*
Group 1:		Group 5:	
55/–	90/–	187/6	232/6
57/6	92/6	190/–	235/–
60/–	95/–	196/6	237/6
62/6	97/6	195/–	240/–
65/–	100/–	197/6	242/6
67/6	102/6	200/–	245/–
70/–	105/–	Group 6:	
72/6	107/6	197/6	242/6
75/–	110/–	202/6	247/6
77/6	112/6	207/6	252/6
Group 2:		212/6	257/6
65/–	100/–	217/6	262/6
67/6	102/6	222/6	267/6
70/–	105/–	225/–	270/–
72/6	107/6	Group 7:	
75/–	110/–	232/6	282/6
77/6	112/6	237/6	287/6
80/–	115/–	242/6	292/6
82/6	117/6	247/6	297/6
Group 3:		252/6	302/6
77/6	112/6	257/6	307/6
80/–	115/–	260/–	310/–
82/6	117/6	Group 8:	
85/–	120/–	257/6	307/6
87/6	122/6	262/6	312/6
90/–	125/–	267/6	317/6
92/6	127/6	272/6	322/6
Group 4:		282/6	332/6
90/–	130/–	292/6	342/6
92/6	132/6	302/6	352/6·
95/–	135/–	305/–	355/–
97/6	137/6	Special Group:	
100/–	140/–	325/–	375/–
102/6	142/6	335/–	385/–
105/–	145/–	345/–	395/–
		355/–	405/–

Source: *Report and Award of the Arbitrator C. W. Guillebaud* (Lusaka, January 1953).

NOTES

File references in the notes are preceded by a notation indicating the archival source. These notations are as follows:

AA	Anglo-American Corporation of South Africa
AMAX	American Metal Climax
CBM	Archives of the Missionary Societies in Great Britain and Ireland
CISB	Copper Industry Service Bureau, Kitwe.
IAS	Institute for African Studies, University of Zambia
LMS	London Missionary Society
MCM	Mufulira Copper Mine
MMS	Archives of the Methodist Missionary Society
NCCM/CSD	Nchanga Consolidated Copper Mines (Centralized Services Division), Kitwe.
NRCM	Northern Rhodesian Chamber of Mines
PRO	Public Records Office, London.
R	Rhokana Division.
RACM	Roan Antelope Copper Mine.
RCM/CSD	Roan Consolidated Mines (Central Services Division), Ndola.
RST	Rhodesian Selection Trust International Metals, London.
SEC	Secretariat files, National Archives of Zambia, Lusaka.
SNA	Secretary of Native Affairs
UMCB	United Missions in the Copperbelt
UW	University of Wyoming, American Heritage Collection
ZA	National Archives of Zambia, Lusaka

INTRODUCTION

1. Arthur Tuden and Leonard Plotnicov, eds., *Social Stratification in Africa* (London, 1970); P. L. van den Berghe, ed., *Africa: Social Problems of Change and Conflict* (San Francisco, 1965), p. 348; P. C. Lloyd, *The New Elites of Tropical Africa* (Oxford, 1966); J. Clyde Mitchell, ed., *Social Networks in Urban Situations* (Manchester, 1969).

2. William Elkan, *Migrants and Proletarians* (Oxford, 1960); H. Jack and Ray Simons, *Class and Colour in South Africa* (Harmondsworth, England, 1969), p. 616.

3. R. Sandbrook and R. Cohen, eds., *The Development of an African Working Class* (London, 1975); Peter C. W. Gutkind, Robin Cohen, and Jean Copans, eds., *African Labor History* (Beverly Hills, California, 1978); Richard Jeffries, *Class, Power and Ideology in Ghana: The Railwaymen of Sekondi* (Cambridge, England, 1978).

4. Charles Perrings, *Black Mineworkers in Central Africa* (New York, 1979); Robert H. Davies, *Capital, State and White Labour in South Africa* (Atlantic Highlands, New Jersey, 1979).

5. E. P. Thompson, *The Making of the English Working Class* (New York, 1963), pp. 8–10; G. Carchedi, "On the Economic Identification of the New Middle Class," *Economy and Society* 4, no. 1 (1975); N. Poulantzas, *Classes in Contemporary Capitalism* (London, 1975).

6. Some well-known advocates of this approach are: Thompson, *English Working Class*; István Mészáros, ed., *Aspects of History and Class Consciousness* (London, 1971); Gareth Steadman Jones, "Working-Class Culture and Working-Class Politics in London, 1870–1900: Notes on the Remaking of a Working Class," *Journal of Social History* 7, no. 4 (Summer 1974): 498; Michael Mann, *Consciousness and Action Among the Western Working Class* (New York, 1973), p. 13; Anthony Giddens, *The Class Structure of the Advanced Societies* (London, 1973), p. 103.

7. Elena L. Berger, *Labour, Race and Colonial Rule* (Oxford, 1974); Ian Henderson, "Labour and Politics in Northern Rhodesia, 1900–1953: A Study in the Limits of Colonial Power" (Ph.D. diss., University of Edinburgh, 1973); A. L. Epstein, *Politics in an Urban African Community* (Manchester, England, 1958); J. Clyde Mitchell, *The Kalela Dance*, Rhodes-Livingstone Paper No. 27 (Lusaka, 1957).

8. In contrast Perrings focuses on "the objective basis of proletarianization . . . and not the consciousness that transforms the worker from rightless proletarian to the lever of social change." In an otherwise excellent study, Perrings too readily equates class membership with consciousness and behavior. Perrings, *Black Mineworkers*, pp. 3–4.

9. Lukács argues that the proletariat has to struggle against itself as well as other classes and that this internal struggle obscures real class interests, thus leading to false consciousness. He predicted that "the proletariat will only have won the real victory when it has overcome these effects within itself." Georg Lukács, *History and Class Consciousness* (London, 1971), pp. 70, 80.

10. K. Marx and F. Engles, *On Britain* (Moscow, 1953); V. I. Lenin, *Imperialism, The Highest Stage of Capitalism* (Moscow, 1968) and *What Is To Be Done?* (Moscow, 1969).

11. Joseph Femia, "Hegemony and Consciousness in the Thought of Antonio Gramsci," *Political Studies* 23, no. 1 (March 1975): 38; Chantel Mouffe, *Gramsci and Marxist Theory* (London, 1979). Ideology is "a set of ideas or beliefs or attitudes characteristic of a group"; John Plamenatz, *Ideology* (New York, 1970), p. 16.

12. Geoffrey Crossick, "The Labour Aristocracy and Its Values: A Study of

Mid-Victorian Kentish London," *Victorian Studies* 19, no. 3 (March 1976); David Lockwood, "The Weakest Link in the Chain? Some Comments on the Marxist Theory of Action," in Richard L. Simpson and Ida Harper Simpson, eds., *Research in the Sociology of Work* (Greenwich, Connecticut, 1981), vol. 1.

13. Poulantzas, *Contemporary Capitalism*, p. 14. Poulantzas defines class struggle as "the antagonistic contradictory quality of the social relations which comprise the social division of labor."

14. Ibid., Introduction. Productive labor produces surplus value and is directly involved in material production.

15. David Stark, "Class Struggle and the Transformation of the Labor Process," *Theory and Society* 9 (1980); E. P. Thompson, "18th-Century English Society: Class Struggle Without Class?" *Social History* 3, no. 2 (1979); Jones, "Working-Class Culture."

16. Richard Johnson, "Three Problematics: Elements of a Theory of Working-Class Culture," in J. Clarke, C. Critcher and R. Johnson, eds., *Working-Class Culture* (New York, 1979).

17. Wright points out that some positions in the class structures have objectively contradictory locations within class relations. Erik Olin Wright, "Class Boundaries in Advanced Capitalist Societies," *New Left Review* 98 (July–August 1976).

18. Mann, *Consciousness*, p. 13; Giddens, *Class Structure*, p. 103; Paul M. Lubeck, "Class Formation at the Periphery: Class Consciousness and Islamic Nationalism among Nigerian Workers," in Simpson and Simpson, *The Sociology of Work*, pp. 52–53.

19. Stark, "Class Struggle"; Terry Johnson, "What Is to Be Known? The Structural Determination of Social class," *Economy and Society* 6, no. 2 (May 1977).

20. Poulantzas, *Contemporary Capitalism*, pp. 24–25; idem, "The Capitalist State: A Reply to Miliband and Laclau," *New Left Review* 95 (January–February 1976).

21. Ralph Miliband, *Marxism and Politics* (Oxford, 1977).

22. Johnson, "Three Problematics," pp. 234, 236–37.

23. Gavin Kitching, *Class and Economic Change in Kenya* (New Haven, 1980); Davies, *Capital, State and White Labour*.

24. B. J. Berman and J. M. Lonsdale, "Crises of Accumulation, Coercion and the Colonial State: The Development of the Labor Control System in Kenya, 1919–1929," *Canadian Journal of African Studies* 14, no. 1 (1980); Michael Burawoy, "The Hidden Abode of Underdevelopment: Labor Process and the State in Zambia," *Politics and Society* 11, no. 2 (1982): 196.

25. Burawoy, "Hidden Abode," pp. 161–63; Ken Good, "Settler Colonialism: Economic Development and Class Formation," *Journal of Modern African Studies* 14, no. 4 (1976).

26. Kitching, *Change in Kenya*, p. 455. Kitching cites the following examples: "Peter C. W. Gutkind and Peter Waterman, *African Social Studies: A Radical Reader* (London, 1977), especially pp. 226–94; also nearly all the work of Cliffe, Saul and Arrighi and others in the early 'Dar es Salaam School', a representative selection of which is found in G. Arrighi and J. S. Saul (eds.),

Essays on the Political Economy of Africa (New York, 1973). See also Issa Shivji, *Class Struggles in Tanzania* (London, 1976); and M. Mamdani, *Politics and Class Formation in Uganda* (London, 1976). For a wider range of literature on Central and West Africa see my 'Concept of Class and the Study of Africa', *The African Review*, no. 3, 1972, pp. 237–50, an article which itself exemplifies this confusion perfectly."

27. Most scholars of the African working class define proletarians as persons solely dependent upon wage labor for their livelihood. Peace disagrees, claiming that "once a worker enters the factory floor he is 'proletarianised'." Adrian Peace, "The Lagos Proletariat: Labour Aristocrats or Populist Militants?" in Sandbrook and Cohen, *African Working Class*, p. 284.

28. Mann, *Consciousness*, p. 51.

29. Frantz Fanon, *The Wretched of the Earth* (New York, 1963), p. 88; John Saul, "The 'Labour Aristocracy': Thesis Reconsidered," in Sandbrook and Cohen, *African Working Class*. Fanon includes all proletarianized workers in Africa in the labor aristocracy. Others tend to limit the definition to the more highly paid and skilled sectors of African workers. For more discussion, see P. Waterman, "The 'Labour Aristocracy' in Africa: Introduction to a Debate," *Development and Change* 6, no. 3 (July 1975).

30. Adrian Peace, "Industrial Protest in Nigeria," in Emanuel de Kadt and Gavin Williams, eds., *Sociology and Development* (London, 1974), p. 142.

31. Robin Cohen, "From Peasants to Workers in Africa," in Peter C. W. Gutkind and I. Wallerstein, eds., *The Political Economy of Contemporary Africa* (London, 1976), p. 162.

32. Arnold Hughes and Robin Cohen, "An Emerging Nigerian Working Class: The Lagos Experience, 1897–1939," in Gutkind, Cohen, and Copans, *African Labor History*, p. 51.

33. Richard Moorsom, "Underdevelopment, Contract Labor and Worker Consciousness in Namibia, 1915–1972," *Journal of Southern African Studies* (JSAS) 4 no. 1 (October 1977); Charles van Onselen, "Worker Consciousness in Black Miners: Southern Rhodesia, 1900–1920," *Journal of African History* 14, no. 2 (1973): 254; Ian Phimister, "African Worker Consciousness: Origins and Aspects to 1953," in I. R. Phimister and C. van Onselen, *Studies in the History of African Mine Labour in Colonial Zimbabwe* (Salisbury, 1978), p. 29.

34. T. Adler, ed., *Perspectives on South Africa* (Johannesburg, 1977); David Hemson, "Dock Workers, Labour Circulation and Class Struggles in Durban, 1940–59," *JSAS* 4, no. 1 (October 1977); Sandbrook and Cohen, *African Working Class*; and Gutkind, Cohen, and Copans, *African Labor History*.

35. Previous work focused on the growth and organizational character of trade unions, their success in wage-bargaining, and their relationship with political parties and governments. E. J. Berg and J. Butler, "Trade Unions," in J. S. Coleman and C. G. Rosberg, eds., *Political Parties and National Integration in Tropical Africa* (Los Angeles, 1964).

36. Paul Lubeck, "Unions, Workers and Consciousness in Kano, Nigeria: A View from Below," and Adrian Peace, "The Lagos Proletariat," in Sandbrook and Cohen, *African Working Class*; Introduction and Sharon Stichter, "Trade Unionism in Kenya, 1947–1952: The Militant Phase," in Gutkind,

Cohen, and Copans, *African Labor History*.
37. Lubeck, "Unions, Workers and Consciousness," p. 156.

CHAPTER 1

1. D. Hywell Davies, *Zambia in Maps* (London, 1971), pp. 10–11.
2. J. F. Holleman and S. Biesheuvel, *White Mineworkers in Northern Rhodesia* (Cambridge, England, 1973), p. 25; Richard Hall, *Zambia* (London, 1965), Chaps. 1 and 8.
3. Davies, *Maps*, p. 44; Hall, *Zambia*, p. 313, Appendix IV.
4. H. W. Langworthy, *Zambia Before 1890* (London, 1972).
5. Andrew Roberts, *A History of Zambia* (New York, 1976), p. 182.
6. Ibid., p. 212; Elena Berger, *Labour, Race, and Colonial Rule: The Copperbelt from 1924 to Independence* (Oxford, 1974), Appendix D.
7. Roberts, *Zambia*, pp. 212–18.
8. For further details see Roberts, *Zambia* or Carolyn Baylies, "The State and Class Formation in Zambia" (Ph.D. diss., University of Wisconsin, 1978).
9. Edmund Davis, born in Tuorak, Australia, 1862, was one of the first speculators for gold at Johannesburg and a friend of Cecil Rhodes. Davis became "the driving force of some 50 companies" in the city. In 1925 he became a board member of the British South Africa Company, and in 1928 of the Anglo-American Company. Died 20 February 1939. *The London Times*, 21 February 1939.
10. Michael Gelfand, *Northern Rhodesia in the Days of the Charter* (Oxford, 1961), p. 124; Kenneth Bradley, *Copper Venture: The Discovery and Development of Roan Antelope and Mufulira* (London, 1952), p. 57; F. L. Coleman, *The Northern Rhodesian Copperbelt 1899–1962: Technological Development up to the End of the Central African Federation* (Manchester, 1971), p. 15. The first orebodies found in Northern Rhodesia had been copper oxide ores with 3.5% copper, as opposed to 15% in the Katanga ore.
11. Sir Alfred Chester Beatty (1875–1968) was an American consulting engineer and assistant general manager of the Guggenheim Exploration Company. He started the pour-free copper method and became interested in Northern Rhodesia through a friend. After moving to England, he established the Selection Trust Ltd. in December 1914 and was knighted in 1956.
12. Coleman, *Northern Rhodesian Copperbelt*, pp. 32–33, 44–45.
13. Sir Ernest O. Oppenheimer (1880–1957) formed the Anglo-American Company of South Africa Ltd. in September 1917 and was knighted in 1921. He became chairman of DeBeers, the South American diamond company, in 1929. He had important interests in the Rand gold mining industry, and helped develop the Orange Free State gold fields.
14. By the end of 1925, Anglo-American had acquired interests in all the concession companies and had become consulting engineers to them and the British South Africa Company. Coleman, *Northern Rhodesian Copperbelt*, p. 43; Simon Cunningham, *The Copper Industry in Zambia: Foreign Mining Companies in a Developing Country* (New York, 1981).
15. Bradley, *Copper Venture*, pp. 82–83; Raymond Brooks, "How the Rhode-

sian Coppers Were Found," *Engineering and Mining Journal* (May 1944), p. 81.

16. Prosser Gifford, "The Framework for a Nation: An Economic and Social History of Northern Rhodesia from 1914 to 1939" (Ph.D. diss., Yale University, 1964), p. 241; Thomas R. Navin, *Copper Mining and Management* (Tucson, Arizona, 1978), Chaps. 11 and 23.

17. American Metal Company sent Otto Sussman to investigate an old South African copper mine. Sussman visited Northern Rhodesia and advised the company to invest there. As a result, American Metal swapped 20% of its shares to Selection Trust for its holdings in RST. John Payne, Jr., interview in Old Lyme, Connecticut, 13 July 1981; Walter Hochschild to L. H. Gann, cited in Gifford, "Framework," p. 229. Hochschild and his brother Harold were chairmen of American Metal Company (later AMAX when American Metal and Metal Climax merged in 1957). Harold was particularly interested in Northern Rhodesia and made numerous visits there.

18. Sir Ronald Prain, *Reflections on an Era* (Surrey, England, 1981), p. 27; Erwin Weill, interview in New York, 15 July 1981. Former secretary of American Metal, Weill emphasized Harold Hochschild's role in securing African advancement on the mines in the 1950s.

19. Theodore Gregory, *Ernest Oppenheimer and the Economic Development of Southern Africa* (Oxford, 1962), pp. 416–17.

20. Sir Auckland Geddes (1879–1954) was a medical doctor. In 1919–20 he was President of the Board of Trade and Principal of McGill University. In 1920 he was appointed British Ambassador in Washington. He was chairman of Rio Tinto from 1923 and chairman of Rhokana Corp. after January 1931.

21. Leslie Pollak (died 1934) was E. Oppenheimer's brother-in-law and business associate. In 1927 he was made managing director for Rhodesian Anglo-American. S. S. Taylor was the second managing director for RAA in 1930. In 1931 he became managing director for RAA and in 1934 he became RAA's chief spokesman in London. He was a London director for DeBeers.

22. Roberts, *Zambia*, p. 186; Gregory, *Oppenheimer*, pp. 31, 404–15.

23. L. H. Gann, *A History of Northern Rhodesia* (London, 1964), p. 251; Charles Perrings, "Black Labour in the Copper Mines of Northern Rhodesia and the Belgian Congo 1911–1941" (Ph.D. diss., University of London, 1976), p. 280; Navin, *Copper Mining*, Chap. 12

24. Gifford, "Framework," p. 256; Report on the Copper Industry, U.S. Federal Trade Commission (Washington: U.S. Government Printing Office, 1947), pp. 108–09; O. C. Herfindahl, *Copper Costs and Prices: 1870–1957* (Baltimore, 1959), p. 174, Table 14. A long ton equals 2,240 lbs.

25. Gregory, *Oppenheimer*, pp. 442–43; Rhokana Corporation, *Annual Report*, 1935; Roan Antelope Copper Mine, *Annual Report*, 1935.

26. American Metal Company, *Annual Report*, 1934; Rhokana Corporation, *Annual Report*, 1933.

27. The free world is the world minus U.S.S.R. and Yugoslavia. W. J. Barber, *The Economy of British Central Africa* (Stanford, 1961), p. 127, Table 11.

28. Gifford, "Framework," pp. 258–62; Herfindahl, *Copper Costs*, p. 112.

29. A. Pim and S. Milligan, *Report of the Commission Appointed to Enquire into the*

Financial and Economic Position of Northern Rhodesia (Colonial No. 145 of 1938), p. 20 (*The Pim Report*); Robert E. Baldwin, *Economic Development and Export Growth: A Study of Northern Rhodesia* (Los Angeles, 1966), p. 33.

30. SEC/MG/44, Commissioner for the Mines to the Chief Secretary (CS), 14 December 1946.

31. Perrings, "Black Labour," p. 321; Baldwin, *Economic Development*, pp. 32–33.

32. *The Economist* (1941–45); *Northern Rhodesia Chamber of Mines Year Book* (Kitwe, 1956), p. 60.

33. Sir. R. L. Prain, "Copper Pricing Systems: Address to the Organization for European Economic Cooperation," in Prain, *Selected Papers, 1958–60* (London, 1961), vol. 2, pp. 34–35.

34. Baldwin, *Economic Development*, p. 33. CISB, 100:30:20, Chronological List of Events, submitted by the mining companies to the Commission Appointed to Inquire into the Unrest in the Mining Industry in Northern Rhodesia in Recent Months (Lusaka, 1956) (The Branigan Commission); the commission report is *The Branigan Commion Report*.

35. Berger, *Labour*, p. 6; American Metals Company, Ltd., *Annual Report*, 1935 and 1937; R. J. B. Moore, evidence presented to The Commission Appointed to Enquire into the Disturbances on the Copperbelt of Northern Rhodesia (London, 1935), Cmd. 5009, p. 744 (The Russell Commission).

36. Eric C. Bromwich, "African Advancement," RST mimeograph, 5 February 1962.

37. In 1957 copper was £181 per ton; *Northern Rhodesia Chamber of Mines Book 1957* (Kitwe, 1957). Profit for the four mines was £15 million in 1958 as compared to £41.2 million in 1956; annual company reports in *The Economist*, 1956–58.

38. *The Central African Examiner*, 13 August 1960.

39. Hall, *Zambia*, p. 265.

40. For more details on nationalization of the industry see Marcia Burdette, "The Dynamics of Nationalization Between Multinational Corporations and Peripheral States" (Ph.D. diss., Columbia University, 1979).

41. In 1928, Sussman and Field never mentioned the cheap labor available in Northern Rhodesia as a reason for entering the Northern Rhodesian copper field. Cunningham, *Copper Industry*, p. 126; Payne interview (*see* note 17).

42. Epstein, *Politics*, p. 63.

43. RCM/CSD/RACM c.201.3.3(R11): Memorandum on the classification of native labor, 8 January 1941.

44. A. L. Epstein, *Politics in an Urban African Community* (Manchester, 1958), pp. 15–16.

45. *The Branigan Commission Report*, pp. 16–17.

46. Berger, *Labour*, p. 220; *Report of the Commission Appointed to Inquire into the Mining Industry in Northern Rhodesia* (Lusaka, 1962), pp. 19–20, 22 (*The Morison Report*).

47. Baldwin, *Economic Development*, p. 36.

48. After the war a new double taxation agreement allowed the Northern Rhodesian Government to retain income taxes from the mining companies

to the fullest extent of the Northern Rhodesian rate (7/6 in the £); only the balance due at the higher British rate went to the United Kingdom. *The Pim Report*, pp. 134–35.

49. Berger, *Labour*, pp. 8–10.
50. The British South Africa Company royalties were a large drain on Northern Rhodesian revenues. After prolonged pressure from the Legislative Council, in 1950 the Company agreed to give the territorial government one-fifth of their royalties. In return, the Company's mineral rights were confirmed until 1986. The Company still made handsome profits, with total payments of £160 million by 1963. *The Northern Rhodesia Chamber of Mines Year Books 1955–63*; Garry Allighan, *The Welensky Story* (Cape Town, 1962), pp. 161–86.
51. Baylies, "Class Formation," pp. 95–96.
52. Ann Seidman, "The Economics of Eliminating Rural Poverty," in Robin Palmer and Neil Parsons, eds., *The Roots of Rural Poverty in Central and Southern Africa* (Los Angeles, 1977), pp. 412–15; Baldwin, *Economic Development*, pp. 193–95.
53. Robert Rotberg, *Black Heart: Gore-Browne and the Politics of Multiracial Zambia* (Los Angeles, 1977); T. Ranger, "Making Northern Rhodesia Imperial: Variations on a Royal Theme, 1924–1938," *African Affairs* 79, no. 316 (July 1980): 351. For example, Governor Stanley in 1924 apologized for "the uncouthness of the settlers."
54. Doris J. Dodge, *Agricultural Policy and Performance in Zambia* (Berkeley, 1977), pp. 6–9.
55. Maud Muntemba, "Thwarted Development: A Case Study of Economic Change in Kabwe Rural District of Zambia, 1902–70," in Palmer and Parsons, *Roots*, pp. 351–61; Terence Ranger, "Growing from the Roots: Reflections on Peasant Research in Central and Southern Africa," *JSAS* 5, no. 1 (1979).
56. Ranger points out that "because of the minimal demands it made on its subjects, the colonial administration did not need to foster any very strong or elaborate ideology. It did not have opportunities to do this anyway. What was required was the idea of a benevolent Imperial Monarchy, which succeeded till the late 1940s." Ranger, "Northern Rhodesia," p. 350.
57. "In 1929–30, the revenue from Africans was £125,270, about one-fifth of the total revenue. Direct expenditure on services for Africans in the same year amounted to £12,028, with a further £11,471 at headquarters—altogether a very small proportion of the total government expenditure of £554,527." Colonial Office (C.O.) 795/47/36150: Governor Maxwell to Secretary of State for the Colonies, 24 April 1931.
58. George Chauncy, Jr., "The Locus of Reproduction: Women's Labour in Zambian Copperbelt, 1927–1953," *JSAS* 7, no. 2 (April 1981); Baldwin, *Economic Development*, pp. 86–93; Helmuth Heisler, *Urbanisation and the Government of Migration* (London, 1974).
59. Ranger, "Northern Rhodesia"; Robert Rotberg, "Race Relations and Politics in Colonial Zambia: The Elwell Incident," *Race* 7, no. 7 (July 1965).
60. D. D. Keet, "The African Representative Council 1946–1958: A Focus on African Political Leadership and Politics in Northern Rhodesia," (M.A. thesis, University of Zambia, 1975).

61. Baylies, "Class Formation," Chap. 5; Ken Good, "Settler Colonialism: Economic Development and Class Formation," *Journal of Modern African Studies* 14, no.4 (1976).

CHAPTER 2

1. Frederick Johnstone, "Class Conflict and Colour Bars in the South African Mining Industry," Institute of Commonwealth Studies, Collected Seminar Papers, No. 10 (London, 1970).
2. Charles van Onselen, *Chibaro: African Mine Labour in Southern Rhodesia 1900–1933* (London, 1976); John Rex, "The Compound, The Reserve, and The Urban Location: The Essential Institutions of Southern African Labour Exploitation," *South African Labour Bulletin* (SALB) 1, no. 4 (July 1974): 4–17; Sean Moroney, "The Development of the Compound as a Mechanism of Worker Control," *SALB* 4, no. 3 (May 1978).
3. Charles Perrings, *Black Mineworkers in Central Africa* (New York, 1979), pp. 110–11. A stope is any underground production chamber.
4. ZA/7/1/14/7, Provincial Commissioner, Luangwa Province, *Annual Report*, 1931.
5. L. H. Gann, *A History of Northern Rhodesia* (London, 1964), p. 209.
6. Ibid., p. 209; ZA1/9/18/49/1, J. W. S. Horne, Acting Secretary for Native Affairs to Chief Secretary, 18 May 1931.
7. ZA/7/1/12/7, Provincial Commissioner, Luangwa Province, *Annual Report*, 1929.
8. CBM Box 1211, Sydney Ball (UMHK mining engineer) to B. Willis of Stanford University, 22 October 1930.
9. RCM/CSD/KHB41, general manager MCM to RST, 30 January 1930.
10. van Onselen, *Chibaro*, pp. 115–41.
11. Perrings, *Black Mineworkers*, pp. 27–28; Charles Coulter, "The Sociological Problem," in J. Merle Davis, ed., *Modern Industry and the African* (London, 1933), p. 53; Bruce Fetter, *The Creation of Elisabethville* (Stanford, 1976), p. 129.
12. Northern Rhodesia, *Annual Report upon Native Affairs*, 1930.
13. van Onselen, *Chibaro*, pp. 115–41; Alfred Mwalwanda, interview in Luanshya, 13 September 1976; Perrings, *Black Mineworkers*, Chaps. 1 and 5.
14. C. F. Spearpoint, "The African Native and the Rhodesia Copper Mines," Supplement to the *Journal of the Royal African Society* 36, no. 144 (July 1937): 7–8, 10.
15. A. Pim and S. Milligan, *Report of the Commission to Enquire into the Financial and Economic Position of Northern Rhodesia* (Colonial No. 145 of 1938) (*The Pim Report*).
16. J. L. Vellut, "Rural Poverty in Western Sheba c. 1890–1930," in R. Palmer and N. Parsons, eds., *The Roots of Rural Poverty in Central and Southern Africa* (Los Angeles, 1977), p. 334; Perrings, *Black Mineworkers*, pp. 88–89; ZA1/9/18/43/1, J. Moffat Thomson, SNA, to Chief Secretary, 23 September 1929.
17. RCM/CSD/WMA 65(205.5), Spearpoint to general manager RACM, 16 November 1938; *Annual Report upon Native Affairs*, 1930.

18. The mines saved from £3 to £4 per voluntary worker. Robert E. Baldwin, *Economic Development and Export Growth: A Study of Northern Rhodesia* (Los Angeles, 1966), p. 85.
19. In 1932, only 10,492 men out of 30,000 were recruited. ZA1/9/18/36/2, Thomson to Provincial Commissioner, Kasama, 2 April 1931.
20. Perrings, *Black Mineworkers*, pp. 90–93; Coulter, "Sociological Problem," p. 53.
21. Theodore Gregory, *Ernest Oppenheimer and the Economic Development of Southern Africa* (Oxford, 1962), pp. 442–45; Prosser Gifford, "The Framework for a Nation: An Economic and Social History of Northern Rhodesia from 1914 to 1939" (Ph.D. diss., Yale University, 1964), pp. 258–62.
22. Coulter, "Sociological Problem," p. 60.
23. RCM/CSD/WMA 19, C. F. Spearpoint, compound manager, to F. Ayer, general manager, RACM, 16 September 1936; NCCM/CSD, L. A. Pollack, Report, 4 July 1929.
24. *Annual Report upon Native Affairs*, 1931; RCM/CSD/WMA 3, general manager, RACM to RACM, London, 4 January and 1 February 1930.
25. RCM/CSD/KHB41, RST, London, to general manager MCM, 30 January 1930; *Annual Report upon Native Affairs*, 1931.
26. RCM/CSD/W(2)HA 58, L. Eaton, "Report," October 1929.
27. ZA1/9/18/34/1, H. Y. Willis, "Report on Rhodesian Natives in Katanga," 31 December 1931; Willis was British Vice-Consul in Elisabethville. Spearpoint, "African Native," p. 8.
28. RCM/CSD/KHB41, E. E. Barker to A. D. Storke, 27 November 1929.
29. *Annual Report upon Native Affairs*, 1929; RCM/CSD/KMA 18, Report on African earnings per shift, all mines, 1930–48.
30. To cope with Copperbelt competition, UMHK introduced a separate, and higher, wage scale for experienced Northern Rhodesians. Perrings, *Black Mineworkers*, pp. 88–89; PRO/CO/795/18/18254, 1926 Native Reserves Commission, evidence of H. E. Scott, I, 206, and delegates from the Broken Hill Mining Conference, Exhibit 5, IV.
31. Northern Rhodesians working at UMHK were paid in British sterling which kept pace with the falling value of the franc. In 1926, Northern Rhodesian wages were worth twice the real wage of a Congolese working at UMHK. Consequently, after the fall of the franc in 1927, the cost of Northern Rhodesian labor in Katanga rose. This was a factor pushing UMHK towards stabilization. Fetter, *Elisabethville*, p. 85.
32. In 1932, Roan's married miners worked on average 20.25 months, while single men stayed 9.79 months. Nkana averaged 12.9 months for married workers and 8.6 months for single men. Coulter, "Sociological Problem," p. 61.
33. In 1936, the Roan compound manager said he needed 30% of the black work force working longer than 18 months. In contrast, the Rhokana compound manager only needed 16%. RCM/CSD/WMA 139, Spearpoint to Frank Ayer, 16 November 1936. Rhokana Corporation, notes for NILAB meeting, 11 February 1937.
34. Spearpoint, "African Native," p. 54. Many couples were not formally married; for statistical purposes they will be treated as married. George

Chauncy, Jr., "The Locus of Reproduction: Women's Labour in the Zambian Copperbelt, 1927–1953," *JSAS* 7, no. 2 (April 1981).

35. David Irwin, "Notes for a Talk Given to the RST Group Executive Gathering, Lusaka, 25–26 September 1959," University of Wyoming Archives.

36. John Payne, Jr., interview in Old Lyme, Connecticut, 13 July 1981. "In the fall of 1928, Luanshya consisted of eight or ten Kimberley brick houses, some Rondavels, three prospect shafts with wood burning steam hoists, a pilot mill, carpenter shop, combined General and Survey Office, a tennis court, a doctor without a hospital, no adequate water supply nor sanitation system, an embryo brick plant, three shot drill crews in the bush across the Luanshya drift, and Jimmy Moore and C. F. Spearpoint. The railroad was on the way from Ndola, but proceeding very cautiously"; "Notes for a Talk", p. 8.

37. Spearpoint, "African Native," pp. 34–35; RCM/CSD/file 210.6, Roan Monthly Compound Report, 30 November 1932.

38. ZA/7/1/16/7, Luangwa Province, *Annual Report*, 31 December 1930; RCM/CSD/KSN 3/1/4, District Commissioner, Ndola, *Annual Report*, 1932.

39. *The Pim Report*, p. 45; Coulter, "Sociological Problem," p. 61.

40. Dennis Etheredge, interview in Johannesburg, 12 October 1976.

41. SEC/LAB/1, W. J. Scrivener, "Native Labour as Affecting the Copper Industry of Northern Rhodesia," 17 August 1934; PRO/CO/795/43/36043, H. S. Munroe, Rhodesian Anglo-American to Permanent Under-Secretary of State, C. O., 30 January 1931.

42. Spearpoint, "African Native," p. 4.

43. *The Pim Report*, pp. 55–56.

44. J. S. Moffat, evidence to The Commission Appointed to Enquire into the Disturbances on the Copperbelt of Northern Rhodesia (London, 1935), Cmd. 5009, 74 (The Russell Commission); the commission report is *The Russell Report. The Pim Report*, p. 164.

45. ZA/KSN/3/1/3, Provincial Commissioner, Luangwa Province, *Annual Report*, 1929.

46. Some provincial officials anticipated "the growth of a class of stabilized mineworkers living with their families in or near mine compounds"; ZA/KSN/3/1/3, P. C., Luangwa Province, *Annual Report*, 1929. William Stubbs, interview in Oxford, England, 25 October 1976.

47. Henry Carlisle, "David D. Irwin: An interview," *Mining Engineering* (June 1964), p. 89.

48. The 1932 Mine Township Ordinance formalized mine control over their townships. *The Pim Report*, pp. 55–56.

49. Spearpoint, "African Native," p. 18.

50. G. St. J. Orde Browne, *Labour Conditions in Northern Rhodesia* (Colonial No. 150 of 1938), p. 31 (*The Orde Brown Report*).

51. Gabriel Musumbulwa, interview in Luanshya, 30 August 1976; SEC/LAB/2, General Manager, RACM to Labor Commissioner, 15 November 1941.

52. Stubbs interview (*see* note 46).

53. Chris Cook and Mavis Lloyd Leith, interview in East London, South Africa, 4 October 1976; Joseph Mubita, interview in Mufulira, 7 September 1976.

54. John V. Taylor and Dorothea S. Lehmann, *Christians of the Copperbelt: The Growth of the Church in Northern Rhodesia* (London, 1961), p. 32. Spearpoint

believed "the general attitude of the native towards the European is that of a child looking to a teacher to impart to him all the necessary knowledge essential to his progress"; Spearpoint, "African Native," p. 15.

55. When Ashton Kabalika's (a hospital clerk) house was searched, he complained to the compound manager, Mr. Gabbitas, who discharged the offending police. "The clerks and hospital clerks had some respect, so could demand their rights. It was harder for other people." Ashton M. Kabalika, interview in Kitwe, 29 August 1976.

56. By 1940 Spearpoint had been a Compound Manager for 16 years: eight at Roan, seven in Southern Rhodesia, and the rest in Northern Rhodesia on other properties; Mwalwanda interview (*see* note 13).

57. Benjamin Schaefer, Compound Manager at Mufulira from 1930–36; he was in the Native Labor Department of UMHK and before that in the Panda-Shituru compound. A. B. K. Kaniki, interview in Kitwe by Dr. Ian Henderson, 19 August 1970; Schaefer, evidence to the Commission Appointed to Inquire into the Disturbances in the Copperbelt, Northern Rhodesia, July, 1940 (Lusaka, 1941), 30 (The Forster Commission).

58. Chembe Phiri, interview in Luanshya, 3 September 1976.

59. William J. Scrivener: 1912–19, employed by Robert Williams and Co.; 1919–24, employed by the Union Minière Native Labor Department; 1924–29, Compound Manager at Bwana Mkubwa; 1929–60, Compound Manager at Rhokana. Dr. A. Charles Fisher, interview in Kitwe, 21 August 1976.

60. Matthew Mwendapole, interview in Ndola, 3 August 1976.

61. Terry and Chella Ndhlovu, interview by D. Lehmann, Nchanga, 1958. Gabbitas was Compound Manager at Nchanga from 1945; before that he spent eight years in the Rhokana Personnel Department and six years in the police.

62. Etheredge interview (*see* note 40); N. R. K. Davis, interview in Kitwe, 15 September 1976.

63. RCM/CSD/KHB/41, H. H. Field to manager, Native Labor Association, 22 August 1930.

64. Fetter, *Elisabethville*; Carlisle, "Irwin," p. 90; Coulter, "The Sociological Problem," p. 65.

65. RCM/CSD/W (2) HA 62, A. J. Orenstein, "Report on Health Conditions at Bwana Mkubwa, Nkana, Nchanga, Broken Hill, and Roan," 20 December 1929; RCM/CSD/KHB41, H. H. Field to manager, Native Labor Association, 22 August 1930; a house at Roan in the mid-1930s cost about £25 to build. *The Pim Report*, p. 41.

66. LMS Box 9; A. M. Chirgwin, Report to Central African Committee, May–July 1931.

67. Reverend Fr. S. Siemieski, "The Mine Compound and Its Moral Influence upon the Native," *Proceedings of the General Missionary Conference of Northern Rhodesia*, 1931 (Lusaka, 1931).

68. Carlisle, "Irwin," p. 90.

69. Coulter, "Sociological Problem," pp. 66–67; E. A. G. Robinson, "The Economic Problem," in Davis, *Modern Industry*, p. 166.

70. Coulter, "Sociological Problem," p. 69.

71. Women received 7 pounds of mealie meal and 1 pound of meat per week. Each child received 3 pounds of meal a week. In contrast, each miner received 10½ pounds of mealie meal and 2¾ pounds of meat per week plus nuts, vegetables, beans, salt, drippings, and fruit. W. J. Scrivener, evidence to the Russell Commission 62; Spearpoint, "African Native," p. 38.

72. Chauncy found that in the 1930s women earned from perhaps £1 to £2 per brew after expenses, a significant addition to the family income when starting wages at the mines ranged from 12s6d to 30s per month. Chauncy, "Reproduction," p. 145.

73. Ibid., pp. 30–31; Albert Musakanya, interview in Nkana, 22 September 1976.

74. Spearpoint, "African Native," p. 44.

75. Ibid., pp. 40–46; RCM/CSD file 210.6, Compound Monthly Report, RACM, 31 January 1932.

76. Rev. H. C. Nutter, "Native Welfare Work in the Copperbelt of Northern Rhodesia," *Proceedings of the General Missionary Conference of Northern Rhodesia, 1931* (Lusaka, 1931), p. 123; CBM Box 1211, R. J. B. Moore to A. Cocker Brown, 25 February 1935.

77. NILAB, first meeting, 1935.

78. *Annual Report upon Native Affairs*, 1929 and 1930.

79. Spearpoint, "African Native," p. 10. Musakanya recalled that "if in any group of fifteen people, three died, everyone would run away"; Musakanya interview (*see* note 73).

80. "The native genuinely seeking employment does not remain for very long at one place if he has had no success at such a place; he moves on to other places until he finds it. In the Copperbelt they appear to move around in a circle from one mine to the other until they get work"; Spearpoint, "African Native," p. 50. Musakanya interview (*see* note 73).

81. Scrivener, evidence to the Russell Commission, p. 453.

82. Northern Rhodesia, *Report of the Northern Rhodesian Police Comission of Inquiry* (Lusaka, 1947), 29; Kabilika interview (*see* note 55); Union Minière had no bonus system, making frequent use of fines instead. Coulter, "Sociological Problem," p. 64.

83. Spearpoint, "African Native"; John Dalton, interview in Lusaka, 4 August 1975.

84. Spearpoint, "African Native," p. 21; Phiri interview (*see* note 58); Mubita interview (*see* note 53).

85. Kabalika interview (*see* note 55).

86. "Misbehaving in the compound was not allowed"; V. K. Chisala, interview in Kitwe, 21 September 1976. RCM/WMA 64, RACM, Report, Compound Underground Branch—Supervisors' Duties, 17 June 1947. Scrivener, evidence to the Russell Commission, pp. 442–46.

87. Northern Rhodesia, *Report of the Northern Rhodesian Police Commission of Inquiry* (Lusaka, 1947), p. 29.

88. Spearpoint, "African Native," pp. 18–19.

89. P. J. Law, interview, Oxford, England, 26 October 1976.

90. ZA1/9/18/28/1, D. D. Irwin, general manager, RACM to Thomson, Secretary of Native Affairs, 24 December 1929.

91. Spearpoint, "African Native," pp. 19–20; idem, evidence to the Russell Commission, p. 593.
92. Scrivener, evidence to the Russell Commission, pp. 453–54.
93. *Annual Reports upon Native Affairs*, 1931, 1932; J. H. Holleman and S. Biesheuvel, *White Mine Workers in Northern Rhodesia* (Cambridge, England, 1973), p. 10.
94. ZA)KSN/3/1/4, Ndola District, *Annual Report*, 1932; ZA/KSN/3/1/5, Ndola District, *Annual Report*, 1935.
95. RCM/CSD/RACM 210.65, RACM, monthly labor returns, 1929–41; *Annual Report upon Native Affairs*, 1934; R. Hesom (Assistant Compound Manager, MCM), evidence to the Russell Commission, p. 155.
96. SEC/LAB/34, vol. 1 *Report of the Sub-Committee of the Native Industrial Labour Advisory Board on Administrative Control of the Industrial Population* (Lusaka, 1936); ZA1/9/18/36/2 Report of the Board of Management of the Native Labor Association, Ltd., for the year ending 31 December 1931.
97. RCM/CSD/WMA5, General Manager RACM to RST, London, 13 February 1932; Scrivener, evidence to the Russell Commission, p. 559.
98. In 1935, 34% of the black underground workers at Roan were "skilled." RCM/CSD/WMA 139, Spearpoint to R. M. Peterson, 15 October 1935.
99. *The Pim Report*, p. 45. At Roan in 1935, 66% of the underground miners and 84% of the Nyasa underground miners were married; RCM/CSD/WMA 139, Spearpoint to Peterson, 15 October 1935.
100. RCM/CSD/KHB 41, RACM to RACM, London, 19 July 1935; *Chairman's Report of Meetings of the Native Industrial Labour Advisory Board held at Ndola on November 7th and 8th and December 16th and 17th, 1935* (Lusaka, 1936). The average period of employment at Roan was 416 shifts per worker, the longest on the Copperbelt; RCM/CSD/KHB 41, Colonel Stephenson, "Report," 17 July 1935.
101. Scrivener, evidence to the Russell Commission, p. 75; Scrivener, "Native Labour," 17 August 1934. The percentage of Nyasa miners (generally skilled workers) was 20% at Roan in 1935, while dropping to 7.8% at Nkana; SEC/NAT/66G, Nkana District, *Annual Report*, 1935.
102. Mufulira's turnover rate was 151% in 1935. RCM/CSD/KHB 41, RACM to RST London, 19 July 1935; J. D. Tallant, evidence to the Russell Commission, pp. 374, 377.
103. RCM/CSD/210.6, RACM, Monthly Compound Reports, 30 June 1932; Phiri interview (*see* note 58).
104. ZA1/9/18/28/1, F. Ayer, RACM to E. H. Jalland, Acting Secretary of Native Affairs, 2 August 1934.
105. Married housing was 14' × 14', with iron roofs, good doors, and cement floors. Single housing was smaller and more crowded. ZA1/9/82/10, E. H. Jalland (Acting Secretary of Native Affairs), "Tour Report," 7 August 1934.
106. ZA/KSN/3/1/5, Ndola District, *Annual Report*, 1933.
107. ZA1/9/18/57/1, meeting of Sir Auckland Geddes and Northern Rhodesian Government (NRG), 13 December 1933.
108. ZA/Acc. 72/3, vol. I, P. C., Ndola to General Manager, Rhokana, 28 July 1934; Dr. A. Charles Fisher, evidence to the Russell Commission, p. 545.

109. ZA1/9/82/11, Jalland, "Tour Report," 7 August 1934.

110. *The Russell Report*, p. 62.

111. Nutter, "Native Welfare," pp. 121–23.

112. ZA/KSN 3/1/4, Ndola District, *Annual Report*, 1932.

113. Spearpoint, evidence to the Russell Commission, pp. 595–96.

114. *The Orde Browne Report*, p. 33; ZA 1/5/18/57/1, Geddes and NRG, 13 December 1933.

115. Fisher interview (*see* note 59); George Dunlop, evidence to the Russell Commission, p. 172; *Annual Reports upon Native Affairs*, 1931–35.

116. B. Schaefer, evidence to the Russell Commission, p. 29; Cook interview (*see* note 53).

117. *Annual Report upon Native Affairs*, 1934; Scrivener, evidence to the Russell Commission, p. 464; Spearpoint, evidence, p. 89.

118. ZA1/9/82/9, Secretary of Native Affairs, "Tour Report," October 1933.

119. LMS Box 26, Central Africa, R. J. B. Moore to Chirgwin, 3 November 1933.

120. ZA1/9/18/28/1, F. Ayer to E. H. Jalland, 2 August 1934.

121. Gann, *Northern Rhodesia*, p. 252; Rhodes House Collection, MSS. British Empire s. 345, Autobiography of A. C. Vivian, "A Man of Metal," pp. 144–47.

122. *The Pim Report*, p. 47.

123. Ibid. District Officers at Mufulira and Nchanga were recalled in 1931, leaving only a handful of police and a District Officer at Nkana. Thomas Sandford, Secretary for Native Affairs, evidence to the Forster Commission, p. 7.

124. H. H. Field, evidence to the Russell Commission, p. 184.

125. "The Mine natives and their families are well housed and fed and the Mine Authorities as a rule show a laudable desire to do their best for their social and physical welfare." ZA/4/1/16/2, Luangwa Province, *Annual Report*, 1933.

126. *The Orde Brown Report*, p. 5.

127. One such official claimed management at Nkana "simply wanted to get 2 shillings worth of work for 1 shilling wage out of the bloody nigger." SEC/LAB/16, R. S. W. Dickenson to Harold F. Cartmel-Robinson, 11 October 1933.

128. Sir Auckland Geddes' suggestions for improvements at Nkana had been countered by assertions that the Northern Rhodesian government opposed a settled labor force. His exasperation with government officials, upon being told that stabilization was fine with them, is understandable. ZA1/9/18/57/1, Sir Auckland Geddes meeting with government officials, 13 December 1933; *Legislative Council Debates*, Northern Rhodesia, 12 December 1940, p. 383.

129. ZA/Acc. 72/1/1, District Officer, Nkana to Provincial Commissioner, Ndola, 1933; CBM Box 1211, R. J. B. Moore to T. Cocker Browne, 25 February 1935.

130. Elena Berger, *Labour, Race, and Colonial Rule: The Copperbelt from 1924 to Independence* (Oxford, 1974), Chap. 3.

131. In 1933 the Luanshya Beer Hall made a profit of £3,500. RCM/CSD/203.6, Mine Secretary, RACM to District Officer, Luanshya, 16 April 1932; RCM/CSD/203.6, African Welfare—Beer Halls and Canteens, RACM, 1930–55.

CHAPTER 3

1. Elena Berger, *Labour, Race, and Colonial Rule: The Copperbelt from 1924 to Independence* (Oxford, 1974), p. 34; Ian Henderson, "Early African Leadership: The Copperbelt Disturbances of 1935 and 1940," *Journal of Southern African Studies* (*JSAS*), 2, no. 1 (October 1975), pp. 84, 89–90.
2. Charles Perrings, *Black Mineworkers in Central Africa* (New York, 1979), Chap. 8.
3. Chris Cook, interview in East London, South Africa, 4 October 1976; R. Hesom (Assistant Compound Manager, Mufulira), evidence to the Commission Appointed to Enquire into the Disturbances in the Copperbelt, Northern Rhodesia (London, 1935), Cmd. 5009 of 1935, p. 155 (The Russell Commission); Ben Schaefer, evidence, p. 89. The commission report is *The Russell Report*.
4. F. Ayer, evidence to the Russell Commission, p. 201.
5. LMS Box 29, Central Africa, R. J. B. Moore to T. Cocker Brown, 22 August 1935; Poland Muyumbana (clerk, Nkana), evidence to the Russell Commission, p. 487; J. S. Moffat, evidence, p. 282.
6. The Mbeni dance society was established in the late 1920s on the Copperbelt. At Mufulira, "Mbeni drums were used during the strike to call people together." Mateyo Musiska, evidence to the Russell Commission, p. 252; Amos Mpundu, evidence, p. 341.
7. *The Russell Report*, p. 15; Moffat, evidence to the Russell Commission, pp. 48, 61; Edward S. Fold, evidence, p. 666.
8. W. Scrivener, evidence to the Russell Commission, pp. 454–57; A. T. Williams, evidence, pp. 436–37, 441, 449.
9. Alimoni Juli (Nkana), evidence to the Russell Commission, p. 531; Scrivener, evidence, p. 470. Capitaō were black supervisors.
10. Scrivener, evidence to the Russell Commission, pp. 458, 468; Muyemba Smoke (Nkana), evidence, p. 485.
11. E. Muwamba, evidence to the Russell Commission, p. 872.
12. *The Russell Report*, p. 20.
13. Two different workers tried to start a strike, but were arrested. SEC/LAB/ 67 vol. 1, F. Ayer to C. Dundas, 27 May 1935.
14. RCM/CSD/WHB9, F. Ayer to RACM, London, 30–31 May 1935; Sam Mwase, evidence to the Russell Commission, pp. 753–54; Muwamba, evidence, p. 879; A. B. Knox Kaniki, interview in Kitwe by Ian Henderson, 19 August 1970.
15. *The Russell Report*, Appendix.
16. RCM/CSD/WHB9, F. Ayer to RACM, London, 30–31 May 1935; *The Russell Report*, p. 21.
17. Muwamba, evidence to the Russell Commission, p. 874; J. L. Keith, evidence, pp. 144–46.
18. ZP/10/3/1, J. L. Keith (D.C., Luanshya), "Report on the Strike on the Mines," 31 May 1935, pp. 197–98; Joseph Kazembe (clerk, Roan), evidence to the Russell Commission, p. 811.
19. RCM/CSD/WHB 9, H. H. Field, "Diary of Events from 27 May 1935 to 31 May 1935."

20. Berger, *Labour*; Henderson, "African Leadership"; Perrings, *Black Mineworkers*.

21. Spearpoint claimed that a mass meeting in the dark was led by Bemba, although he wasn't there himself. C. Spearpoint, evidence to the Russell Commission, p. 597; Spearpoint was probably misled by the use of Bemba at large public meetings. At one meeting, for example, a Rozi man spoke in Bemba to the crowd; Muwamba, evidence, p. 875. A compound policeman told Ayer that the meeting on the football field was "a meeting of Bemba mineworkers"; RCM/CSD/WHB 9, F. Ayer to RACM, London, 30 May 1935.

22. Gabriel Musumbulwa, interview in Luanshya, 30 August 1976. Muwamba admitted that people at a big Nkana meeting "were talking in ChiWemba, but I cannot say that they were of the Wemba"; Muwamba, evidence, p. 879.

23. *The Russell Report*, p. 14; Alfred Mwalwanda, interview in Luanshya, 13 September 1976.

24. Moffat, evidence to the Russell Commission, pp. 80–81.

25. *The Russell Report*, p. 20; E. Glyn-Jones (District Officer, Luanshya), evidence to the Russell Commission, p. 34; Keith, evidence, p. 197; Kazembe, evidence, pp. 780–81.

26. CBM Box 1211, R. J. B. Moore to T. Cocker Brown, 12 August 1935.

27. S. Kayela, evidence to the Russell Commission, p. 415.

28. Shiengi Mwepa (miner, Roan), evidence to the Russell Commission, p. 342; Suponi Kombe (Compound Policeman, Mufulira), evidence, p. 150; Albert Musakanya, interview in Kitwe, 22 September 1976.

29. Sylvester Nkoma, interview in Luanshya, 3 September 1976.

30. Knox Kaniki interview (*see* note 14).

31. Dr. A. Charles Fisher, evidence to the Russell Commission, p. 168; Nkoma interview (*see* note 29).

32. Eliti Tuli Phili (Nyasa clerk, Roan), evidence to the Russell Commission, p. 758; Isaac Munkhata (capitaō, Luanshya compound), evidence, p. 324. During the Depression, starting wages fell from 17s6d to 12s6d for surface work, and from 30s to 20–22s6d for underground work; Scrivener, evidence, p. 559.

33. Kazembe, evidence to the Russell Commission, pp. 318–19; Mufulira mineworkers, evidence, p. 239.

34. Lubita Mukubesa (Health Dept., Nkana), evidence to the Russell Commission, p. 482–83; Mufulira mineworkers, evidence, p. 238; Kabuyu (miner, Roan), evidence, p. 340.

35. Muyumbana, evidence to the Russell Commission, p. 102; Samson Chilzia (boss boy underground, Roan), evidence, p. 801; Julius Chattah (Nyasa clerk, Roan), evidence, p. 355.

36. Mukubesa, evidence to the Russell Commission, p. 98; Patson Kambafwile, interview at Mufulira, 9 September 1976.

37. Chola Linyama, former scraper driver, interview by Perrings at NCCM, Chingola, 18 April 1975. Charles Perrings, "Black Labour in the Coppermines of Northern Rhodesia 1911–1941" (Ph.D. diss., University of London, 1976), p. 409; Babu Time (Nkana), evidence to the Russell Commission, p. 115; Dr. A. Charles Fisher, interview at Kitwe, 21 August 1976.

38. Mufulira mineworkers, evidence to the Russell Commission, pp. 238–39; Ngostino Mwambwa (miner, Mufulira), evidence, p. 229; Sergeant Major Kafwilo (Mine Policeman, Nkana), evidence, p. 137.
39. If anything, witnesses underplayed grievances for fear of dismissal. CBM Box 1211, R. J. B. Moore to T. Cocker Brown, 22 August 1935. Moore lived near Mindolo Compound (Nkana), spoke Bemba, and circulated through the mines daily during and after the strike.
40. RCM/CSD/HHB41, Secretary, MCM to RST, 4 April 1930; Kambafwile interview (*see* note 36).
41. C. F. Spearpoint, "The African Native and the Rhodesian Copper Mines," supplement to the *Journal of the Royal African Society* 36, no. 144 (July 1937): 10–16; G. Musumbulwa interview (*see* note 22) and Musakanya interview (*see* note 28).
42. Mwalwanda interview (*see* note 23). Many white underground miners relied heavily on the African supervisors working with them. Brian Goodwin, interview at Lusaka, 26 June 1976.
43. Kambafwile interview (*see* note 36).
44. Fanny Musumbulwa, interview in Luanshya, 1 September 1976; Pascale Sokota, interview in Kitwe, 28 August 1976.
45. Musakanya interview (*see* note 28); A. L. Epstein, "Linguistic Innovation and Culture on the Copperbelt, Northern Rhodesia," *Southwestern Journal of Anthropology* 15 (1959): 235; M. E. Kashoki, "Town Bemba: A Sketch of its Main Characteristics," *African Social Research* 13 (June 1972).
46. Musakanya interview (*see* note 28).
47. Kambafwile interview (*see* note 36).
48. Musakanya interview (*see* note 28).
49. Spearpoint, "African Native," p. 34; Mwalwanda interview (*see* note 23).
50. John Dalton, interview at Lusaka, 4 August 1975; Cook interview (*see* note 3).
51. Mwalwanda interview (*see* note 23); John Chisata, interview at Mufulira, 14 September 1976.
52. R. J. B. Moore, "Native Wages and Standard of Living in Northern Rhodesia," *African Studies* (1942), p. 145. In 1935, African underground workers at Roan received 52s6d per month maximum; Spearpoint, evidence to the Russell Commission, p. 90. In 1929, a European underground timberman made £31.10s per month maximum; F. L. Coleman, *The Northern Rhodesian Copperbelt, 1899–1962: Technological Development up to the End of the Central African Federation*, p. 179.
53. Phili, evidence to the Russell Commission, p. 757.
54. Charles Coulter, "The Sociological Problem," in J. Merle Davis, ed., *Modern Industry and the African* (London, 1933), p. 89.
55. Spearpoint, "African Native," p. 10; Kambafwile interview (*see* note 36). Three men who ran away from the mines claimed they had been beaten at the mine and "that the work was too hard"; they preferred jail to mine work; ZA/Acc.72/3, vol. 1, District Commissioner, Chinsali to District Officer, Nkana, 18 November 1931.
56. The Roan desertion rate was 638.2 per 1,000 in 1929, 377.4 in 1931, and 37.2 in 1935. RCM/CSD/210.65; RACM, Monthly Labor Returns, 1929–41. Nkana had high desertion rates; Dalton interview (*see* note 50).

57. Northern Rhodesia, *Annual Report upon Native Affairs*, 1930.
58. Musakanya interview (*see* note 28).
59. G. Musumbulwa interview (*see* note 22) and Nkoma interview (*see* note 29); Private papers, J. Clyde Mitchell, from his 1952–53 Copperbelt survey.
60. ZA1/9/18/43/1, J. Moffat Thomson, Secretary for Native Affairs to the Chief Secretary, 23 September 1929; Spearpoint, "African Native," p. 22.
61. Spearpoint, "African Native," pp. 23, 34; Coulter, "Sociological Problem," p. 73.
62. Chembe H. Phiri, interview in Luanshya, 3 September 1976.
63. T. O. Ranger, *Dance and Society in Eastern Africa* (Los Angeles, 1975), pp. 71–76, 133; J. Clyde Mitchell, *The Kalela Dance: Aspects of Social Relationships among Urban Africans in Northern Rhodesia*, Rhodes-Livingstone Paper No. 27 (Manchester, 1956).
64. Sholto Cross, "The Watch Tower Movement in South Central Africa 1908–1945" (Ph.D. diss., Oxford 1973), pp. 360–61.
65. *Legislative Council Debates*, 11 May 1936; C.O. 795/77/45103, Despatch from the Governor of Northern Rhodesia to S/S for the Colonies, P. Cunliffe-Lister, 1935.
66. LMS, Box 26, Central Africa, A. J. Cross to A. M. Chirgwin, 31 January 1932.
67. Cross, "Watch Tower," p. 388.
68. Keith, evidence to the Russell Commission, p. 199; Munkonge, evidence, p. 125.
69. CBM Box 1213, Talk by Audrey Richards, Africa Circle, London, November 1934; George Chauncy, Jr., "The Locus of Reproduction: Women's Labour in the Zambian Copperbelt, 1927–1953," *JSAS* 7, no. 2 (April 1981).
70. (R)-A. 11, African Personnel Managers' Annual Report, 1935. Miners spent £764 in 1933, £474 in 1934, and £400 in 1935 for imported clothes; Spearpoint, "African Native," pp. 34–35, 54.
71. Gladys Eastland (welfare worker, Luanshya), evidence to the Russell Commission, p. 503.
72. The Police Inspector, Ndola, evidence, p. 697.
73. Perrings, "Black Labour," 418–19; (R)-A. 11, African Personnel Managers' Monthly Compound Reports, January 1935.
74. Perrings, *Black Mineworkers*, pp. 207–13.
75. Kambafwile interview (*see* note 36) and Mwalwanda interview (*see* note 23).
76. Kambafwile interview (*see* note 36) and Nkoma interview (*see* note 29); Mwase, evidence to the Russell Commission, pp. 753–54.
77. Schaefer claimed that "it is very easy to get labor. At times we find it necessary to discharge many boys"; Ben Schaefer, evidence to the Russell Commission, pp. 29, 112. Scrivener, evidence, pp. 465, 469.
78. Kambafwile interview (*see* note 36). "There is much communication between the natives of Nkana and Luanshya . . ."; Moffat, evidence to the Russell Commission, p. 284.
79. Ian Henderson, "Labour and Politics in Northern Rhodesia 1900–1953" (Ph.D. diss., University of Edinburgh, 1972), p. 153.
80. Williams, evidence to the Russell Commission, pp. 436–37; Scrivener,

evidence, pp. 441, 449, 457; CBM Box 1211, R. J. B. Moore to T. Cocker Brown, 22 August 1935.

81. Mwalwanda interview (*see* note 23); A. H. Goslett (Mufulira police officer, European), evidence to the Russell Commission, p. 348.
82. Musakanya interview (*see* note 28).
83. Chisata interview (*see* note 51); Scrivener, evidence to the Russell Commission, p. 457; Moffat, evidence, p. 82.
84. Silas Mubanga (underground miner, Mufulira) evidence to the Russell Commission, p. 328; Scrivener, evidence, p. 461; Spearpoint, "African Native," p. 34.
85. Knox Kaniki interview (*see* note 14).
86. SEC/NAT/66G, *Annual Report upon Native Affairs*, 1935. Roan had the longest average length of employment and the lowest labor turnover on the Copperbelt; *The Russell Report*, p. 35.
87. *The Russell Report*, p. 29.

CHAPTER 4

1. Elena Berger, *Labour, Race, and Colonial Rule: The Copperbelt from 1924 to Independence* (Oxford, 1974), p. 57; Ian Henderson, "Early African Leadership: The Copperbelt Disturbances of 1935 and 1940," *Journal of South African Studies* (*JSAS*) 2, no. 1 (October 1975); Charles Perrings, *Black Mineworkers in Central Africa* (New York, 1979), pp. 217–24.
2. RCM/CSD 201.33, RACM, Monthly labor returns, 1941.
3. A. Pim and S. Milligan, *Report of the Commission Appointed to Enquire into the Financial and Economic Position of Northern Rhodesia* (Colonial No. 145 of 1938), pp. 36, 52 (*The Pim Report*); H. Heisler, "Target Proletarians," *Journal of Asian and African Studies* 5 (1970): 167–68.
4. W. Stubbs, interview in Oxford, England, 25 October 1976.
5. Honorable W. M. Logan, "Address to Broken Hill Political Association," *Race Relations* 6, no. 2 (1939): 58; E. B. H. Goodall (Provincial Commissioner, Central Province), evidence to the Commission Appointed to Inquire into the Disturbances in the Copperbelt of Northern Rhodesia (Lusaka, 1941), p. 85 (The Forster Commission); the commission report is *The Forster Report*.
6. P. J. Law, interview in Oxford, England, 26 October 1976.
7. SEC/LAB/3, Acting Provincial Commissioner, Ndola (Wickins) to Acting Chief Secretary (Bradley), 23 September 1937; Law interview (*see* note 6).
8. Chairman's Report of Meetings of the Native Industrial Labour Advisory Board, 7–8 November and 16–17 December 1935; SEC/LAB/34, T. F. Sandford to NRCM, 31 March 1941; *The Pim Report*, pp. 48, 205.
9. Chris Cook, interview in East London, South Africa, 10 October 1976.
10. RCM/CSD/202.7 (1 and 2), Acting Compound Manager to Business Manager, RACM, 23 September 1938. The 1940 proportion of married workers in the work force: Nkana—40%, Roan—58%, Nchanga—44.5%, and Mufulira—55%; ZA/Acc.52/3, Recommendations of the Forster Commission.
11. *The Pim Report*, pp. 42, 45. Out of 3,969 workers at Roan, 1,053 had worked

over three years; RCM/CSD/202.7 (1 and 2), Spearpoint to Business Manager, RACM, 23 September 1938.

12. RCM/CSD/KHB41, General Manager, RACM to Secretary, MCM, 8 December 1937; N. R. K. Davis, interview in Kitwe, 15 September 1976.

13. RCM/CSD/WMA 65, C. Spearpoint to Géneral Manager, RACM, 16 November 1938.

14. (R)-A.11, Monthly Compound Reports, June–August 1935.

15. SEC/NAT/66G, Luanshya District, *Annual Report*, 1939; G. Howe (Labour Commissioner), evidence to the Forster Commission, p. 96.

16. ZA/Acc. 72/1/3, District Commissioner, Nkana to Provincial Commissioner, Ndola, 24 November 1937.

17. W. Scrivener, evidence to the Forster Commission, p. 573; SEC/NAT/66G, Chingola Station, *Annual Report*, 1939; RCM/WMA 65 (205.5), General Manager, RACM to District Commissioner, Luanshya, October 1938.

18. Scrivener, evidence to the Forster Commission.

19. LMS Box 32B, Central Africa, B. D. Gibson to J. Soulsby, 3 August 1938; CBM Box 1213, A. Cross to B. D. Gibson, 10 September 1938.

20. MMS/MII.1, Agnes Fraser to B. D. Gibson, 12 May 1938; Monty Graham-Harrison, interview in London, 27 October 1976.

21. The mines even petitioned the government to create schools with high fees for the children of "superior Native employees and semi-permanent employees." CBM Box 1213, A. Cross to B. D. Gibson, 9 February 1937.

22. UMCB, *Annual Report*, 1936–37. Mufulira in 1939 had a self-supporting night school with attendance of 125; LMS Box 32B, Central Africa, Extracts from Minutes of the Team, 20 November 1939. Fifty men signed up at Mufulira in 1938 for the African Lecture and Debating Society; MMS BI.1, W. H. Harrison to G. Ayre, MMS, London, 19 May 1938.

23. UMCB, *Annual Report*, 1938–39, p. 7; David Greig, evidence to the Forster Commission, p. 328.

24. LMS Box 30, Central Africa, R. J. B. Moore to LMS, London, 7 June 1937; LMS Box 32B, Central Africa, Moore to LMS, London, 22 November 1938.

25. CBM Box 1213, Pamphlet prepared for the Anti-Slavery and Aborigines Protection Society, Africa Conference, "The Industrialization of the African," November 1937; SEC/LAB/1, Parliamentary Debates, Extract from the Official Report of 8 July 1937.

26. G. St. J. Orde Browne, *Labour Conditions in Northern Rhodesia* (Colonial No. 150 of 1938), pp. 3–4, 23–24, 28, 33, 72 (*The Orde Brown Report*); *The Pim Report*, pp. 333–39.

27. SEC/LAB/92, Governor John Maybin to Chief Secretary, 4 March 1940; Ian Henderson, "Workers and the State in Colonial Zambia," in *The Evolving Structure of Zambian Society*, Proceedings of a Seminar held in the Centre of African Studies, University of Edinburgh, 30–31 May 1980 (Edinburgh, 1980).

28. CBM Box 1213, A. Cross to B. D. Gibson, 10 September 1938; Joseph Pierce, interview in Luanshya, 2 September 1976.

29. ZA/Acc. 52/6, G. Howe, Labor Commissioner, views on *The Forster Report*, 9 March 1940.

30. RCM/CSD/WMA 65 (205.5), C. Spearpoint to General Manager, RACM, 16 November 1938.

31. Scrivener, evidence to the Forster Commission, pp. 560, 562; (R)-A.11 Compound Monthly Report, January 1936.

32. Arthur J. Cross, evidence to the Forster Commission, p. 286.

33. Scrivener, evidence to the Forster Commission, p. 609.

34. Ibid., p. 609; C. F. Spearpoint, "The African Native and the Rhodesia Copper Mines," supplement to the *Journal of the Royal African Society* 36, no. 144 (July 1937): 22.

35. Scrivener, evidence to the Forster Commission, pp. 560, 562.

36. Cross, evidence to the Forster Commission, p. 286.

37. Scrivener, evidence to the Forster Commission, p. 609.

38. Ashton Kabalika, interview in Kitwe, 29 August 1976.

39. *The Forster Report*, pp. 47–52, Appendix IV; RCM/CSD/KMA 94, A. R. Harrison, Rhokana to Chief Secretary, 27 March 1940.

40. Henderson, "African Leadership," pp. 90–91; RCM/CSD/KMA 94, H. H. Field to R. M. Peterson, 17 April 1940, diary of events between 17 March and 8 April 1940.

41. Perrings, *Black Mineworkers*, p. 221; Albert G. Musakanya, interview in Nkana, 22 September 1976.

42. Thomas Muhongo, evidence to the Forster Commission, p. 375; Edward Sampa, evidence, p. 343.

43. T. F. Sandford, evidence to the Forster Commission, p. 367.

44. *The Forster Report*, Appendix.

45. Morton Mwinifumba, evidence to the Forster Commission, p. 367; Musa-kanya interview (*see* note 41).

46. Julius N. Chattah (clerk, Mufulira), evidence to the Forster Commission, p. 439; Howe, evidence, p. 108; A. T. Williams, evidence, p. 180.

47. R. J. B. Moore, "Native Wages and Standard of Living in Northern Rhodesia," *African Studies* 1, no. 2 (June 1942); Frank Bedford, evidence to the Forster Commission, pp. 499–500.

48. Williams, evidence to the Forster Commission, p. 191; Mufulira Committee of Seventeen, evidence, p. 518; Kabalika interview (*see* note 38).

49. NCCM/CSD/KMA 94, R. M. Peterson, Memorandum on the Strike, 27 April 1940; *The Forster Report*, pp. 16, 18–20.

50. Chattah, evidence to the Forster Commission, p. 436.

51. William Stubbs, evidence to the Forster Commission, p. 399.

52. Yaphat Gerusi (Ngoni miner, Mufulira), evidence to the Forster Commission, p. 445; Stubbs, evidence, p. 394.

53. Mufulira Committee of Seventeen, evidence to the Forster Commission, p. 509.

54. Greig, evidence to the Forster Commission, pp. 321–22.

55. Lama Kabuka (worked nine years on mine, tribal elder), evidence to the Forster Commission, p. 362; Henry Mulenga, evidence, pp. 333–34.

56. Stubbs, evidence to the Forster Commission, pp. 402, 404, 406–07; Josiah Imbowa, evidence, p. 338; Williams, evidence, p. 197; Sampa, evidence, p. 346.

57. Stubbs, evidence to the Forster Commission, p. 422.

58. Sandford, evidence to the Forster Commission, pp. 26, 42.

59. Sampa, evidence to the Forster Commission, p. 345.

60. LMS Box 32B, Central Africa, Julius Lewin, Report on a Visit to the Copperbelt, May 1940.
61. Sandford, evidence to the Forster Commission, p. 11.
62. Stubbs, evidence to the Forster Commission, pp. 420–21; Sandford, evidence, p. 31.
63. Howe, evidence to the Forster Commission, p. 82; Sandford, evidence, p. 17; Robert I. Rotberg, *Black Heart: Gore-Browne and the Politics of Multiracial Zambia* (Berkeley, 1977), p. 219.
64. Howe, evidence to the Forster Commission, p. 79. Gore-Browne walked around Nkana after the shooting with the permission of some strike leaders; Rotberg, *Black Heart*, pp. 221–22.
65. LMS Box 32B, Central Africa, Julius Lewin, "Report," May 1940.
66. LMS Box 32B, Central Africa, Lewin, "Report," May 1940; Williams, evidence to the Forster Commission, p. 227; Bedford, evidence, p. 501.
67. *The Pim Report*, p. 47.
68. MMS/MII.1, Agnes Fraser to B. D. Gibson, 5 December 1938.
69. LMS Box 32B, Central Africa, A. Cross to Cullen Young, 4 August 1939.
70. R. J. B. Moore and J. R. Shaw, "Marriage and Temporary Unions," and Monty Graham-Harrison, "Women and Girls' Work in the Urban Areas," *Proceedings of the General Missionary Conference of Northern Rhodesia, 1939*. The ratio of men to women at Chingola mine was 2:1; SEC/NAT/66G, Chingola Station, *Annual Report*, 1939.
71. Malcolm Watson, "A Conquest of Disease: Hygiene in Northern Rhodesia," in Malcolm Watson, ed., *African Highway: The Battle for Health in Central Africa* (London, 1953), p. 70; MMS/MII.1, Agnes Fraser to B. D. Gibson, 5 December 1938.
72. (R)-A.11, Compound Report, January 1939.
73. CBM Box 1213, LMS, London to Agnes Fraser, 15 March 1935.
74. Ernest Muwamba, evidence to the Forster Commission, pp. 531–32.
75. Julius Lewin, evidence to the Forster Commission, p. 170. In Copperbelt schools, one out of ten children aged twelve to seventeen years had never been to their parents' home village. Half of them had been brought up in the urban areas. For children under ten years, the proportion was about three-quarters. R. J. B. Moore, *These African Copper Miners* (London, 1948), p. 60.
76. Herkos Sikwanda (miner of three years, Nkana), evidence to the Forster Commission, p. 524.
77. Muwamba, evidence to the Forster Commission, p. 530.
78. H. H. Field, evidence to the Forster Commission, p. 624. In 1942, Saffery concluded that "Africans working on the mines are becoming increasingly conscious of the great gap between the wages paid to Europeans and those which they themselves receive. I have been impressed by the bitterness with which Africans speak of their wages. They declare openly that although it is they who do the work, it is the Europeans who get the money." A. Lynn Saffery, "A Report on Some Aspects of African Living Conditions on the Copper Belt of Northern Rhodesia," mimeograph (Lusaka, 1943), p. 20.
79. Chattah, evidence to the Forster Commission, p. 441.
80. In 1941, wage increases established grade C (unskilled labor) at a wage

from 25s to 50s per ticket, grade B (semi-skilled) from 40s to 70s per ticket, and grade A (skilled) from 50s to 100s per ticket. Surface labor could make a maximum of 30s per ticket for grade C, 50s for grade B, and 80s for grade C. Special Grade workers, like clerks, could make £2.10s per month. Saffery, "Report," p. 11.

81. Cook interview (*see* note 9).
82. Matthew Mwendapole, interview in Ndola, 3 August 1976.
83. Perrings, *Black Mineworkers*, pp. 220–22. Perrings emphasizes ethnicity in the clash between strike leaders and clerks. Many clerks were Nyasa. While ethnicity may have enhanced this antagonism, the strike leaders clearly understood that the issue was collaboration with management, *not* ethnicity. Accusations were leveled against *any* black workers who allied themselves with management, not one particular ethnic group.
84. Spearpoint, "African Native," p. 34.
85. R. J. B. Moore, *Man's Act and God's in Africa* (London, 1940), p. 65.
86. Moore believed "the Bantu wants . . . to be treated as people, not only by the few who know them, but by the man in the street." Moore, *Copper Miners*, p. 60.
87. Cross, evidence to the Forster Commission, p. 286. Bedford was accused of wanting to fashion clever Africans; MMS, BI.1, Arthur Slater to W. J. Noble, 27 February 1935; Bedford, evidence, p. 496.
88. LMS, Box 30, Central Africa, Memo regarding the work of the Literature Superintendent with the Inter-Mission Team in Northern Rhodesia, 24 June 1937; J. V. Taylor and D. Lehmann, *Christians of the Copperbelt* (London, 1961), p. 44.
89. UMCB, *Annual Reports*, 1937–40; LMS Box 5, Africa Reports, David Greig, "On the Copperbelt 1936–1937."
90. Musakanya interview (*see* note 41). Musakanya was sports organizer for the Kitwe Management Board.
91. Alfred Mwalwanda, interview in Luanshya, 13 September 1976.
92. Chembe Phiri, interview in Luanshya, 3 September 1976; Patson Kambafwile, interview at Mufulira, 9 September 1976.
93. Godwin Lewanika: worked in the compound office at Nkana; active in early African associations; President of the Kitwe African Society in the 1940s, the Federation of African Societies of Northern Rhodesia 1946–48, the African National Congress 1948–51, and the Mines African Salaried Staff Association 1953–64; Litunga of Barotseland 1968.
94. David Greig recruited Europeans to coach and referee, UMCB, *Annual Reports*, 1936–37, 1937–38.
95. Kabalika interview (*see* note 38); Sylvester Nkoma, interview in Luanshya, 3 September 1976.
96. Stubbs, evidence to the Forster Commission, p. 389; Howe, evidence, p. 67.
97. European Mineworkers, evidence to the Forster Commission, pp. 751–52. Goodwin was a miner at Nkana. He was president of the European Mineworkers' Union in the 1940s; member of the Legislative Council 1944–48. He left the Copperbelt to begin farming near Lusaka.
98. European Mineworkers, evidence to the Forster Commission, p. 719.
99. SEC/LAB/3, Provincial Commissioner, Ndola to Chief Secretary, 2 November 1938; Hodgson, evidence to the Forster Commission, p. 761.
100. *The Forster Commission Report.*

101. NCCM/CSD/Native Strike, 1940, N. J. Nairn to Anglo-American Corporation, Johannesburg, 16 April 1940.

CHAPTER 5

1. Northern Rhodesia, Department of Labor, *Annual Report*, 1944; SEC/LAB/45; Department of Labor, Nchanga and Nkana Reports, March 1944.
2. Scrivener believed "the married employee is undoubtedly more contented than the single, he is better fed, looked after and clothed and has the rudiments of a sense of responsibility which tends to make him a more stable and efficient worker." Married labor was also "an insurance against a labor shortage." RCM/CSD/202.7 (1 and 2), W. Scrivener to general manager, Rhokana, 20 March 1943.
3. Mr. Stratford (Counsel for the mining companies), evidence to the Commission Appointed to Inquire into the Disturbances in the Copperbelt of Northern Rhodesia (Lusaka, 1941), pp. 568, 638 (The Forster Commission).
4. RCM/CSD/202.7 (1 and 2), W. Scrivener to General Manager, Rhokana, 20 March 1943; RCM/CSD/KMA 17, NRCM, memo on Native Labor Policy, September 1944.
5. A. Lynn Saffery, "A Report on Some Aspects of African Living Conditions on the Copper Belt of Northern Rhodesia," mimeograph (Lusaka, 1943), pp. 49–50. Saffery was a special labor officer brought in to investigate conditions in the urban areas.
6. SEC/LAB/45, Labor Department, Mufulira Report, April 1945.
7. RCM/CSD 202.7 (2A), C. F. Spearpoint, Memo on Native Labor Policy, 25 August 1942, and H. H. Field, Memo on Native Labor Policy, 1 September 1942; P. J. Law, interview in Oxford, England, 26 October 1976.
8. Spearpoint and Field, Memos on Native Labor Policy; Law interview (*see* note 7).
9. ZA/Acc.52/6, General Manager, RACM to Chief Secretary, Lusaka, 4 January 1941; Stratford, evidence to the Forster Commission, pp. 542–43.
10. RCM/CSD/KHB 14, Johannesburg Conference, 1946.
11. T. F. Sandford, evidence to the Forster Commission, p. 619; Scrivener, evidence, p. 611.
12. ZA/Acc. 52/17; Labor Commissioner to Chief Secretary, 9 October 1942.
13. Absenteeism fell by 50% after the Emergency Powers were amended to include Africans. SEC/LAB/45, Labor Officer, Report on RACM, 7–10 July 1942.
14. *Mutende*, 30 July 1943 and 26 August 1943.
15. RCM/CSD/KMA 23, General Manager, RACM to Secretary, RACM, London, 2 September 1940.
16. N. R. K. Davis, interview in Kitwe, 15 September 1976.
17. Sandford, evidence to the Forster Commission, p. 10; William Stubbs, interview in Oxford, England, 25 October 1979.
18. CISB, 100:20:7A, W. A. Pope, General Manager, Nchanga to Secretary, NRCM, 25 July 1941.
19. ZA/Acc.52/17, Stubbs to Labor Commissioner, 24 November 1943.

20. Stubbs interview (*see* note 17).
21. In 1941, W. Stubbs was labor officer at Kitwe, and P. J. Law was stationed at Mufulira. ZA/Acc.52/17, Meetings between the Department of Labor and NRCM, 28–29 September 1942.
22. Creech Jones Papers: ACJ/22/3/1, Harold Macmillan to Arthur Creech Jones, 6 May 1942.
23. CISB 100:60:1, Estimates on Social Welfare Expenses submitted at the 5th Executive Committee Meeting, NRCM, 1945.
24. RCM/CSD/202.7 (1 and 2), Scrivener to General Manager, Rhokana, 31 January 1944. NRCM Memo on African Labor Policy, 29 June 1945. McPherson, a UMCB missionary, found the welfare facilities at Mufulira "in a state of decay" in 1946; Fergus McPherson, interview in Lusaka, 26 September 1975.
25. RCM/CSD/202.7 (2A), C. Spearpoint, Memo on Native Labor Policy, 25 August 1942; R. J. B. Moore, evidence to the Forster Commission, p. 72; Francis J. Bedford, evidence, p. 495.
26. CBM Box 1213, Memo from NRCM, 17 June 1943.
27. LMS Box 32B, Central Africa, R. J. B. Moore to T. Cocker Brown, 20 December 1940; Hugh Theobald, *Moore of the Copperbelt: The Man and the Work* (London, 1946).
28. CBM Box 1213, A. Cross to B. D. Gibson, 3 February 1941.
29. RCM/CSD/202.7 (no. 1), C. Spearpoint, Notes on Saffery's Report, 14 July 1943. Field wrote "between the pages of this Report—Part I—there are some very impressive and true photographs, and much has been put into print which I feel is to be true. . . . Part I is of far-reaching importance, and will live to be quoted in the event of industrial trouble"; RCM/CSD/KMA 20, H. Field to General Manager, MCM, 29 June 1943; SEC/LAB/71, Comments on the Saffery Report, NRCM, October 1943.
30. SEC/LAB/71, R. Hudson, "Comments on the Memorandum of the NRCM on the Saffery Report," 25 October 1943; Acting Chief Secretary to South African Institute of Race Relations, 12 September 1946.
31. CISB, 100:60:1, A. H. Elwell, "Memorandum on the Development of African Social Welfare Services in the Urban Areas of the Copperbelt of Northern Rhodesia," 1945.
32. SEC/NAT/311, Gore-Browne, Notes, 24 September 1946; CISB, 100:60:1, Native Affairs Advisory Committee meeting, 19 February 1946.
33. A. Mwalwanda and G. Musumbulwa, interviews in Luanshya, 13 September and 22 September 1976, respectively.
34. "One result of the proposed cut has been a great increase in the efficiency of the labor both European and African, complaints, assaults, and absentees have shown a marked decrease in the last three weeks. This has also happened at Mufulira"; SEC/LAB/45, Department of Labor, Nchanga Report, February 1944. At Nkana, the labor officer reported that "all employees with unsatisfactory records are being dismissed"; SEC/LAB/45, Labor Officer, report on Nkana, 29 February 1944.
35. SEC/LAB/45, Labor Officer, Report on Visits to Roan, 7–10 July 1942 and 29–31 December 1941; RCM/CSD/KMA 5, Tribal Representative Meeting, MCM, 3 May 1943, 21 April 1942, and 4 December 1944.
36. RCM/CSD/KMA 5, Tribal Representative Meeting, MCM, 2 October 1944, and 5 March 1945.

37. Law interview (*see* note 7).

38. RCM/CSD/KHB 41, Meeting between the Labor Department and the African Wages Sub-Committee of NRCM, 28–29 September 1942.

39. ZA/Acc. 52/17, Labor Commissioner to Secretary, NRCM, 9 September 1943; ZA/Acc. 7, W. Stubbs to NRCM, 5 August 1942.

40. Stubbs interview (*see* note 17) Law interview (*see* note 7).

41. ZA/Acc. 52/17, NRCM Memo on the establishment of Boss Boy Associations, 29 September 1942; ZA/Acc. 52/17, Chief Secretary to Labor Commissioner, 29 October 1942.

42. ZA/Acc. 52/17, Meeting of the Sub-Committee of Labor Officers and Compound Managers, Kitwe, 22 December 1943. Labor Commissioner to Stubbs, 2 December 1943.

43. ZA/Acc. 52/17, Labor Officer, Nkana to Labor Commissioner, 28 October 1943. Labor Commissioner to Stubbs, 2 December 1943.

44. Elena Berger, *Labour, Race, and Colonial Rule: The Copperbelt from 1924 to Independence* (Oxford, 1974), p. 87; Epstein, *Politics*, pp. 89–90; Ian Henderson, "Wage-Earners and Political Protest in Colonial Africa: The Case of the Copperbelt," *African Affairs* 72, no. 288 (July 1973): 294–95.

45. ZA/Acc. 52/17, Boss Boys' Committee, MCM, 10 June 1943 and 12 March 1945.

46. Robert I. Rotberg, *The Rise of Nationalism in Central Africa: The Making of Malawi and Zambia, 1873–1964* (Cambridge, Massachusetts, 1965), pp. 200–07; Epstein, *Politics*, pp. 67–68.

47. F. M. N. Heath, "The Growth of African Council on the Copperbelt of Northern Rhodesia," *The Journal of African Administration*, 5, no. 3 (1953): 2. Gore-Browne went to welfare society meetings of 1,000 at Mufulira, 720 at Luanshya, and a large crowd in Kitwe; SEC/LAB/311, Gore-Browne, "Notes on Copperbelt Meetings with Africans," 1946.

48. Unskilled workers still protested conditions by absenteeism, especially at Roan, "mainly attributable to expansion resulting in some labor shortage and to Natives being put to strenuous work before being hardened." Department of Labor, *Annual Report*, 1941. One night-gang took turns being absent because the work was too hard to do fourteen days straight and the pay was not good enough; SEC/LAB/45, Labor Officer, Report on Roan, 3–6 December 1940.

49. Mwalwanda interview (*see* note 33).

50. ZA/Acc. 52/7, Law to Labor Officer, Ndola, 3 August 1942; Stubbs, "Report on Meetings with Nkana and Mindolo Boss Boys," 21 October 1942; SEC/LAB/45, Department of Labor, Monthly Report, Mufulira, October 1942.

51. SEC/LAB/45, Department of Labor, Mufulira, May 1943; RCM/CSD/KMA 5, Boss Boys' Committee, MCM, 12 March 1945 and 2 November 1942.

52. ZA/Acc. 52/7, Law to Labor Officer, Ndola, 3 August 1942; RCM/CSD/ KMA 5, Boss Boys' Committee, MCM, 18 June 1945.

53. Law interview (*see* note 7).

54. RCM/CSD/KMA 5, Boss Boys' Committee, MCM, 18 June 1945; ZA/Acc. 72/1/6, Labor Department, Report on Nkana and Mindolo, 23 and 30 October and 3–5 November 1942.

55. RCM/CSD/KMA 202.2, Compound Managers' Committee, NRCM, 26 September 1944.

56. SEC/LAB/45, Labor Officer, Report on Roan, July–August 1943; ZA/Acc. 52/17, Stubbs to Labor Commissioner, 6 April 1943.

57. Saffery estimated an urbanized African family of four needed a £6.1s7d per month income. The average African miner made £4.14s.7d per month including benefits. Thus, only married workers in high income brackets could support families. Saffery, "Report," pp. 12–13.

58. *Final Report of the Commission of Enquiry into the Cost of Living* (Lusaka, 1947), p. 41.

59. Law interview (*see* note 7).

60. RCM/CSD/KMA 8, Boss Boys' Committee, RACM, 28 November and 25 July 1946; Saffery, "Report," p. 20.

61. Department of Labor, *Annual Report*, 1944.

62. CISB, 100:23 vol. 1, P. H. Truscott to Mine Managers, 4 October 1946; RCM/CSD/KMA 8, Meeting of the Clerks and Boss Boys' Representatives, RACM, 28 November 1947.

63. RCM/CSD/KMA 18, Boss Boys' Committee, RACM, 28 November 1947.

64. ZA/Acc. 52/17, P. J. Law to Labor Commissioner, 23 May 1945.

65. ZA/Acc. 52/17, NRCM to Labor Commissioner, 25 April 1945. Spearpoint believed "the possibility of serious trouble in this Territory . . . will be lessened just so soon as we have a Native Trade Union." He worried about the possibility of a multi-racial union. RCM/CSD file 202.7(2A), C. Spearpoint, Native Labor Policy, 25 August 1942.

66. Sir Richard Luyt, interview in Cape Town, South Africa, 7 October 1976.

67. Matthew Mwendapole, interview in Ndola, 3 August 1976.

68. *Legislative Council Debates*, 20 December 1945 and 6 April 1946; SEC/LAB/150, D.C., Luanshya to Senior Provincial Commissioner, Ndola, 5 July 1947.

69. Law interview (*see* note 7) and Stubbs interview (*see* note 17).

70. Epstein papers, interview with Chambeshi, 27 December 1953; Report of the Department of Labor, February 1943.

71. SEC/LAB/71, P. C., Western Province to Chief Secretary, 2 February 1944; Law interview (*see* note 7) and Stubbs interview (*see* note 17).

72. Albert Musakanya, interview in Nkana, 22 September 1976.

73. ZA/Acc. 52/17, Department of Labor, Draft: Development of Machinery for African Workers in the Copper Mines, 13 May 1946.

74. Arthur Turner, "The Growth of Railway Unionism in the Rhodesias, 1944–55," in R. Sandbrook and R. Cohen, eds., *The Development of an African Working Class: Studies in Class Formation and Action* (Toronto, 1975).

75. Department of Labor, *Annual Report*, 1946, 1947; Evidence to the Commission of Enquiry into the Cost of Living (Lusaka, 1947), pp. 203, 256, 261.

76. RCM/CSD/KMA 8, Boss Boys' Committee, RACM, 29 May 1947. The government did eventually set up a commission.

77. *Legislative Council Debates*, 20 December 1945.

78. Brian Goodwin, interview in Lusaka, 26 June 1976.

79. *Legislative Council Debates*, 6 May 1946 and 9 March 1948; Berger, *Labour*, p. 100.

80. Goodwin interview (*see* note 78).

81. Berger, *Labour*, pp. 89–96; Epstein, *Politics*, pp. 89–90; Anirudha Gupta, "Trade Unionism and Politics on the Copperbelt," in William Tordoff, ed., *Politics in Zambia* (Manchester, England, 1974).

82. Pascale Sokota, interview at Kitwe, 28 August 1976.
83. Law observed that "in some ways, some of the boss boys were very close to the European contract miners in their own gangs. Some of these European miners took a tremendous interest in their own gang. Often relationships between boss boys and Europeans right over them were very good." Law interview (*see* note 7). Kabalika supported equal pay for equal work; he got the idea from Brian Goodwin, whom he described as "a good person, [he] wanted Africans to get better pay and houses." Ashton Kabalika, interview in Kitwe, 29 August 1976.
84. Stubbs interview (*see* note 17), Kabalika interview (*see* note 83), and Mwendapole interview (*see* note 67).
85. SEC/LAB/125, A. Bevan, Report to the Department of Labor, 13 April 1946; SEC/LAB/125, Labor Commissioner to Secretary of Native Affairs, 25 April 1946.
86. SEC/LAB/125, Labor Commissioner, Hudson, to Chief Secretary, 28 April 1946.
87. *Legislative Council Debates*, 7 May 1946; Berger, *Labour*, pp. 90–91.
88. J. R. Hooker, "The Role of the Labour Department in the Birth of African Trade Unionism in Northern Rhodesia," *International Review of Social History* 10, no. 1 (1965): 17; Stubbs interview (*see* note 17).
89. RCM/CSD/KHB 14, The Johannesburg Conference, December 1946.
90. Berger, *Labour*, p. 93.

CHAPTER 6

1. Elena Berger, *Labour, Race, and Colonial Rule: The Copperbelt from 1924 to Independence* (Oxford, 1974); A. L. Epstein, *Politics in an Urban African Community* (Manchester, England, 1958); S. Zelniker, "Changing Patterns of Trade Unionism: The Zambian Case 1948–64" (Ph.D. diss., UCLA, 1970); Ian Henderson, "Wage-Earners and Political Protest in Colonial Africa: The Case of the Copperbelt," *African Affairs* 72, no. 288 (July 1973).
2. William Stubbs, interview in Oxford, England, 25 October 1976.
3. RCM/CSD/KHB 14, Conference at Johannesburg between AA and RST, 9–14 December 1946.
4. Epstein papers, History of Works Committees, 7 December 1953. In 1948 the works committees held ten meetings at Nchanga, ten at Nkana, and eight at Roan Antelope during a period of eleven months. At Mufulira only three meetings took place.
5. Department of Labor, *Annual Report*, 1947; RCM/CSD/KMA 18, 56th Executive Committee Meeting, NRCM, 19 December 1947.
6. Brian Goodwin, interview in Lusaka, 26 June 1976; SEC/LAB/125, W. Comrie, Monthly Report, December 1947.
7. P. J. Law, interview in Oxford, England, 26 October 1976.
8. SEC/LAB/125, Meeting held at Government House to discuss African policy, Lusaka, 19 February 1947; G. St. J. Orde Browne, *Report on Labor Conditions in East Africa* (London, 1946), p. 193.
9. SEC/LAB/125, Labor Commissioner to NRCM, 21 January 1948.
10. SEC/LAB/126, W. Comrie, Monthly Report, March 1948.
11. Joseph Mubita, interview in Mufulira, 7 September 1976.

12. Epstein papers, interview with L. Katilungu, 6 October 1953.
13. Goodwin interview (*see* note 6).
14. SEC/LAB/125, Meeting at Lusaka, 19 February 1947.
15. Law interview (*see* note 7); SEC/LAB/125, meeting at Lusaka, 19 February 1947.
16. Stubbs interview (*see* note 2); Sir Ronald Prain, interview in Weybridge, England, 1982; Law recalled that "Comrie was regarded with a good deal of suspicion by the Administration"; Law interview (*see* note 7).
17. Law interview (*see* note 7).
18. SEC/LAB/125, Labor Commissioner to W. Comrie, 19 January 1948.
19. Sir Richard Luyt, interview in Cape Town, South Africa, 7 October 1976.
20. Zelniker, "Patterns," pp. 126, 129.
21. John Chisata, interview in Mufulira, 14 September 1976.
22. Gabriel Musumbulwa, interview in Luanshya, 30 August 1976.
23. RCM/CSD/KMA 18, Executive Committee, NRCM, 16 July 1948.
24. Labor and Mines Department, *Annual Reports*, 1950, 1951.
25. In 1951, Mufulira had 8,426 miners of whom 2,321 had worked over four years, and 4,586 over two years. RCM/CSD/202.7, no. 2, African Timekeeper, MCM, to Assistant Mine Secretary, MCM, 30 October 1951.
26. J. Clyde Mitchell, *African Urbanization in Ndola and Luanshya*, Rhodes-Livingstone Communication no. 6 (Manchester, 1954), p. 19.
27. Labor and Mines Department, *Annual Reports*, 1950, 1951; J. Clyde Mitchell, tabulations from the Nchanga Staff Records for 30 April 1951, Table 1. Another table from Mitchell concerning Nchanga workers is the following:

Nchanga Survey

Worker's Status	Length of Employment		Total
	Less Than 1 Year	*Over 1 Year*	
Married	1,080	1,927	3,007
Single	1,790	852	2,642
Total	2,870	2,779	5,649
Worker Group 1 (Unskilled)	2,124	1,177	2,201
Worker Group 2 (Some Skill)	746	1,602	2,348
Total	2,870	2,779	5,649

28. CISB, 100:60:1, J. D. Rheinnalt Jones, "The Welfare of African Workers," 1951; CISB, African Statistics, NRCM, September 1952.
29. Matthew Mwendapole, interview in Ndola, 3 August 1976.
30. SEC/LAB/50, Labor Commissioner to Chief Secretary, 13 November 1947.
31. SEC/LAB/125, W. Comrie to Labor Commissioner, 17 November 1947.
32. Zelniker, "Patterns," pp. 136–39; S. Nkoma, interview in Luanshya, 3 September 1976. Epstein papers, interview with Comrie, 17 December 1953.
33. Ian Henderson, "Labour and Politics in Northern Rhodesia, 1900–1953:

A Study of the Limits of Colonial Power" (Ph.D. diss., University of Edinburgh, 1973), p. 226; Alfred Mwalwanda, interview in Luanshya, 13 September 1976.

34. Fanny Musumbulwa, interview in Luanshya, 1 September 1976.

35. Ibid.

36. Pascale Sokota, interview in Kitwe, 28 August 1976; Epstein papers, interview with miner, 10 December 1953.

37. Lawrence Katilungu (1914–61): employed as teacher; underground worker at Nkana 1936–40; paymaster for fish transport in the Belgian Congo; reengaged as clerk, then senior interpreter at Nkana 1947–49; chairman, Kitwe branch, National African Congress 1948; president, African Mineworkers' Union 1946–60; president, African Trade Union Congress 1950; deputy-president of the African National Congress 1961. R. Segal, *Political Africa* (London, 1961) pp. 128–30.

38. Henderson, "Labour," p. 226; Albert Musakanya, interview in Kitwe, 22 September 1976.

39. Epstein papers, interview with Nkoloma, 14 December 1953.

40. Epstein, *Politics*, p. 93. A union paper, the *African Miner*, started in 1953.

41. SEC/LAB/125, Department of Labor, Meeting about organizing African mineworkers' union branches, 22 January 1948.

42. RCM/CSD/KMA 18, meeting between the Labor Department and NRCM, 19 April 1948; SEC/LAB/126, W. Comrie, Monthly Reports, May–June and July 1948. The boss boy in charge of the sanitary cleaners was Nashon, a Lala, with over twenty years on the mines. He and Chambeshi won over the department, which was the first to accept the union. "Since that time the sanitary members have been strong members." Epstein papers, interview with Chambeshi, 25 December 1953.

43. Department of Labor and Mines, *Annual Report*, 1949; SEC/LAB/126, W. Comrie, Monthly Report, May–June 1948.

44. Zelniker, "Patterns," pp. 132–34.

45. Matthew R. Mwendapole, *A History of the Trade Union Movement in Zambia up to 1968*, University of Zambia, Institute for African Studies, Communication No. 13 (Lusaka, 1977), p. 9.

46. Wage increases varied from 2s6d to 30s per month. Department of Labor, Annual Report, 1948.

47. RCM/CSD/202.7, no. 2, MCM African Labor Policy, 15 November 1951; N. R. K. Davis, interview in Kitwe, 15 September 1976.

48. RCM/CSD/202.7 (1 and 2), Memorandum on the Industrial Relations Conference, 8 May 1947. MCM, London to NRCM, 9 June 1947.

49. Prain interview (*see* note 16); *Report of the Commission Appointed to Enquire into the Advancment of Africans in Industry* (Lusaka, 1948), pp. 35–41 (*The Dalgleish Report*).

50. David C. Mulford, *Zambia: The Politics of Independence* (London, 1967), pp. 11–13.

51. Berger, *Labour*, pp. 99, 108. Sir Roy (Roland) Welensky (b. 1907): member of the Legislative Council of Northern Rhodesia, 1938–53; Minister of Transport, Communications and Posts, Federation of Rhodesia and Nyasaland, 1953–56; Federal Prime Minister, 1956–63.

52. Sir Roy Welensky, *Welensky's 4,000 Days* (London, 1964), pp. 21–26.
53. CISB, 100:15, vol. 2, P. H. Truscott, conference at Kitwe, 30 August–1 September 1948.
54. SEC/LAB/125, P. J. Law to Labor Commissioner, 21 April 1948.
55. SEC/LAB/125, meeting at Lusaka, 19 February 1947; RCM/CSD/202.5, no. 2, NRCM to AMWU, 23 July 1951.
56. RCM/CSD/WMA 64, Executive Committee, NRCM, 24 May 1949; RCM/CSD/KMA 19, Meeting of NRCM, Comrie, AMWU and APMs, 22 February 1949; (R)-H.2, general manager, Rhokana to department heads, 20 January 1951.
57. RCM/CSD/205.2, no. 1, Government Gazette, 12 November 1948. Executive Committee, NRCM, 3 March 1949.
58. Stubbs interview (*see* note 2).
59. SEC/LAB/125, labor officer, MCM to W. Comrie, 8 December 1948; RCM/CSD/KMA 18, H. H. Field, compound manager, to general manager, MCM, 2 May 1949.
60. ZA/NR3/48, labor commissioner to labor officer, Ndola, 9 February 1950; RCM/CSD/KMA 19, NRCM, Meeting of Comrie, CMs and AMWU, 22 February 1949.
61. Mwalwanda interview (*see* note 33).
62. SEC/LAB/61, Labor Officers' Conference, 24–25 June 1948; ZA/NR3/66, Labour Officers' Conference, 7–9 July 1947.
63. Mubita interview (*see* note 11); P. Mubanga, interview in Kitwe, 16 September 1976; Zelniker, "Patterns," p. 174.
64. Department of African Affairs, *Annual Report*, 1949, 1952.
65. J. Clyde Mitchell, Nchanga Staff Records, Table 6.
66. Mwendapole, *History*, p. 13; *Northern News*, 9 December 1954.
67. CISB, 100.20.5, Vol. 1, meeting of Roan Branch, 30 December 1954; Mwendapole, *History*, pp. 12–14.
68. F. M. N. Heath, "No Smoke from the Smelter," *Corona* (April 1953), p. 149.
69. In January 1953, a tribunal headed by I. C. W. Guillebaud, Professor of Economics at Cambridge, awarded substantial wage increases to black miners. (*See* Appendix F). Berger, *Labour*, pp. 120–21.
70. The AMWU apparently agreed that when a European job was broken down, pay could be broken down as well. CISB, 100:15, vol. 2, P. H. Truscott to Secretary, MCM, London, 14 October 1950.
71. RCM/CSD/KHB/83/8.F, Tribal Representatives Meeting, MCM, 3 and 4 November 1947.
72. RCM/CSD file 202.9, Meeting of the Council of all Tribal Representatives with the APM, Wusikili, 11 December 1952.
73. RCM/CSD/202.7, no. 3, Executive Committee, NRCM, 30 December 1952. Telegram NRCM to RST, London and AA, Johannesburg, 13 March 1953.
74. Mulford, *Zambia*, Chap. 1. Nkumbula studied at Makerere College and London, taught school on the Copperbelt, and was a member of the Western Province Regional Council.
75. Robert H. Bates, *Unions, Parties, and Political Development: A Study of the Mineworkers in Zambia* (New Haven, 1971), p. 126.
76. Robinson Puta was Nchanga's branch chairman. Chapoloko was a branch secretary. Bates, *Unions*, p. 130; Mwendapole interview (*see* note 29).

77. Epstein papers, interview with Chapoloko, 5 October 1953.
78. Katilungu believed "the African people had most to gain from economic advancement and the Trade Union was the body which could best achieve this." ZA/HA/43, vol. 4, Department of Labor, Monthly Report, July 1953; Mwendapole, *History*, Chap. 2.
79. Epstein, *Politics*, Chap. 7; Henderson, "Wage-Earners," pp. 292, 295; Berger, *Labour*, pp. 96, 134, 137.
80. Mwendapole interview (*see* note 29).
81. Mwalwanda interview (*see* note 33) and G. Musumbulwa interview (*see* note 22).
82. Epstein, *Politics*, pp. 115, 119.
83. Mubita interview (*see* note 11) and Mubanga interview (*see* note 63); RACM, file 2/2, Minutes of the meeting of the APM and AMWU, 16 May 1951.
84. F. Musumbulwa interview (*see* note 34).
85. Epstein, *Politics*, pp. 120–21. Nkoloma claimed "Africans have noticed that the Bwanas are now respecting the Africans working for them. All this is due to the union." RCM/CSD/202.5, no. 3, Notice by M. D. Nkoloma, acting general secretary of the union, 25 July 1952.
86. F. Musumbulwa interview (*see* note 34).
87. RCM/CSD/202.5, no. 3, Notice by M. D. Nkoloma, 25 July 1952.
88. RCM/CSD/KMA 16, conciliation proceedings between the companies and the AMWU, 23 September 1949.
89. RCM/CSD file 202.3, no. 2, meeting of the AMWU and the APMs, 11–12 January 1950.
90. Mwendapole interview (*see* note 29).
91. Hortense Powdermaker, *Copper Town: Changing Africa* (New York, 1962), Chap. 8.
92. Mubita interview (*see* note 11) and Mwendapole interview (*see* note 29). Epstein interviewed a large number of miners in 1953–54. They consistently supported the union. For example, one miner joined because "all mineworkers are members of the union. I do not remember anyone who is not a member." Epstein papers, interview with Leo Chikambala, 22 January 1954.
93. The companies feared "Maybank and Williams [may] have engineered this between them so that the European Union can appear to be friendly with the African Union knowing perfectly well that the question of African progression is bound to come up sooner or later and with the hope that the two Unions can get together with some interested outside party such as the Mines International Federation and come up with some working arrangement at the expense of the Companies." CISB: 100:20:9; Guillebaud Award. Telegram RST, London to NRCM, 12 January 1953, and from NRCM to RST, London, 12 January 1953.
94. CISB, 100:20:9, Guillebaud Arbitration, NRCM, "Social and Economic Conditions of Africans, a Comparison of Copperbelt and Village Conditions," 19 December 1952.
95. Mubita interview (*see* note 11), Mwendapole interview (*see* note 29), and Mwalwanda interview (*see* note 33).
96. Charles Perrings, *Black Mineworkers in Central Africa* (New York, 1979); Peter C. Gutkind, *The Emergent African Urban Proletariat*, Occasional Paper

Series, No. 8, Center for Developing Area Studies (Montreal, 1974).

97. E. J. Berg and J. Butler, "Trade Unions," in James S. Coleman and Carl G. Rosberg, eds., *Political Parties and National Integration in Tropical Africa* (Los Angeles, 1964); Bates, *Unions*, Chap. 7; *see* note 1.

98. Mwendapole interview (*see* note 29).

99. Epstein papers, Annual Conference of the AMWU, 25 September 1953.

100. Lameck Chisanga, interviewed by Dr. Carolyn Baylies, in Zambia, 11 January 1973.

101. Chembe Phiri, interview in Luanshya, 3 September 1976.

102. Mwalwanda interview (*see* note 33).

103. P. Kambafwile, interview in Mufulira, 9 September 1976.

104. Mwendapole interview (*see* note 29).

105. Mwalwanda interview (*see* note 33), Mwendapole interview (*see* note 29), and Sokota interview (*see* note 36).

106. Rhodesia Study Club, Newsletter, 1, no. 13 (October 1949). David Mulford, personal communication to Robert Bates, 17 June 1968, cited in Bates, *Unions*, p. 128.

107. Mwendapole interview (*see* note 29).

CHAPTER 7

1. Elena Berger, *Labour, Race, and Colonial Rule: The Copperbelt from 1924 to Independence* (Oxford, 1974); A. L. Epstein, *Politics in an Urban African Community* (Manchester, England, 1958); S. Zelniker, "Changing Patterns of Trade Unionism: The Zambian Case 1948–64" (Ph.D. diss., UCLA, 1970); Ian Henderson, "Wage-Earners and Political Protest in Colonial Africa: The Case of the Copperbelt," *African Affairs* 72, no. 288 (July 1973).

2. Berger, *Labour*, p. 124. The Guillebaud Award, along with a sharp rise in production costs, cut into post-1949 profit margins; *The Economist*, 5 December 1953, p. 764.

3. For more detail, see Charles Perrings, "A Moment in the 'Proletarianization' of the New Middle Class: Race, Value and the Division of Labour in the Copperbelt, 1946–1966," *Journal of Southern African Studies (JSAS)*, 6, no. 2 (April 1980).

4. Sir Ronald Prain, interview in Weybridge, England, 27 August 1982.

5. N. R. K. Davis, interview in Kitwe, 15 September 1976.

6. Dennis Etheredge, interview in Johannesburg, 12 October 1976; Prain interview (*see* note 4).

7. The Capricorn Africa Society, established in 1949 by Colonel David Stirling, advocated multi-racial alliances with the "right kind of blacks," i.e., those westernized Africans willing to cooperate with liberal Europeans. This movement attracted a considerable following in Northern Rhodesia in the mid-1950s. Dr. A. Charles Fisher, interview in Kitwe, 21 August 1976; Robert I. Rotberg, *Black Heart: Gore-Browne and the Politics of Multiracial Zambia* (Berkeley, 1977), pp. 304–05.

8. Sir Theodore Gregory, *Ernest Oppenheimer and the Economic Development of Southern Africa* (Oxford, 1962), pp. 463, 473–83; R. L. Prain, "The Problem

of African Advancement on the Copperbelt of Northern Rhodesia," in Prain, *Selected Papers 1953–57* (London, 1958).

9. *Legislative Council Debates*, 29 July 1954; RCM/CSD 202.17, no. 1, Executive Committee Meeting, NRCM, 23 November 1954.

10. Prain interview (*see* note 4); Harold K. Hochschild, "Labour Relations in Northern Rhodesia," *Annals of the American Academy of Political and Social Science* 206 (July 1956), p. 47.

11. Taylor Ostrander, interviewed at AMAX headquarters, Greenwich, Connecticut, 14 July 1981. Harold Hochschild telegramed Prain giving American Metal's unqualified support for the advancement fight.

12. Berger, *Labour*, pp. 123–30; Prain interview (*see* note 4).

13. Hortense Powdermaker, *Copper Town: Changing Africa* (New York, 1962), pp. 89, 118. Helmuth Heisler, *Urbanisation and the Government of Migration* (London, 1974), p. 120.

14. *Report of the Commission of Inquiry into the Mining Industry* (Lusaka, 1966) (*The Brown Report*).

15. Andrew Torrance, interview in Kitwe, 23 August 1976; (R)-A.11, African Personnel Manager's Report, April 1950.

16. CISB, 100:20:9A, vol. 1, Summary of meeting with the Secretary of State for the Colonies, 6 January 1953.

17. Richard Bendix, *Work and Authority in Industry* (Los Angeles, 1963), p. 312; Belinda Bozzoli, "Managerialism and the Mode of Production in South Africa," *South African Labour Bulletin* 3, no. 8 (October 1977): 29–41; Mike Hough, interview at Fort Hare University, Alice, South Africa, 4 October 1976.

18. CISB, 100:60:1, J. D. Rheinnalt Jones, "Health and Social Welfare Services for African Mineworkers and Their Families on Nkana, Nchanga, and Broken Hill," 22 August 1949. This was a typical Human Relations strategy, focusing on conditions requiring less capital expenditure, such as welfare.

19. CISB, 100:60:1, J. D. Rheinnalt Jones, Report on a visit to Broken Hill, Rhokana, and Nchanga, April 1952.

20. Sir Ronald Prain, "The Responsibilities of a Mining Industry to the Community," in Prain, *Selected Papers 1953–57*, p. 165; RCM/CSD/203.2.1, no. 1 H. R. Finn to R. L. Prain, 31 July 1951.

21. Etheredge interview (*see* note 6); Prain interview (*see* note 4).

22. CISB, 40.4, vol. 1, Executive Committee, NRCM, 17 July 1952; Minutes of the APMs Committee, NRCM, 2 July 1952 and 29 August 1952.

23. ZA/NR3/66, Department of Labor and Mines, Report on the Annual Conference, 9–10 October 1953.

24. Chris Cook, interview in East London, South Africa, 4 October 1976.

25. SEC/LAB/61, Labor Officers' Conference, 24–25 June 1948; RCM/CSD/ KMA 19, general manager, MCM to secretary, MCM, London, 20 August 1948.

26. RCM/CSD/202.5, no. 5, Executive Committee, NRCM, 16 April 1955.

27. RCM/CSD/202.17, no. 1, NRCM to all general managers, 5 May 1953; (R)-W.9, Welfare Officer, Nchanga, to APM, Nchanga, 5 December 1952.

28. Secretary General Simon Kaluwa, who had defeated Jameson Chapoloko

(Chairman of Nkana branch) in the union's first elections, refused to give Chapoloko a paid union post after his dismissal for leading an irregular strike. Robinson Puta, the union's vice-president, rallied support for Chapoloko, and Kaluwa was dismissed. *Northern News,* 10 July 1952.

29. Berger, *Labour,* p. 137.
30. "The leaders [of MASA] are those who are friends with the Personnel Manager." Epstein papers, interview with Kabuka, an Ngoni market capitaō with 200 tickets, 27 February 1954.
31. RCM/CSD/202.17, no. 1, NRCM to all general managers, 27 October 1954.
32. *The Brown Report,* p. 57; RCM/CSD 300.40.3, NRCM, African Housing, position at March 1958.
33. In 1953, 75% of housing was category 2; RCM/CSD/202.7, no. 4, Conditions of Employment, July 1953. By 1956, only 50% of the married workers lived in two-room houses (category 2); (R)-H.8, Executive Committee, NRCM, 20 April 1956.
34. (R)-A.9, A. Norton, Johannesburg to J. Phillemore, 16 April 1953; Richard Howie, interview in Johannesburg, 10 October 1976.
35. As Bromwich explained, "The primary objective of African Welfare is to create a stable, contented, and productive labor force. . . . It is not a charity, bonus, or bribe, but a logical means of achieving a definite result." RCM/CSD/203.5, no. 2, Memorandum from chief of study to general manager, RACM, 9 July 1955.
36. "A discussion group was started earlier in the year, but because it developed political leanings was discontinued." (R)-W.9 Rhokana, Report on welfare activities, 1954. Welfare Supervisor, Rhokana, to APM, Rhokana, July 1957.
37. (R)-W.9, W. Scrivener to GM, Rhokana, 7 April 1952; (RA), File on Training African Personnel Officers, "Duties of APOs in the African Township," 18 November 1957.
38. CISB, 100:60:7, Native Affairs Dept., Johannesburg, to J. Phillemore, 13 March 1953; Sanford Chiwila, interview in Kitwe, 27 November 1975.
39. *Horizon* 1, no. 3, March 1959; RCM/CSD/203.5, no. 1, Welfare Report ending August 1954.
40. ZA/NR3/66, Minutes of a meeting of the Senior Labor Officer and the Labor Officers, 18 March 1953; Powdermaker, *Copper Town,* pp. 281–82.
41. Passmore reported 457 arrests for loafing in 1953 as opposed to 6,697 arrests in 1955. IAS, Passmore, "Report on the Loafer Problem on the Copperbelt," 14 March 1956, 9. "Checks on unauthorized persons were made daily except Saturday and Sunday"; RCM/CSD/202.7, no. 6, African personnel manager, MCM, to general manager, MCM, 8 August 1955.
42. Gabriel Musumbulwa, interview at Luanshya, 30 August 1976; (R)-A.10, APM, Confidential Report, Rhokana, 30 May 1956.
43. Sylvester Nkoma, interview in Luanshya, 3 September 1976; Epstein, *Politics,* p. 146.
44. By May 1954, union membership was down to one-third of the labor force. *Northern News,* 7 May 1954; Nkoma interview (*see* note 43).
45. Mineworker commitment to political action has been questioned because of incidents such as the Roan miners' refusal to support Congress's boycott of the Luanshya butchers in 1954. The miners refused to cooperate because

the boycott was badly organized, not because they rejected political action. They realized that ineffective collective action would damage the nationalist cause. Epstein, *Politics*, pp. 142–47.

46. At the first meeting, Chapoloko told everyone he was pleased that "Luanshya was at last becoming conscious." Epstein, *Politics*, p. 164.

47. Matthew Mwendapole, interview in Ndola, 3 August 1976; David C. Mulford, *Zambia: The Politics of Independence 1957–1964* (Oxford, 1967), p. 43.

48. CISB, 100:20:5, vol. 1, meeting of the Roan Branch, AMWU, 30 December 1954.

49. CISB, 100.20.5, vol. 1, telephone conversation between F. B. Canning-Cooke and C. E. Cousins, labor commissioner, 4 January 1955.

50. CISB, 100:20:5, vol. 1, meeting of the Roan Branch, AMWU, 30 December 1954; Matthew Mwendapole, *A History of the Trade Union Movement in Zambia up to 1968*, University of Zambia, Institute for African Studies, Communication No. 13 (Lusaka, 1977), pp. 20–22.

51. RCM/CSD/202.5, no. 4, NRCM, 1955 Strike Diary.

52. RCM/CSD/202.7, no. 5, Executive Committee, NRCM, 19 February 1955.

53. The 1954 Annual Conference of the AMWU discussed the possibility of amalgamating with the European MWU. Chindele said, "We gave them hard conditions. One was that if we amalgamated no member of the union shall encourage the company to discharge his fellow member." Epstein papers, interview with trade union leaders, 27 April 1954.

54. CISB, 10:27, vol. 10, Executive Committee, NRCM, 22 February 1955. Telegram RST, Lusaka to NRCM, 28 February 1955.

55. CISB, 100.20, Meeting between the African personnel managers and the AMWU, 5 December 1955; Patson Kambafwile, interview at Mufulira, 9 September 1976.

56. *The Report of the Commission Appointed to Inquire into the Unrest in the Mining Industry in Northern Rhodesia in Recent Months* (Lusaka, 1956), pp. 16–17, 30 (The *Branigan Report*).

57. *The Branigan Report*, pp. 18–22, 44.

58. Mwendapole interview (*see* note 47); P. Mubanga, interview in Kitwe, 16 September 1976.

59. Mwendapole interview (*see* note 47).

60. RCM/CSD/202.5, no. 7, meeting between AMWU, NRCM, and the Labor Department, 19 July 1956.

61. Fanny Musumbulwa, interview in Luanshya, 1 September 1976.

62. Davis interview (*see* note 5).

63. Mwendapole interview (*see* note 47).

64. Epstein papers, interview with W. Munthali, 27 February 1954.

65. RCM/CSD/202.17, no. 1, Secretary, MASA to NRCM, 31 May 1954; RCM/CSD/202.17, no. 2, NRCM to RST and AA, Salisbury, 16 March 1955; Lameck Chisanga, interviewed in Lusaka by Carolyn Baylies, 11 January 1973.

66. R. H. Bates, *Unions, Parties and Political Development: A Study of Mineworkers in Zambia* (New Haven, 1971), pp. 111–19.

67. John Chisata, interview in Mufulira, 14 September 1976.

68. Chembe Phiri, interview on Luanshya, 3 September 1976; Mwendapole, *History*, pp. 21–22.

69. The AMWU was affiliated with the International Confederation of Free Trade Unions (ICFTU), while other unions in Northern Rhodesia maintained ties with the World Federation of Trade Unions (WFTU). The WFTU was more radical about political activism. Bates, *Unions*, pp. 131–32, 142.

70. *Northern News*, 24 October 1955; *The Branigan Report*, p. 40.

71. CISB, Evidence to the Branigan Commission: Companies' Statement of Case, Appendix 29 and 30, pp. 220–27.

72. Philip Mason, *The Birth of a Dilemma: The Conquest and Settlement of Rhodesia* (London, 1958), p. 116.

73. *The Branigan Report*, p. 20.

74. *The Branigan Report*, pp. 17, 20–22, 25–26; Mwendapole, *History*, pp. 27–28.

75. Rhokana welfare programs dropped in attendance by 75%. RCM/CSD/203.5, no. 2, NRCM, Report on African Labor Boycotts, 30 August 1956.

76. Nkoma interview (*see* note 43). These songs chanted "the Makobo [deadfish, a word used to describe MASA members] are finished, the Union is all powerful"; RCM/CSD/203.2, no. 2, Sectional APM to Acting APM, 17 August 1956.

77. Henderson, "Wage-Earners," p. 297; Bates, *Unions*, pp. 272–76, 484–85.

78. Mwendapole interview (*see* note 47).

79. Davis interview (*see* note 5).

80. *Legislative Council Debates*, 30 November 1956, 177; CISB, 100:20:25, Executive Committee, NRCM, 27 June 1957.

81. The African National Congress memorandum to the Branigan Commission, 29 October 1956. *The Branigan Report*, pp. 38, 53–55.

82. CISB, 100:20:20, vol. 1, NRCM to RST and AA, Salisbury, 14 September and 20 September 1956.

83. RCM/CSD/202.5, no. 8, NRCM and AMWU, informal discussion, 14 March 1957.

84. "Congress leaders now appeared to be taking the lead in Union affairs" (at Roan); RCM/CSD/202.5, no. 9, Executive Committee, NRCM, 30 April 1957.

85. *The Central African Examiner*, 8 November and 1 March 1959; Evidence to the Commission Appointed to Inquire into the Mining Industry in Northern Rhodesia (Lusaka, 1962) (The Morison Commission). Companies' statement of case, appendix I: Agreement of the companies and the AMWU, 12 March 1958 and 29 September 1959.

86. Mwendapole interview (*see* note 47).

87. R. Philpott, evidence to the Branigan Commission, 24 November 1956; (RA) file 33/1, L. C. Katilungu to AMWU members, 5 September 1956.

88. In 1957, union membership dropped to 6,560. Berger, *Labour*, p. 161; Kambafwile interview (*see* note 55).

89. Mwendapole interview (*see* note 47), Nkoma interview (*see* note 43), and Chisata interview (*see* note 67).

90. Chisata interview (*see* note 67).

91. CISB, 40:4, vol. 3, APMs Committee Meeting, NRCM, 21 December 1956 and 28 November 1958.

92. Langford Chibambo, interview in Luanshya, 12 September 1976.

93. Boniface Koloko, interview in Luanshya, 30 August 1976.

94. (R)-W.11, APM Monthly Report, October 1957; (R)-T.15, Meeting of the Township Area Committee, 14 January 1958; S. K. Ndhlovu, interview in Mufulira, 8 September 1976; Howie interview (*see* note 34).

95. RCM/CSD/202.28, no. 1, Inter-group Committee Meeting, Salisbury, 27 March 1957; (R)-H.8, O. B. Bennett, general manager, Rhokana, to consulting engineer, AA, Johannesburg, 31 May 1955.

96. *Central African Examiner*, 27 September 1958; Department of African Affairs, *Annual Report*, 1958; CISB, 100:51, vol. 2, R. Gabbitas, APM, to GM, Nchanga, 8 March 1960.

97. Davis interview (*see* note 5) and Etheredge interview (*see* note 6); Torrance interview (*see* note 15).

98. IAS, H. Franklin, "African Absenteeism," mimeograph, 1959, pp. 1–3.

99. CISB, 100:60:7, vol. 1, John I. Hawkins, security officer, to NRCM, 13 January 1958.

100. Chiwila interview (*see* note 38).

101. Domeniko Chansa, youth club organizer, Nchanga, interviewed by D. Lehmann, 19 February 1958; H. Franklin, "An Investigation into the Social Background of the Advancees," RACM, 1958, 3.

102. Information from the Office of the Registrar of Trade Unions, Lusaka, 2 October 1967; Kambafwile interview (*see* note 55).

103. The companies asked the Honeyman Commission to recommend ending the European union's closed shop. The Commission refused but recommended that trade union members with a closed shop agreement should not strike before negotiating procedures had been exhausted. *Report of the Commission Appointed to Inquire into the Stoppage in the Mining Industry in Northern Rhodesia in July, 1957, and to Make Recommendations for the Avoidance and Quick Settlement of Disputes in the Industry* (Lusaka, 1957), pp. 32–33 (*The Honeyman Report*).

104. Berger, *Labour*, pp. 178–83; John Chisata, evidence to the Morison Commission.

105. Unlike Nkumbula, Kaunda rejected the 1958 elections set up by the Benson Constitution. Election disturbances were blamed on ZANC, which was subsequently banned. In 1959, Kaunda formed a new party, UNIP; David C. Mulford, *Zambia: The Politics of Independence* (London, 1967), pp. 85, 100. In the first six months of 1963, UNIP held 17 meetings with 42,350 people, while ANC had 3 meetings with 840 people. M. J. Adams, D. C., Kitwe, evidence to the Commission of Inquiry into Unrest on the Copperbelt, July–August 1963 (Lusaka, 1963), p. 212 (The Whelan Commission).

106. Pascale Sokota, interview in Kitwe, 28 August 1976; J. Malik Chipako, interview in Kitwe, 14 September 1976.

107. Ndhlovu interview (*see* note 94).

108. Sir Ronald Prain, *Reflections on an Era* (Surrey, England, 1981), p. 143. The Monckton Commission was set up to review the Federal constitution Mulford, *Zambia*, p. 116.

109. Mwendapole interview (*see* note 47). John Chisata believed Katilungu political behavior antagonized the mines; Chisata interview (*see* note 67

110. Chisata interview (*see* note 67). UNIP decided to fight the 1962 Gener Election. UNIP leaders believed a strike during the election campaig

would alienate European voters, so asked the union not to strike. Union leaders reluctantly agreed, but this sacrifice caused some hard feelings. Berger, *Labour*, p. 215.

111. Chisata interview (*see* note 67). In 1959 the Trade Union Congress split into two sections, one dominated by AMWU and MASA. In 1961 Chisata agreed to reunify the two sections, and the new organization was called the United Trade Union Congress (UTUC). The AMWU fell out with the UTUC in 1963 over the issue of political control. Mulford, *Zambia*, pp. 173–74. Bates described the UTUC as "the labor wing of UNIP"; Bates, *Unions*, p. 132.

112. *Zambia Pilot* (June 1963), p. 9.

113. Peter Harries-Jones, *Freedom and Labour: Mobilization and Political Control on the Zambian Copperbelt* (Oxford, 1975), pp. 166–67; Chisata interview (*see* note 67).

114. In 1964, more than 2,000 miners left the AMWU for the new union. CISB, 100:47, vol. 8, N. R. K. Davis to the general managers, 30 August 1963.

115. Harries-Jones, *Freedom*, p. 168; Chisata interview (*see* note 67).

116. Davis interview (*see* note 5); *Northern Star*, 31 May 1963.

117. On the eve of independence, the companies adopted a dual wage scale with separate rates for Africans and Europeans; *The Brown Report*, pp. 21–22, 33–35, 45–46.

Expatriate and Local Wages in 1966

Group	Position	Expatriate (£)	Local (£)	Local % of Expatriate
Group A (Staff/ Supervisors/ Technicians)	Shift Boss Underground	212	125	59%
	Cave/Draw Control Officer I	177	94	53%
	Surveyor I	180	100	56%
	Surface Foreman	162	91	56%
Group B (Operatives)	Winding Engine Driver	183	67	37%
	Power Shovel Operator	165	67	41%

Source: *The Brown Report*, Appendix 19, pp. 163–64.

118. Alfred Mwalwanda, interview in Luanshya, 13 September 1976.

119. *Zambia Pilot* (June 1963), p. 9.

120. Several informants stated that trade union leaders would be running the government if they had cooperated with the party, and suggested that workers would be treated better.

CONCLUSION

1. Charles Perrings, *Black Mineworkers in Central Africa* (New York, 1979).
2. Robert H. Bates, *Unions, Parties and Political Development: A Study of the*

Mineworkers in Zambia (New Haven, 1971); Elliot Berg and Jeffrey Butler, "Trade Unions," in James S. Coleman and Carl G. Rosberg, Jr., eds., *Political Parties and National Integration in Tropical Africa* (Los Angeles, 1964).

3. Douglas G. Anglin and Timothy M. Shaw, *Zambia's Foreign Policy: Studies in Diplomacy and Dependence* (Boulder, Colorado, 1979). Shaw has subsequently moved away from this position. T. M. Shaw, "The Political Economy of Zambia: Recession without Resolution" (mimeograph, 1981).

4. See the works of Sharon Stichter, Charles van Onselen, and Ian Phimister in the Bibliography.

5. John S. Saul, "The 'Labour Aristocracy' Thesis Reconsidered," in R. Sandbrook and R. Cohen, *The Development of an African Working Class* (Toronto, 1975); Richard Jeffries, "The Labour Aristocracy? Ghana Case Study," *Review of African Political Economy* 3 (May–October 1975); Robert Davies, *Capital, State and White Labour in South Africa* (Atlantic Highlands, New Jersey, 1979).

6. Charles van Onselen, *Chibaro: African Mine Labour in Southern Rhodesia, 1900–1933* (London, 1976); Jim Silver, "Class Struggles in Ghana's Mining Industry," *Review of African Political Economy*, 12 (1978); Paul M. Lubeck, "Class Formation of the Periphery: Class Consciousness and Islamic Nationalism among Nigerian Workers" (mimeograph, 1980); R. Sandbrook and J. Arn, *The Labouring Poor and Urban Class Formation: The Case of Greater Accra*, Monograph Series No. 12, Center for Developing-Area Studies, McGill University (Montreal, 1977).

7. Frederick A. Johnstone, "Racially Structured Capitalism and South African Labour History," seminar paper, Center for Developing-Area Studies, McGill University, 29 November 1979.

8. R. I. Rotberg, *The Rise of Nationalism in Central Africa: The Making of Malawi and Zambia, 1873–1964* (Cambridge, Massachusetts, 1965); Thomas Hodgkins, *Nationalism in Colonial Africa* (London, 1956).

SELECTED
BIBLIOGRAPHY

UNPUBLISHED PRIMARY MATERIAL

Company Archives

The Archives of RST in Britain

These are located at Rhodesian Selection Trust International Metals, 1 Noble Street, London EC2V7DA. The material consists primarily of secretary's files containing reports from the field management of RACM, MCM, and RST between 1928 and the outbreak of the war. The notation used to indicate material from this source is "RST."

The Archives of RST in Africa

These are held by Roan Consolidated Mines, Central Services Division, P.O. Box 1505, Ndola, Zambia. The archives are well organized and extensive. The material is not always complete, but covers most aspects of the mining operations at Roan and Mufulira from the late 1920s. The notation used to indicate this material is "RCM/CSD."

A number of records are held by the personnel department at Roan Antelope Copper Mine. The notation used to indicate material from this source is "RACM."

The Archives of (Rhodesian) Anglo-American in Africa

This is an incomplete collection held by the Nchanga Consolidated Copper Mines, Centralised Services Division Technical Library, P. O. Box 172, Kitwe, Zambia. Much of the material deals with labor, although with a heavy technical bias. The records date back to the early 1930s, and cover a wide range of subjects. The notation used to indicate material at Nchanga is "NCCM/CSD."

Some records are still in the possession of the operating divisions, primarily the personnel department of Rokana Division (the former Rhokana Corporation) in Kitwe. Although incomplete, the records span the period from the early 1930s to independence. The notation used for material at Rokana Division is "(R)."

The Archives of the Northern Rhodesian Chamber of Mines

These are held by the Copper Industry Service Bureau, P.O. Box 2100, Kitwe, Zambia. The material covers primarily the period since 1940. The notation used for this material is "CISB."

Mission Archives

The Archives of the Council for World Missions

Located at the School of Oriental and African Studies, University of London, they include records of the London Missionary Society, the Commonwealth Missionary Society, and the Presbyterian Church of England Overseas Mission. The records include material on the United Missions in the Copperbelt. The notation for this material is "LMS."

The Archives of the Missionary Societies in
Great Britain and Ireland

These records are located at Edinburgh House, 2 Eaton Gate, London SW1. There are five boxes from the UMCB, 1936–46. The notation for this material is "CBM."

The Archives of the Methodist Missionary Society

Located at 25 Marlybone Rd., London NW1, these records include data on the United Missions in the Copperbelt. The notation for this material is "MMS."

Mindolo Ecumenical Center

The Center is located in Kitwe, Zambia. It used to be the central location for the United Missions in the Copperbelt. The Center has some material from the United Missions, but the collection is uneven. There is some material on mine welfare in the 1950s and 1960s.

State Archives

National Archives of Zambia, Lusaka

These archives have a 30-year rule, so material after 1947 was not available. The secretariat files have their own numbers, beginning with "SEC." Other files are identified by the notation "ZA." Some relevant files are:
    African Labour, 1930–45, SEC/LAB/1.
    Investigation of labour conditions, by province, 1936–37, SEC/LAB/ 17–22.

Stabilisation of native labour, SEC/LAB/27.
Native Industrial Labour Advisory Board, 1935–47, SEC/LAB/33–34.
Labour Department organisation, 1939–41, SEC/LAB/36.
Labour Commissioner's reports, 1941–47, SEC/LAB/41–47.
Labour conditions on mines, 1939, SEC/LAB/68.
African strike on the Copperbelt, SEC/LAB/78–79.
Report on Copperbelt strike by Secretary for Native Affairs, 1940, SEC/LAB/104.
The Russell Commission, 1935, ZP/10.
The Forster Commission, 1940, ZP/12.
Boss Boys' Committees, ZA/Acc. 52/17.
Conditions on the mines, 1929–34, ZA1/9/18/43.
Beer in Northern Rhodesia, ZA1/9/83/2–4.

Archives of the British Colonial Office at the Public Records Office, Portugal Street, London ECI

The notation used to indicate material from this source is "PRO."

Evidence to Commissions and Boards of Inquiry

Copies of the evidence given by witnesses before the Russell (1935) and Bledisloe (1938–39) Commissions of Inquiry are deposited at the Commonwealth Office Library, London. The evidence to the Forster Commission (1940) is located at the National Archives of Zambia, Lusaka. Verbatim reports of the evidence given before the following Inquiries are held in the library of the Copper Industry Service Bureau, Kitwe:
Dalgleish Commission of Inquiry, 1948.
Forster Board of Inquiry, 1954.
Branigan Commission of Inquiry, 1956 (incomplete).
Honeyman Commission of Inquiry, 1957.
Morison Commission of Inquiry, 1962.
Brown Commission of Inquiry, 1966.

Miscellaneous Sources

Papers of Arthur Creech Jones, R. R. Stokes, and G. St. J. Orde Browne in the Colonial Records Project collection, Rhodes House, Oxford.

Institute for African Studies, University of Zambia. Assorted papers on Zambia.

Special Collections, University of Zambia. A good collection of Northern Rhodesian government reports. Has data from the Copperbelt oral history project.

Epstein papers. Private papers of Dr. A. L. Epstein at Sussex University, England.

Dissertations and Theses

Baylies, Carolyn. "The State and Class Formation in Zambia." Ph.D. dissertation, University of Wisconsin, 1978.

Burdette, Marcia. "The Dynamics of Nationalization between Multinational Corporations and Peripheral States." Ph.D. dissertation, Columbia University, 1979.

Cross, J. S. W. "The Watch Tower Movement in South Central Africa 1908–1945." D.Phil. thesis, Oxford, 1973.

Gifford, P. "The Framework for a Nation: An Economic and Social History of Northern Rhodesia from 1914 to 1939." Ph.D. dissertation, Yale University, 1964.

Henderson, I. "Labour and Politics in Northern Rhodesia: A Study of the Limits of Colonial Power." D.Phil. thesis, University of Edinburgh, 1972.

Wincott, N. E. "Some Aspects of the Growth and Development of African Urban Society in Zambia." B. Litt. thesis, Oxford, 1966.

Zelniker, S. "Changing Patterns of Trade Unionism: The Zambian Case 1948–64." Ph.D. dissertation, University of California, Los Angeles, 1970.

Unpublished reports and articles

Anglo-American Corporation. "Joint Memorandum on the Companies Operating in Northern Rhodesia of the Anglo-American Corporation and Rhodesian Selection Trust." 11 July 1963.

Bromwich, E. C. "African Advancement." 5 February 1962 (RST).

Franklin, H. C. "African Absenteesim." 1959 (RST).

——. "An Investigation into the Social Background of the Advancees." 1958 (RST).

Waldstein, N. S. "The Struggle for African Advancement within the Copper Industry of Northern Rhodesia." M.I.T. Center for International Studies, Cambridge, Mass., 1957.

PRINTED MATERIAL

Primary Sources

Annual Series

Northern Rhodesia Legislative Council Debates.
Annual Reports of the Department of Labour of Northern Rhodesia.

Annual Reports of the Department of Mines of Northern Rhodesia. Northern Rhodesia Chamber of Mines Year Books. Kitwe, 1956–63.

Official Reports for Northern Rhodesia

Report of the Sub-Committee of the Native Industrial Labour Advisory Board, Administrative Control of Industrial Population. Lusaka, 1936.

Report of the Commission Appointed to Inquire into the Disturbances in the Copperbelt of Northern Rhodesia. (Chairman, Sir John Forster.) Lusaka, 1941.

Statement by the Government of Northern Rhodesia on the Recommendations of the Report of the Copperbelt Commission, 1940. Lusaka, 1941.

A Report on Some Aspects of African Living Conditions on the Copper Belt of Northern Rhodesia. A. Lynn Saffery, Lusaka, 1943.

Report of the Commission Appointed to Enquire into the Advancement of Africans in Industry. (Chairman, A. Dalgleish.) Lusaka, 1948.

Report and Award of the Arbitrator C. W. Guillebaud. January 1953.

Report of the Board of Inquiry Appointed to Inquire into the Advancement of Africans in the Copper Mining Industry in Northern Rhodesia. (Chairman, Sir John Forster.) Lusaka, 1954.

Report of the Commission Appointed to Inquire into the Unrest in the Mining Industry in Northern Rhodesia in Recent Months. (Chairman, Sir Patrick Branigan.) Lusaka, 1956.

Report of the Committee on Trade Testing and Apprenticeship for Africans. Lusaka, 1957.

Report of the Commission Appointed to Inquire into the Stoppage in the Mining Industry in Northern Rhodesia in July, 1957, and to Make Recommendations for the Avoidance and Quick Settlement of Disputes in the Industry. (Chairman, G. G. Honeyman.) Lusaka, 1957.

Report of the Commission Appointed to Inquire into the Mining Industry in Northern Rhodesia. (Chairman, Sir Ronald Morison.) Lusaka, 1962.

Report of the Commission of Inquiry into Unrest on the Copperbelt, July–August, 1963. (Chairman, F. J. Whelan.) Lusaka, 1963.

Report of the Commission of Inquiry into the Mining Industry. (Chairman, Roland Brown.) Lusaka, 1966.

Official Reports for United Kingdom

Report of the Commission Appointed to Enquire into the Disturbances in the Copperbelt, Northern Rhodesia, 1935. Cmd. 5009 of 1935.

Report of the Commission Appointed to Enquire into the Financial and Economic Position of Northern Rhodesia. (Chairman, Sir Alan Pim.) Colonial No. 145 of 1938.

Labour Conditions in Northern Rhodesia. Report by Major G. St. J. Orde Browne, O.B.E. Colonial No. 150 of 1938.

Rhodesia-Nyasland Royal Commission Report. (Chairman, Lord Bledisloe.) Cmd. 5949 of 1939.

Conference on the Federation of Southern Rhodesia, Northern Rhodesia and Nyasaland. Vol. 2. London, 1953.

Newspapers and Periodicals

The African Mail, Lusaka, 1960–62.
The Bulawayo Chronicle, Salisbury, 1892–.
The Central African Examiner, Salisbury, 1957.
The Central African Mail, Lusaka, 1960–62.
The Central African Post, Lusaka, 1948–62.
The Copperbelt Times, Chingola, 1932–43.
Mutende, Lusaka, 1936–52.
The Northern News, Ndola, 1943–63.
The Northern Rhodesian Advertiser, Ndola, 1935–55.
The Rhodesia Herald, Salisbury, 1892–.
The Zambia News, Ndola, 1963–64.

Secondary Sources

Books

Allighan, Gary. *The Welensky Story.* Cape Town, 1962.

Apthorpe, R. J., ed. *Present Interrelations in Central African Rural and Urban Life.* Rhodes-Livingstone Institute, 11th Conference Proceedings. Lusaka, 1958.

Apthorpe, R. J., and Matthews, D., eds. *Social Relations in Central African Industry.* Rhodes-Livingstone Institute, 12th Conference Proceedings. Lusaka, 1958.

Baldwin, R. E. *Economic Development and Export Growth: A Study of Northern Rhodesia, 1920–60.* Berkeley, 1966.

Bancroft, J. A. *Mining in Northern Rhodesia.* London: BSA Co., 1961.

Barber, W. J. *The Economy of British Central Africa.* Stanford, 1961.

Bates, R. H. *Unions, Parties and Political Development: A Study of Mineworkers in Zambia.* New Haven, 1971.

Bendix, R. *Work and Authority in Industry.* Los Angeles, 1963.

Berger, Elena. *Labour, Race, and Colonial Rule: The Copperbelt from 1924 to Independence.* Oxford, 1974.

Bradley, Kenneth G. *Copper Venture: The Discovery and Development of Roan Antelope and Mufulira.* London, 1952.

Brown, T. C. *Copper in Africa: The Copperbelt of Northern Rhodesia.* Edinburgh, 1943.

Burawoy, Michael. *The Colour of Class on the Copper Mines: From African Advancement to Zambianization.* Zambian Papers, No. 7. Lusaka, 1972.

Clarke, J.; Critcher, C.; and Johnson, R., eds. *Working Class Culture: Studies in History and Theory.* New York, 1979.

Cohen, Sir Andrew. *British Policy in Changing Africa.* London, 1959.

Coleman, F. L. *The Northern Rhodesian Copperbelt 1899–1962: Technological Development up to the End of the Central African Federation.* Manchester, 1971.

Cunningham, Simon. *The Copper Industry in Zambia.* New York, 1981.

Daniel, Philip. *Africanisation, Nationalisation and Inequality.* Cambridge, England, 1979.

Davidson, J. W. *The Northern Rhodesian Legislative Council.* London, 1948.

Davies, D. Hywell. *Zambia in Maps.* London, 1971.

Davies, I. *African Trade Unions.* Harmondsworth, 1966.

Davis, J. Merle, ed. *Modern Industry and the African.* London, 1933.

Elliot, Charles, ed. *Constraints on the Economic Development of Zambia.* Nairobi, 1971.

Epstein, A. L. *Politics in an Urban African Community.* Manchester, 1958.

Fetter, B. *The Creation of Elisabethville 1910–1940.* Stanford, 1976.

Forde, D., ed. *Social Implications of Industrialisation and Urbanization in Africa South of the Sahara.* UNESCO, Paris, 1956.

Franklin, H. *Unholy Wedlock.* London, 1963.

Gann, L. H. *The Birth of a Plural Society: The Development of Northern Rhodesia under the British South Africa Company.* Manchester, 1958.

———. *A History of Northern Rhodesia: Early Days to 1953.* London, 1964.

Gelfand, M. *Northern Rhodesia in the Days of the Charter.* Oxford, 1961.

Gidden, Anthony. *The Class Structure of the Advanced Societies.* London, 1973.

Gray, R. *The Two Nations: Aspects of the Development of Race Relations in the Rhodesias and Nyasland.* London, 1960.

Gregory, Sir Theodore. *Ernest Oppenheimer and the Economic Development of Southern Africa.* Cape Town, 1962.

Gutkind, Peter C. W. *The Emergent African Urban Proletariat.* Occasional Paper Series, No. 8. Montreal, 1974.

Hall, R. *Zambia.* London, 1965.

Harries-Jones, Peter. *Freedom and Labour: Mobilization and Political Control on the Zambian Copperbelt.* Oxford, 1975.

Heisler, Helmuth. *Urbanisation and the Government of Migration.* London, 1974.

Herfindahl, O. C. *Copper Costs and Prices: 1870–1957.* Baltimore, 1959.

Hocking, Anthony. *Oppenheimer and Son.* New York, 1968.

Holleman, J. F., and Biesheuvel, S. *White Mine Workers in Northern Rhodesia, 1959–60.* Leiden, 1973.

Johnstone, F. A. *Class, Race and Gold.* London, 1976.

Kay, G. *A Social Geography of Zambia.* London, 1967.

Kitching, G. *Class and Economic Change in Kenya.* New Haven, 1980.

Lewin, J. *The Colour Bar in the Copper Belt.* Johannesburg, 1941.

Mezger, Dorothea. *Copper in the World Economy.* Translated by Pete Burgess. New York, 1980.

Miliband, Ralph. *Marxism and Politics.* Oxford, 1977.

Mitchell, J. C. *The Kalela Dance.* Rhodes-Livingstone Paper No. 27. Lusaka, 1957.

Moore, R. J. B. *Man's Act and God's in Africa.* London, 1940.

———. *These African Copper Miners.* Revised and with appendices by A. Sandilands. London, 1948.

Mulford, David C. *Zambia: The Politics of Independence.* London, 1967.

Obidegwu, F., and Nziramasanga. *Copper and Zambia.* Lexington, Massachusetts, 1981.

Ohadike, P. O. *Development of and Factors in the Employment of African Migrants in the Copper Mines of Zambia 1940–66.* Zambian Papers, No. 4. Manchester, 1969.

Ollowa, P. E. *Participatory Democracy in Zambia.* London, 1979.

Orde Browne, G. St. J. *The African Labourer.* London, 1933.

Palmer, Robin, and Parsons, Neil, eds. *The Roots of Rural Poverty in Central and Southern Africa.* Los Angeles, 1977.

Perrings, Charles. *Black Mineworkers in Central Africa.* New York, 1979.

Phimister, I. R. and Van Onselen, Charles. *Studies in the History of African Mine Labour in Colonial Zimbabwe.* Gwelo, Zimbabwe, 1978.

Poulantzas, N. *Classes in Contemporary Capitalism.* London, 1975.

Powdermaker, Hortense. *Copper Town: Changing Africa.* New York, 1962.

Prain, Sir Ronald. *Copper: The Anatomy of an Industry.* London, 1975.

———. *Reflections of an Era.* Surrey, England, 1981.

———. *Selected Papers 1953–57.* London, 1958.

———. *Selected Papers 1958–60.* London, 1961.

———. *Selected Papers 1961–64.* London, 1964.

Ranger, T. O. *Dance and Society in Eastern Africa 1890–1970.* London, 1975.

Richards, A. *Land, Labour and Diet in Northern Rhodesia.* London, 1939.

Roberts, Andrew. *A History of Zambia.* New York, 1979.

Roberts, B. C. *Labour in the Tropical Territories of the Commonwealth.* London, 1964.

Rotberg, Robert I. *Black Heart: Gore-Browne and the Politics of Multi-Racial Zambia.* Berkeley, 1977.

———. *The Rise of Nationalism in Central Africa.* Cambridge, Massachusetts, 1966.

Sklar, Richard L. *Corporate Power in an African State: The Political Impact of Multinational Mining Companies in Zambia.* Los Angeles, 1975.

Taylor, John V., and Lehmann, Dorothea S. *Christians of the Copperbelt: The Growth of the Church in Northern Rhodesia.* London, 1961.

Thompson, E. P. *The Making of the English Working Class.* New York, 1968.

Tordoff, William, ed. *Politics in Zambia.* Manchester, 1974.

Van Onselen, Charles. *Chibaro: African Mine Labour in Southern Rhodesia 1900–1933.* London, 1976.

Watson, Sir Malcolm, ed. *African Highways: The Battle for Health in Central Africa.* London, 1953.

Welensky, Sir Roy. *Welensky's 4,000 Days.* London, 1964.

Wilson, Francis. *Labour in the South African Gold Mines 1911–1969.* Cambridge, 1972.

Wilson, G. *An Essay on the Economics of Detribalisation.* Livingstone, 1941–42.

Articles

Berg, E. and Butler, J. "Trade Unions." In *Political Parties and National Integration in Tropical Africa*, edited by J. Coleman and C. Rosberg. Los Angeles, 1964.

Bettison, D. "The Poverty Datum Line in Central Africa." *Rhodes-Livingstone Journal* 27 (June 1960).

———. "Factors in the Determination of Wage Rates in Central Africa." *Rhodes-Livingstone Journal* 28 (December 1960).

Bozzoli, Belinda. "Managerialism and the Mode of Production in South Africa." *South African Labour Bulletin* 3, no. 8 (October 1977).

Burawoy, M. "Another Look at the Mineworker." *African Social Research 14 (1972).*

———. *"The Hidden Adobe of Underdevelopment: Labor Process and the State in Zambia" Politics and Society* 11, no. 2 (1982).

Carchedi, G. "The Reproduction of Social Classes at the Level of Production Relations." *Economy and Society* 4, no. 4 (1975).

Chauncy, George, Jr. "The Locus of Reproduction: Women's Labour in the Zambian Copperbelt, 1927–1953." *Journal of Southern African Studies* 7, no. 2 (April 1981).

Clausen, L. "On Attitudes Towards Industrial Conflict in Zambian Industry." *African Social Research* 2 (December 1966).

Clay, G. C. T. "African Urban Advisory Councils in the Northern Rhodesian Copperbelt." *Journal of African Administration* 1, no. 1 (January 1949).

Epstein, A. L. "Linguistic Innovation and Culture on the Copperbelt, Northern Rhodesia." *Southwestern Journal of Anthropology* 15 (1959).

Femia, Joseph. "Hegemony and Consciousness in the Thought of Antonio Gramsci." *Political Studies* 23, no. 1 (March 1975).

Gann, L. H. "The Northern Rhodesia Copper Industry and the World of Copper: 1923–52." *Rhodes-Livingstone Journal* 18 (1955).

Good, Kenneth. "Settler Colonialism: Economic Development and Class Formation." *Journal of Modern African Studies* 14, no. 4 (1976).

Heath, F. M. N. "The Growth of African Councils on the Copperbelt of Northern Rhodesia." *Journal of African Administration* 5 (1953).

Henderson, I. "The Origins of Nationalism in East and Central Africa: The Zambian Case." *Journal of African History* 11, no. 4 (1970).

———. "Wage-Earners and Political Protest in Colonial Africa: The Case of the Copperbelt." *African Affairs* 72, no. 288 (1973).

————. "Early African Leadership: The Copperbelt Disturbances of 1935 and 1940." *Journal of Southern African Studies* 2, no. 1 (1975).

Hochschild, H. K. "Labour Relations in Northern Rhodesia." *Annals of the American Academy of Political and Social Science* 206 (July 1956).

Hooker, J. R. "The Role of the Labour Department in the Birth of African Trade Unionism in Northern Rhodesia." *International Review of Social History*, 10, no. 1 (1965).

Johnson, Terry. "What Is to Be Known? The Structural Determination of Social Class." *Economy and Society* 6, no. 2 (May 1977).

Jones, Rheinnalt D. "The Effects of Urbanization in South and Central Africa." *African Affairs* 52 (1953).

Maxwell, Sir James C. "Some Aspects of Native Policy in Northern Rhodesia." *Journal of the African Society* 29, no. 117 (October 1930).

Menzies, I. R. "Tribalism in an Industrial Community." In *The Multi-tribal Society*, Proceedings of the Rhodes-Livingstone Institute, 16th Conference Proceedings. Lusaka, 1962.

Mitchell, J. C. "The Distribution of African Labour by Area of Origin on the Copper Mines of Northern Rhodesia." *Rhodes-Livingstone Journal* 14 (1954).

————. "A Note on the Urbanization of Africans on the Copperbelt." *Human Problems in British Central Africa* 12 (1951).

Mitchell, J. C. and Epstein, A. L. "Occupational Prestige and Social Status among Urban Africans in Northern Rhodesia." *Africa* 29, no. 1 (1959).

Moore, R. J. B. "Native Wages and the Standard of Living in Northern Rhodesia." *African Studies* 1, no. 2 (June 1942).

Ohadike, P. O. "Migrants in the Copper Mines of Zambia, 1940–66." In *Population Growth*, edited by S. H. Ominde. New York, 1972.

Oppenheimer, Sir Ernest. "The Advancement of Africans in Industry." *Optima* 3, no. 3 (1953).

Oppenheimer, H. "Sir Ernest Oppenheimer: A Portrait by His Son." *Optima* 2, no. 3 (September 1967).

Perrings, C. A. "A Moment in the 'Proletarianization' of the New Middle Class: Race, Value and the Division of Labour in the Copperbelt, 1946–1966." *Journal of Southern African Studies* 6, no. 2 (April 1980).

————. "Consciousness, Conflict and Proletarianization: An Assessment of the 1935 Mineworkers' Strike on the Northern Rhodesian Copperbelt." *Journal of Southern African Studies*, 4, no. 1 (1977).

Prain, Sir Ronald I. "The Problem of African Advancement on the Copperbelt of Northern Rhodesia." *African Affairs* 53 (1954).

————. "The Stabilization of Labour in the Rhodesian Copperbelt." *African Affairs* 55 (1956).

Rotberg, R. I. "Race Relations and Politics in Colonial Zambia: The Elwell Incident." *Race* 7, no. 7 (July 1965).

Spearpoint, C. F. "The African Native and the Rhodesia Copper Mines." Supplement to *Journal of the Royal African Society* 36, no. 144 (July 1937).

Stark, D. "Class Struggle and the Transformation of the Labor Process." *Theory and Society* 9 (1980).

Stichter, S. "The Impact of the Depression on Workers' Movements in East and Central Africa, 1930–1936." Mimeograph, 1981.

Welensky, Roy. "Africans and Trade Unions in Northern Rhodesia." *African Affairs* 45 (1936).

Wright, Erik Olin. "Class Boundaries in Advanced Capitalist Societies." *New Left Review* 98 (July/August 1976).

ORAL EVIDENCE TAKEN

The following is a list of interviews with individuals having long association with the copper mines in various capacities. Interviews were in English unless otherwise stated.

Bowa, J. H. Community Development Section, MCM, interviewed at Mufulira, 7 September 1976.

Bryant, R. B., Personnel Department, MCM, interviewed at Mufulira, 7 September 1976.

Chibambo, Langford D., Personnel Department, RACM, interviewed at Luanshya, 12 September 1976.

Chipako, J. Malik Personnel Department, Rhokana, interviewed at Kitwe, 14 September 1976.

Chisanga, Reverend Joel, Minister in United Church of Zambia, interviewed at Mindolo Ecumenical Center, Kitwe, 29 August 1976.

Chisata, John, former President of AMWU, interviewed at Mufulira, 14 September 1976.

Chishala, V. K., Pesonnel Department, Rhokana, interviewed at Kitwe, 21 September 1976.

Chiwila, Sandford, Personnel Department, Rhokana, interviewed at Kitwe, 27 November 1975.

Cook, Chris, former African Personnel Manager, RACM, interviewed at East London, South Africa, 4 October 1976.

Dalton, John, management, NCCM, interviewed at Lusaka, 4 August 1975.

Davis, N. R. K., management, NRCM, interviewed at Kitwe, 15 September 1976.

Etheredge, Dennis, management, Anglo-American Corporation, interviewed at Johannesburg, 12 October 1976.

Ferreira, Howard H., former Government Welfare Officer, interviewed at Johannesburg, 11 October 1976.

Fisher, A. C., former Chief Medical Officer, RACM, interviewed at Greystone Park, Kitwe, 21 August 1976.

Goodwin, Brian, former president of the European Mineworkers' Union, and member of Legislative Council, interviewed at Lusaka, 26 June 1976.

Graham-Harrison, Monty, former UMCB member, interviewed in London, 25 October 1976.

Hough, Michael, former Advisor on Community Affairs for Anglo-American Corporation, interviewed at Fort Hare University, South Africa, 4 October 1976.

Howie, Richard, former head of African Welfare, RACM, interviewed at Johannesburg, 10 October 1976.

Kabilika, Ashton Musonda, miner and early union leader, Rhokana, interviewed at Kitwe, 29 August 1976. Language, Chibemba.

Kambafwile, Patson, miner and union leader, MCM, interviewed at Mufulira, 9 September 1976.

Katongo, Theresa, welfare worker, RACM, interviewed at Luanshya, 3 September 1976.

Koloko, Boniface, Personnel Department, RACM, interviewed at Luanshya, 30 August 1976.

Law, P. J., former Labor Officer, Northern Rhodesia, interviewed at Oxford, 26 October 1976.

Lehmann, Dorothea, former UMCB missionary, interviewed at Lusaka, 21 April 1976.

Lloyd, Mavis, former Welfare Officer, RACM, interviewed at East London, South Africa, 4 October 1976.

Luyt, Sir Richard, former Labor Officer, later Chief Secretary, Northern Rhodesia, interviewed in Cape Town, South Africa, 7 October 1976.

McCallum, James, formerly with the Personnel Department, Rhokana, interviewed at Cape Town, South Africa, 8 October 1976.

McPherson, Fergus, former UMCB missionary, interviewed at Lusaka, 26 September 1975.

Morris, Reverend Gordon, former UMCB missionary, interviewed at Kitwe, 22 August 1976.

Morris, Sheila, wife of UMCB missionary, teacher, and welfare worker, interviewed at Luanshya, 3 September 1976.

Mubanga, P., miner and early union leader, Rhokana, interviewed at Kitwe, 16 September 1976.

Mubita, Joseph K., Personnel Department, MCM, interviewed at Mufulira, 7 September 1976.

Musakanya, Albert G., Personnel Department, Rhokana, interviewed at Nkana, 22 September 1976.

Musumbulwa, Fanny, welfare worker, RACM, interviewed at Luanshya, 1 September 1976.

Musumbulwa, Gabriel, Personnel Department, RACM, interviewed at Luanshya, 30 August 1976.

Mwalwanda, David Alfred, former miner and union leader, RACM interviewed at Luanshya, 13 September 1976.

Mwendapole, Matthew, former union leader, government minister, interviewed at Ndola, 3 August 1976.

Ndhlovu, S. K., Chief Community Development Officer, MCM, interviewed at Mufulira, 8 September 1976.

Nkoma, Sylvester, miner and union leader, RACM, interviewed at Luanshya, 3 September 1976.

Ostrander, Taylor, Assistant to the Chairman of American Metal Company, Vice-president of AMAX, interviewed in New York City, 14 July 1981.

Payne, John, Jr., former director of AMAX, technical advisor to RST, interviewed in Old Lyme, Connecticut, 13 July 1981.

Phiri, Chembe H., management and former union leader, RACM, interviewed at Luanshya, 3 September 1976.

Pierce, Joseph, Personnel Department, RACM, interviewed at Luanshya, 2 September 1976.

Prain, Sir Ronald, former managing director of RST, interviewed in Weybridge, England, 27 August 1982.

Sokota, Pascale, former teacher in Kitwe and Legislative Council member, interviewed at Kitwe, 28 August 1976.

Stubbs, William, former Labor Commissioner, Northern Rhodesia, interviewed at Oxford, 25 October 1976.

Torrance, Andrew, former Labor Officer, African Personnel Manager, MCM, now at NRCM, interviewed at Kitwe, 23 August 1976.

Vuillequiz, Jean, former director of RST, now with Metal Traders, Inc., interviewed in New York City, 10 June 1981.

Webber, Vernon, 'B' Director, Nchanga Consolidated Copper Mines Ltd., interviewed in Boston, 2 December 1978.

Weill, Erwin, former secretary of AMAX, interviewed in New York City, 15 July 1981.

INDEX

Absenteeism, 47, 103, 153, 197 n.48. *See also* Discipline; Labor control
Accident rate, mine, 42, 49
Advancement, 24, 121–23, 136–38; The Dalgleish Commission, 122; four-way talks of 1954, 137; three-party conference of 1948, 123. *See also* Labor stabilization; Mines African Salaried Staff Association (MASA)
African Mineworkers' Union (AMWU), 17, 24; branch elections (1954), 143; branch offices, 132–33; corporate attitude towards, 116, 120–24, 145, 149–50; demands for housing and compound, 130–31; early collective labor action, 124–25; establishment, 119–21, 201 n.42; and European Mineworkers' Union, 127, 207 n.53; and Labor Department, 116, 124; membership, 120–21, 125, 130, 150, 154, 203 n.92, 208 n.88; politics, 128–29, 150; public meetings, 130–31; Recognition Agreement, 121; after rolling strikes, 151; solidarity, 131–32; structure, 121; and tribal representatives, 127–28. *See also* Political class consciousness
African National Congress, Northern Rhodesian (ANC), 17–18, 128–129, 133–34, 148, 151; Supreme Action Council, 128–29. *See also* Nkumbula, Harry; Political class consciousness
African nationalism: opposition to Federation, 128–29; rise of, 17–18; and trade unions, 134–35, 155–57. *See also* African National Congress; United National Independence Party; Zambia African National Congress
Agriculture, 26; government policy, 26–

27; land reserves, African, 17; white farmers, 16. *See also* Federation; Northern Rhodesian government
American Metal Company (later American Metal Climax, Inc.), 20, 176 n.17
Anglo-American Corporation: establishment of, 20–21; headquarters, 25, 51; labor policy, 37–38, 81–82; paternalism, 138–43; response to AMWU, 112; worker contentment, 55. *See also* Bwana Mkubwa Mine Company; Copper mining companies; Mufulira Copper Mines; Nchanga Consolidated Copper Mines; Rhokana Corporation

Bamba, 16; role in 1935 strike, 57–58
Beatty, Sir Alfred Chester, 20, 175 n.11
Bedford, Rev. Frank, 85, 101. *See also* United Missions in the Copperbelt
Beer brewing, 42, 52, 77, 183, n.72, 185 n.131
Boss boys, 24, 42; boycott, Luanshya, 109–10; committees, 103–4, 106–9; early union leadership, 119; in 1940 strike, 83–84; relations with European miners, 199 n.83. *See also* Labor aristocracy; Labor, skill levels of; Labor stabilization
Bourgeoisie. *See* Classes
Boycott, Luanshya (1946), 109–10, 206 n.45. *See also* Boss boys
British Labor government, 105; trade union policy, 111–12. *See also* Colonial office
British South Africa Company, 13, 16–17, 178 n.50; mineral rights, 17, 19, 25–26. *See also* Rhodes, Cecil